a handbook for student writers and researchers

ERIC HIBBISON

J. Sargeant Reynolds Community College
and
Consulting Editor for Prentice-Hall

Prentice-Hall, Inc.
Englewood Cliffs, New Jersey 07632

Library of Congress Cataloging in Publication Data

Hibbison, Eric.
A handbook for student writers and researchers.

Includes index.
1. English language—Rhetoric. 2. Report writing.
3. Research. 4. English language—Grammar—
1950– —Handbooks, manuals, etc. I. Title.
PE1408.H4785 1984 808'.042 83-24742
ISBN 0-13-382507-8

Cover design: Lundgren Graphics, Ltd.
Manufacturing buyer: Harry Baisley

Printed in the United States of America

10 9 8 7 6 5 4 3 2 1

ISBN 0-13-382507-8

Prentice-Hall International, Inc., *London*
Prentice-Hall of Australia Pty. Limited, *Sydney*
Editora Prentice-Hall do Brasil, Ltda., *Rio de Janeiro*
Prentice-Hall Canada Inc., *Toronto*
Prentice-Hall of India Private Limited, *New Delhi*
Prentice-Hall of Japan, Inc., *Tokyo*
Prentice-Hall of Southeast Asia Pte. Ltd., *Singapore*
Whitehall Books Limited, *Wellington, New Zealand*

*For Elleanor: Together we bore our
continuing studies, two more boys,
and this book.*

*For Mark, Joey, and Paul: We learned
that old manuscripts make good paper
airplanes and drawing paper.*

*For my parents, George and Mary: You showed
me the values of pride and persistence.*

Eric Hibbison has been Consulting Editor for the following Prentice-Hall texts:

Richard C. Baggett, *A Programmed Approach to GOOD SPELLING!* (1981)

Anne Agee and Gary D. Kline, *The Basic Writer's Book* (1981)

Delaware Technical and Community College English Department, Southern Campus, *Writing Skills for Technical Students* (1982)

Kathleen Macdonald, *When Writers Write* (1983)

Rebecca Burnett Carosso and Judith Dupras Stanford, *The Writing Connection* (1983)

Chopeta Lyons, *Discover Writing* (1984)

Kristbjorg E. O'Harra, *Vocabulary Development Through Language Awareness* (1984)

Contents

2   RESEARCH WRITING   46

Preface

Writing this text and working with other Prentice-Hall authors to develop their texts has changed my image of the writing process. Now, I view writing not as a single process, but as consisting of a variety of processes that people engage in, more or less capably, in a wide range of styles for a wide range of purposes.

As much and as often as possible, I have tried in this text to show students the variety and range of writing—and, therefore, its richness and challenge. At the same time, I have kept in mind what students really need—not armchair advice, but clear and practical explanations and demonstrations and realism in examples and exercises.

In each part of the text, practical writing principles are demonstrated using student or professional writing. Each part of the text also contains charts showing significant information to help students use writing principles in their own work.

Part 1 surveys the writing process, emphasizing the need to write successive drafts for complicated writing tasks. The heuristics presented include free writing, the reporter's questions, and a topic grid based on Abraham Maslow's hierarchy of human needs. This variety of heuristics enables students to discover which procedures are best for them—to determine which lend themselves to practical writing, and which to more literary or essayistic writing.

Matching tone and style to audience and purpose is a recurring theme of this text. Through discussion, excerpts, and a "stylistic scoreboard," students learn that writers vary their vocabulary, sentence structure, and sentence length depending on their view of the reader's expectations. In section 1d, a case study of a student writing demonstrates how a student, in successive drafts of an essay, advanced from free writing to pick experiences that could clarify how one of his values developed over the years. Various sections of the alphabetical handbook reinforce the notion of varying tone and wording to fit an audience. The fifteen exercises in Part 1, and many of the 139 exercises in the alphabetized handbook, support this notion of stylistic range.

Part 2, "Research Writing," assumes that the student has virtually no experience with library sources. It helps students select and narrow a topic to show their informed judgment. It demonstrates *how* to start a working bibliography, when to use indexes, which ones to consult, how to tell if a title is relevant, and how much time to spend searching for library sources. Two sample chronicles of research help students to learn a research process from the trials and successes and some errors of other students. Part 2 lays down strict guidelines about fair use of source material, and also demonstrates summarizing, paraphrasing, quoting, attribution, and documentation. In addition, this part shows students how to evaluate the quality, logic, and usefulness of source material and their own writing.

Also included in Part 2 is an explanation of why documentation is important for sharing information and for verifying its credibility. Teachers may select any cf the documentation styles currently used by directing students to follow Figure 2-11 for in-text reference or section 12 for footnotes/endnotes.

Part 3, the alphabetized handbook, is based on both traditional wisdom on principles of good writing and advice selected carefully from current research on writing pedagogy, psycholinguistics, and reading theory. As often as possible, I have designed examples and exercises that ask students to work with contexts longer than single sentences to learn and practice a principle. For instance, in the section on commas, students are asked to proofread a letter written by a lonely girl just starting out on her own and then to write a letter to her in response and proofread it for commas. Over the years, students have responded warmly to this exercise and written letters from the heart; they seem to appreciate practicing with meaningful material—and with full contexts.

Each entry in the alphabetized handbook ends with a "Special Hint." These hints are aimed at helping students use the writing principles of the section in their own writing. The "Special Hint" segments focus on practical points, such as the aspects of a word a person must know in order to use it *in writing*, the exact structure of an active verb, and using inflections in English. The "Special

Hints" also include charts crucial to grammatical usage, such as a list of irregular verbs and a display of verb forms and the meanings of tenses.

Particular sections of the handbook consider basic skills at length, such as the sections on "Irregular Verbs" and "Relationships." Reviewers have remarked that the sections on "Diction and the Dictionary" and "Spelling" are especially complete and creative in helping students study vocabulary, usage, and spelling systematically.

Each part of *A Handbook for Student Writers and Researchers* is designed to teach students what they haven't learned, rather than merely to review what they supposedly have learned. I have made a special effort to use an encouraging tone, to select practical and appropriate topics, and to provide clear explanations and diverse exercises. For their thorough and helpful suggestions in support of this effort, I wish to thank Judith Stanford of Merrimack College, William Peirce of Prince Georges Community College, Linda J. Bowie of Furman University, and James O'Malley of Triton College.

I am grateful to Bill Oliver for initiating this project and to Phil Miller, English Editor at Prentice-Hall, for seeing it through. I wish to express my admiration for the Prentice-Hall staff—for the aid of Fred Bernardi and Barbara Bernstein, and the sagacity of Joyce Perkins and Lisa Femmel. I also wish to thank Judith Rodgers for editorial advice.

I especially wish to thank the students who allowed me to alter their writings for the sentence-combining exercises: Glen de Hart, Bob Ferguson, Jean Ferguson, Kim Ferguson, Kathy Frazier, Steve Heflin, Brad Hood, Kathy Lovell, and two students who did not want their names used.

Finally, I am indebted to all of my students, who have helped me discover intricacies of professional styles, student writing practices, and sensible research procedures. They have honored me with their patient persistence, their openness, and their growth.

Acknowledgments

The following unpublished manuscripts are used by permission of students at J. Sargeant Reynolds Community College:

Karen Blanton Cohen, "An Analytical Report on the Pros and Cons of Gambling."

John Dixon, "Inexpensive Car"
Jean Ellis, "The Terminal Cancer Patient"
Jean Ferguson, "Weekend Parents"
Cheryl Frasher, "Souping Up a Car Is Stupid"
Chris Glave, *"Clamagore"*
Shirley Griffith, adapted from "The Returning Woman in College"
Ann Headley, "Cosmetics"
William Hogan, "Hunting" and "A True Value"
Ellen Holt, sample résumé and cover letter
Debbie Hoover, "My Father's Last Christmas"
Ronda Jones, "Dolphin Talk"
Janet Palmer, "The Reunion"
David Pangburn, "Living the Dawn-to-Dusk Day"
Vic Ripley, *"Eagle* Crashed"
Norma Taylor, "Granpa's Shoes"
Donna Yesbeck, "Child Abuse"

The following published works are quoted or adapted by permission:

From *A Choice of Catastrophes.* Copyright © 1979 by Isaac Asimov. Reprinted by permission of Simon & Schuster, a Division of Gulf & Western Corporation.

From *The Collapsing Universe* by Isaac Asimov. Copyright © 1977 by Isaac Asimov. Used by permission of Walker & Co.

From Frederick Ausubel, Jon Beckwith, and Kaaren Janssen, "The Politics of Genetic Engineering: Who Decides Who's Defective?" *Psychology Today,* June 1974, pp. 30–32. Reprinted by permission of the publisher, Ziff-Davis Publishing Company.

From Ronald N. Bracewell, *The Galactic Club: Intelligent Life in Outer Space.* © 1974, 1975 by Ronald N. Bracewell. Reprinted by permission of W. H. Freeman.

From Crane Brinton, John B. Christopher, and Robert Lee Wolff, *Prehistory to 1715,* Vol. 1 of *A History of Civilization,* 2nd ed. (Englewood Cliffs, N.J.: Prentice-Hall, 1960), p. 180. Reprinted by permission of the publisher.

From Bernard L. Fontana, "Tarahumara: Runners of the West," *Arizona Highways,* May 1979, p 10. Reprinted by permission of the author. Entries for "proud," "proud flesh," and "supercilious." With permission. From *Webster's New World Dictionary,* Second College Edition. Copyright © 1982 by Simon & Schuster, Inc.

Introduction to Students

Many people think that revising means changing their minds. You should probably think of revising as trying out things to help you make up your mind. In a sense, everything you do for a writing from the very start is a kind of revising.

This text offers suggestions and demonstrates actual practices that other students and some professional writers have followed to write.

To get acquainted with this book, take a few minutes to survey it. This means looking at the essential parts so that you can find what you need more easily. Your instructor may suggest sections for you to study or assign sections. Sections are numbered in sequence throughout the book. The handbook is also alphabetized so that you can find informtion by topics. All of the relevant topics in the text are listed in the index. Finally, the listings inside the covers of the book translate common short codes into topic and page references for you. Your instructor may use these notations on your writings so that you can go to the explanations you need to see.

To survey this text, then, glance at the following sections.

- The Preface lists the parts of this text, their purposes, and their special features.
- The Contents lists the major topics in the text and the text exercises.
- The Handbook introduction demonstrates common uses of a handbook and highlights sections that reviewers have mentioned as most helpful.
- The Glossary is a "hit list" of controversial words whose usage has been debated.

- The Index alphabetizes all of the topics in the text that have to do with studying English.
- The inside front and back covers provide a list of common writing problems with references to pages that contain advice on how to handle them.

A few minutes now spent glancing at these parts of the text can save you some frustration later on. The study of writing is hard enough without having to learn to use your resources—such as textbook and dictionary—while you are trying to learn about style or research or organization principles.

But remember that this text is, after all, just a book. In all matters of instruction you should follow the wisdom and the informed preferences of your instructor. With patience and persistence, you can advance your writing abilities along the continuum of growth that began when you first picked up a pen, pencil, or crayon. That continuum of growth will end after a lifetime of writing called forth by your education, your work, your civic and family responsibilities, and your own interests.

Eric Hibbison
Richmond, Virginia

1 | writing processes: an overview

1. GETTING STARTED

F. Scott Fitzgerald reportedly spent several years writing seventeen drafts of one of his novels. Ernest Hemingway reported that he had drafted the ending of one of his novels thirty-nine times. And experienced writers in fields other than fiction mention writing different drafts for different purposes. Not everyone rewrites extensively for all writing tasks, but rewriting apparently gives people a way to choose what to say and how to say it. One researcher makes the distinction: For routine writing tasks, people don't revise very much, but for tasks that are not routine, experienced writers often revise a great deal, have others read their writing, and then rewrite it some more.

To become an experienced writer in your field, you should know some of the advantages and practices of rewriting. Different people use different writing processes, of course. But student writers generally tend to stop writing too soon, before a composition has fulfilled its possibilities.

In this chapter, you'll see how one student wrote a series of drafts to complete an essay. You'll also see some contrasts—among various styles of writing and various patterns of organization. Some of the suggestions, advice, and demonstrations may reveal things about writing you didn't realize before. You may be familiar with other ideas, which you may have used time and time again. But after studying this chapter, you should be able to see more possibilities in your writing, find more things to say on your topics and more ways to say what you want—in ways that will hold your readers' attention, interest, and understanding.

1a. The Writer's Notebook

F. Scott Fitzgerald not only revised his novels a great deal, but over the years he also kept notebooks of things he had seen, realized, and imagined. Yet he used very little of this notebook writing in his stories and novels; for him, this writing was "disposable," or practice writing. Like Fitzgerald, many writers use writing notebooks to jot down ideas for stories and characters, and describe real people and events. Keeping these notebooks sparks their imaginations and provides a pool of ideas to draw from or reject when they write "for real."

For you, a notebook of practice writings has the same advantages for recording interesting ideas, notes on people and places, summaries of class notes on ideas that got you thinking, or just ideas for writing assignments from your courses. By keeping a notebook, you will begin to "think through your pen"—a habit you must form to write fluently.

Figure 1-1 shows excerpts from a notebook written by a student on a trip to Los Angeles. Most of the entries are very short, and there is no attempt to make full sense or fit descriptions into contexts. The complete notebook contains descriptions of landmarks, sights and sounds at Disneyland, people, plus bits of conversations (real and imagined), some inferences from observations and some personal information. The notebook also includes short references to memories, especially previous personal experiences and things the student had heard of. In other words, the notebook was full of things that made sense only to the writer (who knew the contexts of memories and connections of observations), but the excerpts tell us something about the contents of a writer's notebook.

The material in Figure 1-1 was written by a student who had read and written quite a bit in high school and had kept notebooks and journals before beginning this notebook. Of course, if you keep a writer's notebook, you will use it for your own purposes and to record your own observations; but keeping a notebook can make you look at some things, people, and ideas more closely. It can also cause you to consider words more carefully—words like "marshal," "truncated," and even "blaring" don't spring to mind automatically unless there's some reading and writing experience involved. A "good" writer's notebook doesn't have to contain profound experiences and deep thoughts. All you need to do is

Figure 1-1. Excerpts from a Student's Writer's Notebook

—"discussing the cause of family heart attacks, gesturing with a Wiley Ceyote (sp?) doll, w. the Thanksgiving Day parade blaring on the television, and three children and a cat clambering in a group on the floor"

—"the way my feet press the sand dry and a circle of lighter colored sand spreads out fr. my feet as I walk slowly along the shore"

—"a clock that reads 12:00 noon during the day and 12:00 midnight at night"

—"'maids' = girls brought fr. Mexico to live in, w. one day off per week"

—"a freight train w. one hobo. It is not possible to open a freight car door from the top of the car."

—"28 % of Ariz. = Indian reservations, wh. business leaders want to have taxed and developed by oil, timber, and mining (*Tucson Daily Citizen*)"

—"Reverence for something is useful only when it does not obscure truth; irreverence is useful when it dispels the clouds of sentiment from the truth."

—"The elevator bell rings every now and then to announce the arrival of the elevator on the sixth floor, but nobody punched the button. It opens onto a red carpeted lobby with four rooms to the left and the main part of the hotel to the right. No one gets off and the door closes. The hallway stands empty while the traffic noise and the yells of sailors and men looking for thrills drifts up from the street. The artificial plants imagine themselves growing in a planter circled by a black-cushioned, circular lounge in the center of the lobby. The black and white splotches in the carpet marshal themselves in pattern with no one to review them. The elevator rattles in its coccoon, guarded by a stalwart, green ashcan banded with gold at head and foot. The two newer elevators rush while the two older elevators across the lobby are at rest for the night. The air blisters the paint. The ceiling on one side buckles so the sideboards don't reach it. There are no sideboards on the other side and the ceiling is met securely by the wall. The elevator rattles by. Above the sign indicating the direction of rooms 636 to 662, 645 to 663, someone has heavily marked in ballpoint pen 'also 666.' The elevator bell rings and the elevator rattles to a stop and opens, closes, and sneaks off. A light gleams in the ladies room at the end of one of the wings in the truncated H."

look closely at what's around you and look a little beneath the surface.

1b. The Writer's Journal

A variation on the writer's notebook is the journal. Spend ten to fifteen minutes each day writing about anything that comes into your mind. Or write about what's been on your mind lately. Writing in a journal lets you see what you think, and so can help you think things through.

Some things that go into a writer's notebook (maybe all of them—don't worry too much about definitions right now) could be written in a journal. But a journal often includes things that might be first drafts, not just bits and pieces of experiences but contexts, too. Figure 1-2 shows passages from students' journals. As you can see, these journal entries record personal experiences and information important to the students. Any subject can be right for a journal, but the best journal entries make us think and feel, sometimes very deeply.

You may have noticed that the writing in Figure 1-2 shows a range of "polish," but the content of the writing is really the focus of a journal. A journal, since it is basically a private document, does not need to be carefully edited for the public eye. A journal is a place to think. It's also a place to experiment, try combinations of ideas, argue with yourself, try out new words and new writing techniques and new information. Most of all, a journal is more than a collection of experiences and random thoughts. It's a place to reflect on your experiences so that you can discover their meaning and importance for you.

EXERCISE 1. A Writer's Notebook

For at least one week, keep a writer's notebook. That is, each day write down at least five things that you have noticed, thought about, or realized that day. (See Figure 1-1 for a sample.)

EXERCISE 2. A Journal

For at least one week, keep a journal. Try to fill at least one side each day. (Most people use 8½″ × 11″ notebooks for journals.) (See Figure 1-3 in the next section if you have trouble thinking of what to write.)

Figure 1-2. Sample Journal Entries

GRANDPA'S SHOES

When I think about Christmas, I have to remember the year 1961 when I was eight years old and knew beyond a reasonable doubt that there was no Santa Claus.

My brothers and I were helping my Grandma, whom we lived with, decorate the tree a few days before when all hell broke loose. I was mad because Paul wouldn't let me put the angel on the top so I yelled out, "Well, there's no need to put this stupid thing up anyway 'cause there ain't no Santa Claus!" Just then Pete and Paul got all upset; and, of course, I was punished.

So anyway, the three of us were not really looking forward to Christmas.

Then to my amazement, on Christmas Eve I was woken by a loud thumping noice. I was the bravest of the three of us, so I got up, opened the door to a crack, peeked out, and was so shocked by what I saw. I ran back to my bed to calm my thumping heart and slow my breathing down. After I calmed a little, I told Pete to look out there. He wouldn't go unless I got up and went with him, and Paul was scared to stay alone so he came too.

When Pete saw what I did the first time, he got all excited and told Paul, who was hiding behind me, "It's Santa." But Santa heard him and came over to the door as we were scurrying back to our beds, and invited us to get up and have some cocoa and cookies with him.

After a long time of talking about the North Pole and such, we were all getting tired and Santa told us to give him a kiss and get back to bed so we wouldn't be too tired to open our gifts in the morning. Pete kissed him, Paul shook his hand, and then I kissed him and dropped the plate the cookies were on in the process. As I looked down and saw the plate in a million different pieces on the floor, I noticed that Santa had Grandpa's shoes on.

I never told the boys or Grandpa what I saw, but Santa did get two kisses and two hugs that very special night.

Oh yeah, that loud thumping noice was something we didn't even ask for. Bicycles.

(Norma Taylor, student)

INEXPENSIVE CAR

I drive a '71 Gold Duster. I don't know much about engines, and when it broke down, I had a hard time fixing it. When it started to blow oil out of the dipstick, I thought my rings had gone bad. I asked about having it rebuilt, but it was suppose to be less expensive to have it replaced with a new rebuilt engine. I called around for another, but does anyone have $500 I can have?

In one of my classes I had a mechanic, and so I asked him. He said it might be the screen for the oil pump is clogged. He told me to change the oil a couple of times. I did, but it did not work so I got him to look at it. When he looked at it, he said, "Replace 'that.'" "That" turned out to be the crank case ventilation valve, which cost about $5.

(John Dixon, student)

CLAMAGORE

You step down a ladder into a small metal room with wires and pipes covering the ceiling. The walls are covered with shelves and racks except for the one with four tubes sticking from it. On the wall across from the four tubes, there is a sink and a door. The door is about four feet in diameter. Step through the small door and you're in another room with dials and controls on every wall and another door like the first on the wall across from the other door. In the next room you walk on a narrow passage between two long diesel engines with instruments and controls all around. You walk through another door into a room like the one you just left; walk across the room to the next, which is a kitchen with food freezers and everything a well equipped kitchen should have. Next, you enter the radio room with radios everywhere. After that, you enter the control room where you find instruments for controlling the depth and course of the ship. Next, you enter the officer quarters and Wardroom, where the officers live and work. After the room, you are in the last room of the ship. This room is like the first room except it is larger. This ship, if you have not guessed, is a submarine. The last diesel powered submarine in the U.S. Navy. She was commissioned in June, 1945 and decommissioned in 1975. Her name is *Clamagore*. Her length is 325½ feet, her speed was 20 knots on the surface and 10 submerged. She carries 10 torpedo tubes and had a crew of 8 officers and 72 men.

(Chris Glave, student)

MY FATHER'S LAST CHRISTMAS

There is for me a memory so clearly etched upon my mind that each time I recall it, it is as if time has been standing still, and I am living it all once again. Two years ago at Christmas time my father, the wisest, kindest, and most gentle man I have ever known, was suddenly taken ill. He had been operated on the previous September for lung cancer, and had been given an excellent prognosis.

Our lives had returned to a normal routine, and we were all looking forward to Christmas, always a very special family time, primarily due, I think, to my Dad's almost child-like love of holidays.

On a morning in early December our lives were suddenly turned upside down, never to be quite the same again. I was diligently cleaning house while my husband slept, after working a night shift, when we received a call that my father had collapsed in the street, having seizures, and had been rushed to a nearby hospital. The hours and days that followed are a jumble of complicated tests, a steady stream of unfamiliar doctors, sleepless nights, gallons of coffee, and, permeating it all, fear.

Finally we learned that the lung cancer they thought cured, had metastasized in the left frontal lobe of Daddy's brain, and, if lucky, he had about three months to live. The doctors recommended radiation therapy to alleviate the pain, so Daddy was transferred to another hospital with the proper facilities and began the treatments a few days before Christmas.

On Christmas Eve, with false gaiety, already perhaps feeling a sense of our impending loss, we all gathered in Daddy's room. The scene that unfolded there remains captured in my mind, much as an artist captures a certain expression on canvas.

A hospital room, well decorated, and accented with seasonal decorations, but nevertheless, an alien place to be on Christmas Eve. The sound of Christmas carols filling the air from carollers stopping to spend a few minutes in each room, and, finally, my father, weak and terminally ill, but sitting up in bed singing and clapping his hands along with the carollers, and on his face the happiest, most peaceful smile I have ever seen.

(Debbie Hoover, student)

1c. Where Do Topics Come From?

Much of what we write for school, for work, or for other purposes is done to fit someone's demands. We are given a set task, we know the reader or readers, and we know basically what to say. All we have to worry about is what approach to take. For example, a writer who has to draft a memo to his boss's supervisor on the company's new telephone system has a specific task for a known reader. The writer summarizes the data on how effective the new system is and sends it on to the boss for review and initials.

Even the tasks we set for ourselves often involve known readers and given expectations. For example, a note of sympathy sent to a friend involves a set task for a known reader.

Sometimes, however, our writing tasks are less clearly defined. Writing for practice—for ourselves or for others—is often done within a larger context. For instance, keeping a writer's notebook or a journal does not require us to focus in on one topic. And sometimes essays are assigned and the student is asked to choose the topic. Even professional writers and scholars may feel the need to write before they have a clear subject in mind—like a newspaper columnist facing a deadline or a college professor whose position depends on writing for academic journals. When the topic is not given to us, where do topics come from?

Writers who have to provide their own topics must draw from their own interests and experiences. Sometimes it seems impossible to find a workable topic in your interests and memories. At other times, you may have two or three ideas, but no direction for any of them. This section concerns what to do when you are "stuck" for a topic or what to do with a topic.

Imagining Your Reader For school writing, at least one teacher will read your writing. That means you are guaranteed of one reader, but you should probably include the rest of your class in your idea of who will read your writing. In other words, your image of your reader should not be too narrow. If more than one reader is involved, you'll need to give more details. A larger audience also works to your advantage—you'll have more of a chance to interest someone in your topic.

What's interesting to a reader? You'd be surprised. Any topic can be interesting, if you give enough details and if you let your own enthusiasm show. You don't have to be an astronaut or an Arctic explorer to hold a reader's interest. You just have to be interested yourself.

Reading Very often people are provoked to write because of something they have read or heard about. For instance, suppose someone hears that an estimated 1.5 to 2 million people in greater Los Angeles are starving each year. That shocking number might provoke the person to do more reading (who's starving? what exactly does "starving" mean? why aren't they being helped?). It might provoke an initial reaction worth writing into a journal. It might eventually provoke someone to want to take action to help hungry Americans.

As you learn from your own reading, you form new interests. Some things stand out—positive and negative things, achievements and outrages. Anything you read or experience personally that makes you feel some strong emotion could be a "topic."

Free Writing   One way to tap your interests is to write for ten, fifteen, or twenty minutes a day on anything that comes to mind. This writing is "free" because you can wander from idea to idea without worrying about anything, including punctuation and spelling. You just write as fast as you can—but then you look back at what you have written to find a focus. Free writing is rarely orderly or coherent—it depends on what's on your mind and how you react to what you are writing.

Focused Free Writing   Suppose you have a topic or two in mind, but no direction. What do you do? Try writing about each topic for ten minutes or so; then look back to find the main idea of what you have written. Try to summarize all or part of the writing in a single sentence. You might use that main idea as the focus for another ten-minute writing or as the beginning of a rough draft, depending on how enthusiastic you are about it.

The Topic Grid   Some people need a system for finding topics. Figure 1-3 shows one system for finding topics by searching your own experiences and knowledge. The trick to using such a system effectively is to practice enough so that you ask helpful questions. For instance, even though your survival may not be threatened, you certainly have heard about threats to others—such as in news reports of murders, wars, diseases, famine, and negligence that causes accidents. Perhaps the murder rate alarms you. Perhaps the cancer rate concerns you. You might start with a ten-minute writing on either topic. Some questions you may write on could include: Why do people kill others? Does the state have the right to kill killers? If smoking leads to cancer, why do people smoke? How can smokers quit? Whom do they hurt—only themselves or others, too?

The grid also includes time. History, the way things are now,

Figure 1-3. A Grid for Finding Your Own Topic

| Focus | Needs or Achievements | | |
	Survival	Security	Self-Concept
Self			
People I Know			
People I Have Heard or Read About			

PAST   PRESENT   FUTURE

Survival includes food, shelter, clothing, heating, and care for physical and mental health.

Security includes emotional stability, financial safety, civil rights, and other things that make our world safe.

Self-Concept includes feelings of self-worth, goals, influences on our personalities, and other things that help us define ourselves.

Self, in this case, is you.

People I Know includes relatives, friends, acquaintances, and even people you see every day but don't speak to.

People I Have Heard or Read About includes every person (and idea) in your textbooks, your novels, the magazines or newspapers you read, the television and radio news and programs, as well as real people.

and guesses about what the future holds can fit any topic—and suggest quite a few. For instance, one thing that influences children's self-concepts is the "role models" they see. Recently, role models have become less rigid—an "athlete" is not always a man, a "nurse" not always a woman. The diversity of role models threatens some people; others see it as a new kind of freedom. How do you feel about it? Do your friends fit the traditional stereotypes?

H5W   Once you have a topic, what do you do with it? The answer often grows out of the topic. Your idea might be that smokers kill not only themselves but others as well, or that smokers hurt no one, despite the claims of links to lung cancer. The examples you come up with to illustrate your idea will depend on your own experiences and reading. But, to be systematic, you may wish to use a simple formula to sort out what you know: *who, what, where, when, why,* and *how.* Questions often start with these words. Apply them to your topic. Who smokes? Why do they smoke? Where is smoking allowed? Where should it be allowed? When do people smoke? When did smoking begin, and how? How much smoking does it take to cause cancer?

As you try to piece together answers for these questions and others like them, you may gather so much information that you will have to narrow your focus to a smaller topic. For instance, if you wanted to convince people to ban smoking in public places, you would have to provide quite a bit of information.

Even when you start with nothing more than a need to write *something,* you can search your experiences to find a topic.

1d. Finding a Thesis and Organizing Principles Through Drafting

The last section showed ways to find a topic and to see the possibilities for developing it in an essay. This section concerns where to go from here. Figure 1-4 is a first draft of a student's essay. It's really a free writing that was done in about fifteen minutes. The notes following it were added just after the free writing. These notes indicate other ideas that could go into the essay, directions to explore, relationships between the writer and his topic. This first draft demonstrates the following advice.

Figure 1-4.   A Student's First Draft

HUNTING

Hunting, is the sport of capturing or killing wild animals, at one time man could get his food only if he haunted for it. Sonetimes it is both sport and survival of man.

I myself started hunting about five years ago as a means of both. Not to say that I didn't have any money but to cut down on food expenses, are to take advantage of where I lived. Hunting is quite different for all. As for me I've found a true contest between the hunter and the hunted.

My first adventure started on a cold January morning deer hunting. Around six thirty in the morning, with the temperature lagging at fifteen degrees. I thought to myself "You could be still in bed and warm" at that Passing the time, waiting for the sound or sight of a deer./ All of a sudden, something caught my eye. Around two hundreds off a deer had come out of the woods onto the open field. As I watched each step of his movements, I could feel the excitement in me. Coming closer, watching his movements in smell and sight, interested me in his survival techniques.

HOW
I'm
changed
in
technique
_____
ULtra
sportsmanship

1.)   HUNting/ WHAT is?
2.)   weapons AND metHoDs
3.)   kinds of HUNNtiNg
4.)   WHATs makes Hunting a sport
5.)   Hunting Techniques
6.)   GAME LAWS
7.)   ANimals Hunt other ANimals   RelationsHip to MEN
8.)   Experience's

1.   When you have a topic in mind, write down all you can about it in fifteen minutes (focused free writing).
2.   Take stock of what you have written, perhaps by underlining or summarizing a main idea.
3.   List additional ideas: What else could be included?
4.   Don't stop to fix grammar or spelling while you're getting ideas. You're not being graded on your rough drafts.

It seems from the rough draft in Figure 1-4 that the writing went smoothest when the writer was telling an incident. But even the incident is not sharply focused. Also, the "true contest" idea that ends the second paragraph only hints at what the student means.

Three drafts and much discussion followed this first draft. Three classmates read the second draft and reacted to it by summarizing the main idea and picking out the best sections. I read the third draft and discussed it with the student. He and I focused on the main incidents in his hunting experiences and what they meant to him. The first draft (Figure 1-4) mentioned a deer-hunting episode. The second draft mentioned flushing out wild rabbits on one farm and the deer-hunting incident in more detail. The third and fourth drafts went still further, by describing in detail a deer hunt done with bow and arrow. Figure 1-5 shows the fourth draft of this essay. Notice how the writer uses the incidents to demonstrate how he formed his definition of sportsmanship.

The growth of this writing so far has been *organic*. In other words, as the idea took shape—that his values had changed over the years—this student located experiences that showed the change. First he chose the rabbit hunt of his youth; and he showed how the rabbit was as good at avoiding the hunter as the hunter was at hunting—actually, the rabbit was better, the hunter needed luck. But even though both the rabbit hunt and the deer hunt had involved guns, it was the deer hunt that made it clear to the student that he had mixed feelings. By the third draft, he realized that he had to add the incident of the bow hunt to make his essay complete.

But is the essay complete? Much of the writing could be improved, especially the paragraphs between incidents. The first page does not contain an obvious thesis, such as "Three hunting incidents in my life helped me decide the meaning of sportsmanship." A sentence like that would signal directly the organizing principle of the essay. Some wording improved from the third to fourth drafts, and some spelling and word choices were corrected, mainly by the student. A few items simply need to be checked; for instance, what is the plural form for "doe"? Is it "does" or "doe's"?

Nevertheless, this is the draft the student chose to hand in for a grade. As a draft it shows that the student took the following

A TRUE VALUE

To this day, I remember at the age of six, hunting became an influence in my life! My grandparents had a three hundred and fifty acre farm outside of Chase City, Virginia, where my father would take me hunting with him sometimes.

There was nothing mor fun than tagging along, traveling the countryside looking for a wild rabbit. Sometimes we would spend hours intercrossing the field hoping to flush out a rabbit. If we were lucky, one would make its move.

I even recall one day, while flushing out a rabbit, realizing how smart this animal was—traveling almost faster than you could think, zig-zagging, as though anticipating the next move my father would make, the rabbit far superior! Only if we were lucky would we return home with a kill to make a stew.

As time passed in my life, the occasion for the sport became infrequent. School, dating girls, and my friends became the center of my activities; I forgot almost what influence hunting had on me. Every once in a while I would have a memory to reflect back on but never the time to go hunting.

Finally, at the age of twenty-four, I had settled down and was working and living on a six hundred and fifty acre farm. It was a place where wildlife was abundant and enjoyable to be around. Every day there was something to watch and notice about wild animal behavior.

One day, a good friend of mine dropped by to visit, and in talking we found we shared the same childhood experiences, his in deer hunting, mine with rabbit. Our interest sparked by the memories, we planned a Saturday morning to go deer hunting, following the week of work ahead of us.

I must say the week went by slowly. Although I was looking forward to the hunt, I was puzzled at the same time; my values had changed. Guns were too easy, not offering my prey the chance it should have to survive. My idea of sportsmanship had become different from the image I had formed in my youth.

At last Saturday came. Up by five o'clock in the morning and out the door, I went to meet my friend, George. It was a cold, January morning, with the temperature lagging at fifteen degrees. As we headed out into the woods we could see and feel the stillness of the morning as the sun rose. Most people would probably rather still be in bed, but to George and me there couldn't be anything more beautiful. There was so much freedom in this feeling.

Taking our tree stands, we separated, waiting for a deer to come close. Sitting in my stand, I was really becoming involved with my surroundings when suddenly a deer headed our way. The experience of taking aim and watching every movement this animal made was unbelievably tense. Every step this buck made he would look and hold his head high to try to smell any fear in the air. Luck was on our side; he got into range of my gun. Off with my shot, down with the deer, and we had plenty of meat for the remainder of winter.

The adventure was astonishing! To get that close is something rarely accomplished. Still, in the back of my mind, I thought guns were not fair, not really hunting as a sport. On another deer hunt, I was introduced to the bow and arrow.

After practicing some time with the bow, I thought I had become skilled enough to take it out in the field. On this particular occasion, it was late in the evening, an hour or two before sunset. As I sat in the tree stand, my mind wandered. The complete silence was broken by the rattling of leaves. Maybe a deer was heading my way, I thought. The sound would come and go, getting closer to the edge of the woods. A deer was coming; I knew from experience it was stepping to pause, seeing or smelling my fear in the air. It seemed like hours listening to every sound it made. I was standing up in my tree stand, arrow drawn back on the bow, when two doe's walked out into the opening twenty-five yards away. My adrenalin was flowing so fast that I could hear my heart beat. My confidence told me at last that more skill was required, as I edged the arrow off the deer. If I missed and did not get her in the right place, she would run for a couple of days wounded, if not dying. Watching the two doe's walk out of sight, going to the other side of the hill, I knew I would be back!

From that day on, I knew that I had found the ultra sport. My attitude, values, and even justification came into focus. Hunting with a bow has given me the greatest excitement ever! There is so much more involved than eyeing an animal down a gun barrel! I have found a set of laws in hunting that govern me. It's a good feeling; nature has its fair chance as much as I do.

(William Hogan, student)

advice:

1. As your idea takes shape, you need to choose information and memories to support it. That means leaving out things that you had considered using and had wanted to use because they don't really fit the idea.

2. Your essay will grow in detail and length as you probe your topic more deeply.
3. Getting other people to read your early drafts can help you see what needs to be changed, added, or left out.

This student was writing personally, and he was writing organically—that is, letting the form of his writing emerge with his idea. This example shows rather informally some of the methods experienced writers use to find ideas, and develop ideas, with a kind of organizing principle—something they discover as they move from draft to draft.

Yet experienced writers also know how to write to specifications. They have a pool of common organizing principles to draw from, principles they know that readers can recognize. The next section looks at the standard theme as a task of writing to specifications, and then demonstrates common organizing principles. This is not the only basis of an experienced writer's organizing principles, however—as you will see later, in the discussion of style.

EXERCISE 3. Free and Focused Writing with a Planned Draft

Write for ten minutes without stopping; try to fill a notebook-sized page. You don't have to write on a single topic—just write about anything that comes to mind.

After ten minutes, look back over your work for ideas that seem worth developing, such as things that bring back memories or things you consider important. List at least three possible topics.

Write for ten minutes on the topic you most want to try out. Then underline what you consider your main or best idea—or write it down in one sentence. Then list what more you could say about this main idea. (See Figure 1-4 for an example.)

EXERCISE 4. Draft and Show

Begin this exercise a day or two after completing Exercise 3. Begin by trying to write two to three pages about your topic, following or ignoring your list of what to say. Does your draft seem organized? If not, what's missing? Show your draft to someone whose judgment you trust; ask your reader for a summary statement, plus a list of best parts and weakest parts. Assess your

reader's judgments and revise the writing again. Repeat this process of seeking advice and revising until you are satisfied that you have a clear organizing
principle. Then read the section on "Revising for Style."

2. WRITING THE STANDARD THEME

The task of writing a standard school theme is to specify a
thesis by developing topic sentences that are supported in detail.
Writing a standard theme is good training in the rigors of writing
in an exact pattern. As well, knowing how to write a standard
theme can be very useful in your essay exams and impromptu
writings. That is, if you are grounded in a set form, you're free
to concentrate on your essay's content and style. Little if any
professional writing follows this particular rigid structure, but
practice here can make you more aware of other common organizing principles that prevail in professional writing—writing that
you will have to read and do for your job and other pursuits.
Here are a few parts of the standard school theme:

1. *The thesis:* Usually this is a statement of what your topic is *and* what
   you intend to say about the topic. The thesis also sets up your
   organization by listing subtopics, and it sets the tone of your writing.
   So the thesis need not be restricted to one sentence—a thesis stated
   in one sentence can be too bulky at times.
2. *Topic sentences:* Since the subtopics of your essay will probably be
   listed in your thesis, you are likely to develop those topics one by
   one. Your thesis commits you to develop your essay in the order
   stated. Your topic sentences are also commitments to your reader
   to develop the smaller sections of your theme—usually paragraphs.
   Topic sentences usually come first in a paragraph; everything in a
   paragraph relates back to the topic sentence.
3. *Support:* Since topic sentences are general, they do not explain
   themselves fully. Therefore, each paragraph between the thesis and
   conclusion must detail, explain, and justify its topic sentence.
4. *Transitions:* For an essay to be clear, it must contain phrases (sometimes whole sentences) designed to get readers from one idea to
   another. Specifically, essays have at least three major levels of
   detail—the thesis is the most general statement in the essay; the
   topic sentences give the thesis some focus; and the support sentences
   add even closer focus. Also, the supporting sections may contain

sentences of more than one or two levels of detail. Transitions do two things: they signal shifts in levels (as done by words such as "specifically"), as well as signalling shifts between sentences and phrases on the same level (as done by words such as "also" and "as well as"). (For a list of transitions and their value as signals, see the entry "Relationships" in the handbook.)

The standard school theme usually consists of about five paragraphs and is about 500 words long, but can easily be expanded by adding more parts to the thesis. After an introduction, which customarily ends with the thesis, the middle paragraphs treat the topics listed in the thesis one by one. The length of the theme can be expanded by writing more than one paragraph on each topic. The thesis is reemphasized in a concluding paragraph, often after the most significant details in the essay are summarized. The sample outlines in "Outlining" illustrate the structure of an expanded standard theme. Figure 1-6, right, shows a sample essay that follows the structure of a standard school theme.

The essay in Figure 1-6 shows a reasonable attempt at following the format of a standard theme. Following the introduction of the thesis, three topics are described in detail in the middle paragraphs, in the order given in the thesis, and then there is a concluding paragraph. This draft (not the first draft of this essay by the student) was submitted for a grade. You may notice that the topics are developed in order of importance, ending with the central point—the most serious difficulty posed by cosmetics.

The essay in Figure 1-6 does not have very obvious and heavy-handed transitions between paragraphs, such as "The first difficulty is," etc. The topic sentences do, however, pick up the main words of the thesis. In fact, the thesis was probably written into the rough draft after the topic sentences were done. To signal the order-of-importance arrangement of the middle paragraphs, this student writer might have begun the fourth paragraph with a sentence such as: "The financial costs of cosmetics and their toll on a woman's self-image are serious considerations, but the most serious difficulty with cosmetics is the health risks they pose." Such an obvious transition would emphasize the final point more than the word "even" does in the current topic sentence for the fourth paragraph.

Figure 1-6. An Essay Written in the Form of a Standard School Theme

COSMETICS

Cosmetics are thought of by millions of women as the miracle wonder that will transform them from ugly ducklings into beautiful swans. Cosmetics may be wonder products that create great beauty, but they also can create great difficulties. These difficulties are the cost of the beauty products, the false sense of beauty they give, and the danger they can cause to those who wear them.

THESIS

Thousands of dollars are spent by each woman during her lifetime to become beautiful and desirable. An average of two hundred to four hundred dollars a year is spent by a woman for cosmetics. The foundation base for a woman's face can run from two dollars to forty dollars. Women can buy Mabelline lipstick for a couple of dollars, but Merle Norman lipstick costs eight dollars per tube. Esteé Lauder and Merle Norman are two of the most expensive brands of cosmetics. Mabelline, Max Factor, and Love's are three of the less expensive brands of cosmetics.

Topic Sentence

In truth, cosmetics are a mask, changing the looks and identity of many women—or so they think. Cosmetics give women a false sense of beauty. Women think that by applying makeup they will become as beautiful as models. In reality, they are not. According to an article in *TV Guide*, the average woman is depressed by all the beautiful models she sees in advertisements. She feels inadequate for the simple reason that she is not as beautiful as a model like Jacklin Smith or Cheryl Tiegs.

Topic Sentence

Cosmetics can even be dangerous to women's health. Many labels on cosmetics warn women that they may be dangerous to their health. Cosmetics can cause dry skin, rashes, chapping, and infection, and if the cosmetics get into the eyes of women, they can sometimes cause blindness. Hypoallergenic cosmetics were created to eliminate these dangers, but many women do not like hypoallergenic cosmetics. Many women believe these do not enhance beauty since they tend to cake. Some women prefer beauty to safety.

Topic Sentence

Women should always be careful of cosmetics they buy. They should take into consideration the cost, the false sense of beauty they provide, and the danger they can cause to their health. Women should also realize that the true beauty they have is their own and not created by cosmetics.

THESIS REVIEW

(Ann Headley, student)

EXERCISE 5. "Found" Themes in Textbooks

Select one of your textbooks that uses subheadings throughout a chapter. (A biology, psychology, economics, or history text will do.) Pick a section of several paragraphs under one subheading. Can you find one sentence that controls the content of this section? Do the paragraphs generally begin with topic sentences? Do paragraphs begin or end with transitions? Try one or two more sections or another book that has subheadings. How can this "theme" structure help you study textbooks?

EXERCISE 6. Summary and Comparison

Do Exercise 5 with a textbook that has chapter summaries. Write down the "thesis" of the section you use; write down the topic sentences from the paragraphs in the section. Summarize these in fifty words or less. Then try to find in the author's chapter summary the part that goes with the section you read. How is the author's summary different from yours?

EXERCISE 7. Practice Essay Answers

After you finish reading a chapter from one of the subjects in your other courses, make up five or six essay exam questions for yourself. Pick the one you think the teacher is most likely to emphasize (even if the teacher does not use essay exams), and write a five-paragraph answer in standard theme form.

EXERCISE 8. "Found" Themes in Magazines

Try Exercise 5 with a magazine article that includes several subheadings.

3. COMMON ORGANIZING PRINCIPLES

There are many systems for categorizing writing. A common system separates writing into narration, description, exposition, and persuasion. Figure 1-7 gives simple definitions and some

Figure 1-7.   Organizing by Purpose: The Four Modes of
                  Writing and Common Applications

Narration: Telling a story

Book-Length Applications	*Shorter Applications*
biography and autobiography	anecdote (similar to "incident" and
novels	"extended example") and scenario
	(see Figure 2-9)

Description: Detailing physical parts, mannerisms, and personality traits to
set one individual, thing, or place apart from others

Book-Length Applications	*Shorter Applications*
catalogs	thumbnail sketches
travel books	scene settings within stories

Exposition: Explaining (usually as "objectively" as possible)

Book-Length Applications	*Shorter Applications*
textbooks	instructions
reference books	newspaper and magazine articles
training manuals	

Persuasion: Convincing (usually with "subjective" interpretations)

Book-Length Applications	*Shorter Applications*
some nonfiction books	editorials, ads, "junk" mail

applications of these four terms. These types of writing have
different purposes, as shown in the list below:

narration—to entertain

description—to identify

exposition—to explain

persuasion—to cause belief or action

When you sit down to write, these may be your general
purposes. When you revise a draft, though, you should define
your purpose more precisely. Who will read your writing? For
what purpose of theirs? How will they use what you write? What

do you expect of your readers? Every decision you make about your writing will be influenced by these questions. Writers and readers meet on the written page. Both have expectations that influence how they process the writing word by word, sentence by sentence, paragraph by paragraph, and even for the entire writing. One expectation is that at each of these levels some organizing principle will be evident. Whatever purpose you have (whichever of the four "modes" you write in), it's likely in a single writing that you will use several of the organizing principles in Figure 1-8. Some people sometimes use them without realizing it and

---

Figure 1-8.   Common Organizing Principles (*Other words for roughly the same principle appear in parentheses.*)

1. **Analysis into parts** (division, partition, structure).
   What are the "parts" of the mechanism, organization, or human relationship? What do these parts look like separately? How do they work together?
2. **Causes** (reasons, incentives, deterrents).
   Why does this happen? Why do people do this? Why don't they do this?
3. **Circumstances.**
   What things always go with this? What always happens with this? Is this possible or impossible?
4. **Classification.**
   What are the categories of this? Is this a category or type of something?
5. **Comparison** (similarity, analogy, likeness).
   What else is like this, literally or in my imagination?
6. **Contrast** (opposite, paradox, differences).
   How is this different from other things in the same group?
7. **Deduction** (generality to specifics, whole to parts, rule to applications).
   What assumptions, guiding principles, or premises do I (or other people) make about this?
8. **Definition.**
   What is this? What kind of experience, event, person, etc., is this, and what makes it different from others of the same kind?
9. **Details** (specifics).
   What names, dates, places, and other numbers (such as for size, amount, duration) go with or could explain this?

---

10. **Effects** (results, consequences).
    What happens because of this? What will or could happen?
11. **Examples** (precedents).
    What instances do I know of this? Can I list instances, or should I develop one or more in detail?
12. **Illustration** (anecdote, scenario, incident, extended example).
    What happening do I know of (or can I imagine) to portray this?
13. **Importance.**
    Do I use my best evidence first or last? Do I use second-best supporting evidence first?
14. **Induction** (specifics to generalization, parts to whole)
    What instances or items lead me to draw the conclusions I have made? What leads others to their conclusions?
15. **Maxim** (proverb, aphorism, saying, famous quotation).
    How would I apply this saying to a situation I know? Does the usual wisdom hold true for this?
16. **Pros and cons** (advantages and disadvantages)
    What are the (best) things for and against this?
17. **Problems and solutions.**
    What's the problem with this? What solutions have been proposed in the past? What worked or might work?
18. **Process** (procedure, "how-to").
    How does this mechanism, organization, human relationship work? What makes it break down? How should someone make this, including tools, ingredients, and steps?
19. **Space** (physical description).
    How should I describe this person, place, or scene? Left to right? Near to far? Most noticeable thing to least? Top to bottom? Middle to edges? Stationary or moving?
20. **Statistics** (figures, numbers).
    How could I depict this numerically? What are the facts and figures on this? Do I need a graph or table to show this? How should I summarize a graph or table on this?
21. **Time** (chronology).
    How should I present this happening? First thing that happened to last? Past, present, and future? Then and now? Start with a climactic event, look back, and then pick up from the climactic event?
22. **Verification** (documentation).
    What should I use to verify my evidence? Statistics? Expert testimony—quoted, paraphrased, or summarized? Personal experience or eyewitness accounts? Opinion polls or surveys?

certainly without stating it (a writer may not say, "Now I'm writing a comparison"). But when they plan and revise, many people wish they had a "better example" or could "describe this process more clearly." The list is alphabetical because it's a shopping list, a checklist you can use to search out ways to organize essays, paragraphs, and sentences when you get stuck.

Every writing—whether a sentence, paragraph, essay, or even a book—will have as its foundation just about any of these organizing principles. Let's think through an example of how such organizing principles might work in an essay. Figure 1-9 shows a student essay that evolved through a few drafts. The kernel of the essay is a contrast between "weekend" parents and full-time parents. After some tinkering and thinking, the student saw a way to make this contrast a frame for her essay; the contrast gave her a beginning and an ending. The second and third paragraphs describe in detail the apparent advantages of being a weekend parent; the fourth paragraph discusses the often overlooked disadvantages of weekend parenting. The next two paragraphs amplify the disadvantages, disputing the conventional wisdom, or the outward appearance, of the situation. Each of the middle paragraphs uses short sentences to list circumstances of parenting. Within the "speech" in the fifth paragraph, the last three sentences emphasize sharing, teaching, and love. The series of questions works on the reader's emotions. Whether you see an "order-of-importance" or a "parts-to-whole" relationship doesn't much matter. And whether the writer was aware as she wrote that she was using a "cause" structure in her second paragraph isn't the crucial

---

Figure 1-9.   A Sample Essay Demonstrating How Organizing Principles Operate at Several Levels

WEEKEND PARENTS

The scene: It is 3:00 in the afternoon and pouring rain outside. There are toys and books strewn from one end of the house to the other. The television is going full blast. There are cookie crumbs and half-filled glasses of Kool-Aid everywhere. The air is filled with constant cries of "We don't have anything to DO!" At this point, the parent's thoughts shift to Bob Jones down the street. Bob is one of those "lucky" weekend parents.

Oh, what a luxury! Bob sees the kids once a week or so. He and the kids go to the park or to the movies. They go out for ice cream. Because Bob is not the main disciplinarian in the kids' lives, they adore him. No yelling or fussing. Just a day of fun, and then Bob drops the kids off and has the rest of his evening free.

Bob has it made. He does not have to see that the kids have their homework done. He does not have to see that they brush their teeth or take their vitamins. He does not have to force them to eat spinach or clean up their rooms. He does not have to stay up all night when they are sick, or take time off from work to take them to the doctor (dentist, orthodontist, etc.). He does not have to worry about babysitters. All he has to do is entertain them once a week.

But there are a lot of other things Bob does not do. He does not get to see the delight on his children's faces on Christmas morning. He gets a "Christmas" on the following Saturday afternoon. Bob does not get to teach his children how to whistle or snap their fingers. One weekend they just show up able to do it. Bob does not get to help the kids with their homework or share in the excitement of an "A" on a test. He may, however, get to see an occasional report card. Bob does not get to watch the Charlie Brown special with the kids because it comes on television on a weeknight. He does not get to hold and comfort his children when they wake up from a nightmare. He does not get the special hugs one receives from kissing a scraped elbow or knee. He does not share in what happened at school, or after school, or in the evening.

Being a weekend parent is not all it's cracked up to be. It is not fun. It is not a luxury. It is more along the lines of a special torture. Seeing your child once a week (or even less frequently) is nothing more than being teased: "Look, here is your child. Here's a taste of what it's like to be this child's parent. See how much fun it can be to share things with him? To teach him things? See how it feels to give and receive love from this child?

"Uh oh, time's up—must take the child back for another week or two. Go back to your non-parental life. Surely this one afternoon has been plenty for you."

If full-time parents could only know how much Bob would give for the toys and books everywhere and the blasting television. If they could just understand how much the cookie crumbs and Kool-Aid would mean to Bob. And if they only knew how badly Bob would like to hear, "Daddy, we don't have anything to DO!" or "Daddy—" anything, then they would realize that the luxury does not lie in being a weekend parent. The real luxury, the real privilege, lies in being a mommy or daddy all the time.

(Jean Ferguson, student)

point. The point is that people use organizing principles (consciously or unconsciously) at every level of their writing. The contrast came later in revision, after the advantages/disadvantages structure, but it wasn't hard to see once she envisioned the opening scene.

At times, disorganization works. For instance, in the first paragraph of "Weekend Parents," we are led to see a chaotic scene—and later to appreciate the chaos. The fourth paragraph seems to have no typical organization, but it isn't hard to tell that it is bounded by "things that can happen between parent and child during the week or at night." This is a special organizing principle for this subject, an application of the "time" principle. The fourth paragraph is a collection of situations from which the weekend parent is barred because of seeing the children only on one afternoon a weekend.

In short, organizing principles grow out of your work with your topic. Nevertheless, when you get stuck in planning or revising—or even if you get "finished" but you're not satisfied with the content of your writing—turn to Figure 1-8 and run down the list of questions. If you're still open to your writing (not fiercely determined to stop), something should come to mind that you can use.

EXERCISE 9. Detecting Organizing Principles in a Sample Essay

The following essay is compassionate, written from the heart. But it is still organized at each level. Do the following to find the essay's organizing principles.

1. Write a summary of the essay in about 200 words.
2. List the problems associated with cancer that are discussed in the essay.
3. List the nurse's activities in caring for terminal cancer patients, according to the essay.
4. State which of the common organizing principles in Figure 1-8 seems to dominate this essay; explain how you can tell (in about 100 words or less).
5. List five other organizing principles that you see working in the essay at some level. For each principle you see, note the number of the paragraph (second, sixth, etc.), or copy the sentence, and explain how it works (such as by pointing out which words signal the organization).

THE TERMINAL CANCER PATIENT

As a nurse on a medical floor, I have contact with many terminal patients and their families. The majority of the terminal patients on our floor have some type of cancer. Working with the terminal cancer patient is difficult emotionally for the nurses. It requires a lot of compassion, support, and measures of care to provide the greatest amount of comfort possible as the cancer progresses. Caring for the terminal patient is rewarding because of your knowing you are doing the best you can do for them and their knowledge that you care.

Whether the cancer has just been diagnosed or it has progressed to the point where it is destroying the body's vital functions, there are many problems to be faced by the patients, their families, and the nurses.

Depression is probably the most difficult problem to deal with. The patients, as well as family members, have to be given much moral support and encouragement. It is important for members of the nursing staff to sit with patients and family members and listen to their feelings and fears.

Automatically, when patients are told they have cancer which is malignant or has spread from one area of the body to another, they know that it means eventually they will die—in most cases before they are mentally ready to die. The patients have to decide whether or not they will accept treatment such as chemotherapy or cobalt therapy, not knowing if it will arrest the disease. Both intravenous therapy and radiation therapy are expensive and uncomfortable for patients. With or without treatments, cancer patients will experience other physical problems to add to their depression. Weakness, weight loss, and decrease in appetite are problems which never cease until the long, difficult wait is over.

Recently, we had a lady on our floor who was a newly diagnosed cancer patient. The type of cancer she had was in a progressive stage and untreatable. The most difficult problem she had to deal with was, "Who will take care of my children when I die?" She is divorced and has two young children. Her sister was taking care of them while she was hospitalized; however, the sister informed her that she was unable to "handle them." The lady does not want her ex-husband to take care of the children because he molested the youngest child some years ago. Many of the younger, divorced or widowed cancer patients who are terminal have problems such as this one to worry about. Not all family problems are this complicated; nevertheless, family responsibilities are still there for many terminal patients.

The cancer patients also have other problems to face as their health deteriorates. For patients who have progressive cancer of the lung, it becomes more and more difficult to breathe. It is very frightening for people not to be able to breathe as easily as they used to. Some patients with this problem are afraid to go to sleep, not knowing whether their "shortness of breath" will prevent them from seeing another day.

Other systems become affected as the cancer spreads. The urinary, circulatory, nervous, and digestive systems at some point begin to malfunction.

The final problem the terminal cancer patient faces is the acceptance of death. Whether the patient has three months or three years left, it is difficult to accept death. Most of the terminal cancer patients I have worked with accept death because they are tired of fighting, tired of pain and just want relief. I don't believe they ever really accept death; I think it is just the only way out of misery for them.

There are a few patients that I have met who, I find, have an unbelievable amount of faith in God and let Him steer the course of the remainder of their life. When these patients feel that it is close to the time for God to take them away, it is then that they say, "I am ready to die; I have fulfilled my purpose and time on earth."

(Jean Ellis, student)

4. REVISING FOR STYLE: READABILITY OR GRACE?

Readers expect enough information from a writing so that, at the very least, they won't be totally confused by it. Most readers like to have enough information so that they can read with understanding, perhaps enough to read with ease. Readers also expect to find some organizing principle in a writing, and the quicker they can find it, the better. The earlier portions of this chapter concerned ways to get a topic, to search for information and clarify your own ideas on a topic, and to organize your presentation.

Readers also expect a writing to be clearly written, at the very least, and many readers expect a writing to show grace or style. One thing is true: Some readers like it simple, and some don't. Figure 1-10 shows two passages from professionally written articles. The two are obviously written in different styles, and yet both meet the reader's expectations—in what they discuss and in how they are worded—though in very different ways.

In this section we will look very closely at style. There's

Figure 1-10. Two Professional Passages in Two Different Styles

From "The Sun Turns Savage" by Dennis Overbye

Slouched amid a clutter of coffee mugs and enveloped by a haze of cigarette smoke, a dozen or so casually dressed men and women confer twice each day in a small room at the Goddard Space Flight Center outside Washington, D.C., to ponder and outwit the sun. They seem more studious than boisterous and, despite their devotion to the sun, some of them look rather pale. Their windowless sanctum is lined with maps and photographs wired daily from the world's solar observatories; their only view of the sun is televised. That unblinking image, transmitted from a small telescope on the grounds of the center, stares from every corner in the maze of makeshift offices housing the human beings and computers that are the ground-based, thinking half of the Solar Maximum Mission. Meanwhile, 356 miles above the earth, a satellite, affectionately called Solar Max, with electronic eyes squinting in obedience to commands from Goddard, is scanning the sun's surface for seeds of violence.

Every 11 years or so, when the number of dark sunspots on its surface reaches a peak—the so-called solar maximum—the sun gets a little more savage than usual. Huge storms erupt suddenly in its tenuous upper reaches, lashing the solar system with X-rays and spewing billions of tons of sun into

From "Can Technology Prevent Another Ice Age?" by Isaac Asimov

Suppose an ice age comes. How bad a disaster might it be? After all, we've had a million years of glaciers coming and going and here we all are. That's true and, if we stop to think of it, the glaciers creep slowly. They take thousands of years to advance and even at the stage of maximum glaciation, it is surprising how little change important parts of the world undergo.

Right now, some 25 million cubic kilometers (6 million cubic miles) of ice are resting on the various land surfaces of the world, chiefly Antarctica and Greenland. At the height of glaciation there was a monster ice sheet covering the northern half of North America and smaller ice sheets in Scandinavia and northern Siberia. At that time, a total of perhaps 75 million cubic kilometers (18 million cubic miles) of ice rested on land. This means that at the height of glaciation, 50 million cubic kilometers (12 million cubic miles) of water that is now in the ocean was then on land.

The water subtracted from the ocean to feed the glaciers was, even at the height of glaciation, only 4 percent of the total. This means that even at the height of glaciation, 96 percent of the ocean was right where it is now.

From the standpoint of sheer room, therefore, sea life would feel no particular constriction of the environment. To be sure, the ocean

space. This debris can spiral out from the sun and smack the earth with a tidal wave of radiation, electric and magnetic fields, and high-energy particles, causing radio blackouts, electrical damage, and beautiful displays of northern lights, or aurora borealis.

water would, on the average, be somewhat colder than it is now—but what of that? Cold water dissolves more oxygen than warm water does, and sea life depends on oxygen as much as we do. That is why the polar waters are far richer in life than the tropic waters and why the polar waters can support giant mammals that live on sea animals—such as great whales, polar bears, elephant seals, and so on.

If, during an ice age, the ocean water is colder than it is now, that would actually encourage life. It might be *now* that sea life feels the pinch, not then.

nothing mysterious to writing with style, but the particular style you aim for depends on what you judge to be your readers' preferences. You will find that your ability to master style is a measure of your ability as a writer; varying your style to suit your readers is difficult, and is one reason why good writing requires practice.

4a. Common Sentence Structures

There are two common ways to classify sentences—by structure and by "shape." The structure of a sentence is determined by the number of subject–verb pairings it contains. A *simple sentence* contains just one subject–verb pairing:

SIMPLE SENTENCE: Storms erupt.

This sentence is about "storms"; "storms" is the *subject*. The verb that is paired with that subject tells us what storms do, according to the writer. They "erupt"; "erupt" is the *verb*. These two essential parts work as a pair to make a sentence. No matter how many other words are added to this base, as long as there is no other subject–verb pair, the sentence is structurally "simple."

SIMPLE SENTENCE: Huge storms erupt suddenly in its [the sun's] tenuous upper reachers, lashing the solar system with X-rays and spewing billions of tons of sun into space.

This sentence is still about storms and what storms do—that is, they erupt. Do "lashing" and "spewing" have a subject partner the way "erupt" does? No. So they aren't verbs, they're something else very important.

Why worry about such definitions? First, having clear terms, such as "simple," will help us to discuss the sample writings. Second, the sentence structures in the samples contain several "tricks of the trade" that you can learn to use with surprisingly little practice. The ability to write with style is one of the main factors that determine the quality (and grade) of a writing.

A *compound sentence* is a sentence that consists of two simple sentences joined in a special way. When a writer sees that two consecutive sentences are closely related in meaning, the writer may link them together. The joining is done with a semicolon or a coordinating conjunction. (See "Conjunctions" for more details.) That is, only one of the following elements can join two sentences:

**, and , but , for , nor , or
, so , yet ;**

Here is a sample framework for a compound sentence from the Asimov passage in Figure 1-10:

COMPOUND SENTENCE: We have had years, and we are.

Of course, this framework doesn't make much "sense" as a sentence, in the same way that a foundation doesn't "make sense" as a house. But in the framework above, you can see two "simple" sentences: "We have had years," and "We are." You can also see the junction between these two: ", and." (Although many magazine editors do not require a comma with conjunctions like *and*, most teachers prefer this extra marker for joining two sentences.) Here's the complete sentence:

COMPOUND SENTENCE: After all, we've had a million years of glaciers coming and going and here we all are.

Two or more subject–verb pairs in a sentence form *clauses*. Clauses that can stand alone as separate or independent sentences are called *independent clauses*. So compound sentences contain at least two independent clauses.

By contrast, a *dependent clause* could not stand alone as a separate sentence. Clauses like "if we stop to think of it" or "where it is now" or "than it is now" cannot stand alone because each is designed to be attached to (or "depend on") a sentence. The words *if, that*, and *than*, as well as many other "subordinating conjunctions," are signals of dependent clauses. Like a car pulled by a tow truck, a dependent clause must go with an independent clause.

A *complex sentence*, then, is one that has at least one dependent clause, and a single independent clause.

COMPLEX SENTENCE: Water dissolves oxygen than water does.

Again, without other words, this sentence framework makes no sense. But it shows the essential structure of a "complex" sentence—an independent clause that acts as a base for the sentence, "Water dissolves oxygen." This base clause is followed by "than," a signal for the dependent clause, "than water does." Here's the sentence from Asimov's passage:

COMPLEX SENTENCE: Cold water dissolves more oxygen than warm water does. . . .

Why does this sentence end with four periods? (Actually, there's one period plus the form of punctuation known as an "ellipsis.") Some words are left out. Writers (and speakers) easily use more than one structure in a sentence. The ellipsis signals that something has been omitted, in this case, another independent clause, "sea life depends on oxygen" and a clause that depends on it, "as much as we do." So Asimov's sentence is both *compound* (it has two independent clauses) and *complex* (it has at least one dependent clause). So the whole sentence makes a *compound–complex sentence*.

COMPOUND–COMPLEX   Cold water dissolves more oxygen than warm
SENTENCE: water does, and sea life depends on oxygen as
                    much as we do.

4b. Sentence Structures in the Sample Passages

Which of the passages in Figure 1-10 is easier to read? You will probably pick the Asimov passage because it comes right to the point, has generally understandable words, and has shorter sentences. The Overbye passage opens with the human interest picture of the scientists at work, uses some longer words (and more unusual words), and has much longer sentences. Figure 1-11 compares the two passages for style. The Asimov passage has about the same number of syllables, even though the Overbye passage is only about three-fourths as long. The Overbye passage has longer words. It also has more words per sentence. But the surprising fact is in how the sentence structures differ. Half of the Overbye sentences are "simple" in structure, based on a single subject–verb pairing. Fewer than one-third of the Asimov sentences are "simple." In short, "simple" structure does not guarantee simple reading.

To understand the secret to the two writing styles in the sample passages, we need to consider the sentence types in another way.

Figure 1-11.   A Stylistic Scoreboard for the Sample Passages in Figure 1-10.

STYLISTIC FEATURE	OVERBYE	ASIMOV	
1. Number of words in passage	258	347	
2. Number of words longer than one syllable	100	100	(approximately)
3. Number of sentences in passage	8	17	
4. Number of words per sentence	32	20	
5. Numbers of sentences by structure			
a. simple	4	5	
b. compound	1	1	
c. complex	2	7	
d. compound–complex	1	4	
total	8	17	

4c. Common Sentence Shapes

Where in a sentence does the subject–verb pairing occur? When the main subject–verb pairing is toward the end (the period) of the sentence, the sentence is "periodic."

PERIODIC SENTENCE: Every 11 years or so, when the number of dark sunspots on its surface reaches a peak—the so-called solar maximum—the sun gets a little more savage than usual.

In this sample from the Overbye passage of Figure 1-10, the main subject–verb pair, "sun gets," comes after a lengthy introduction. Even if the subject comes early in the sentence but the verb is postponed, the sentence still seems to be hanging, and is still periodic.

PERIODIC SENTENCE: Meanwhile, 356 miles above the earth, a satellite affectionately called Solar Max, with electronic eyes squinting in obedience to commands from Goddard, is scanning the sun's surface for the seeds of violence.

The separation between the subject, "satellite," and the verb, "is scanning," creates a hanging sensation in the sentence. Thus, periodic sentences create tension or suspense, and carry the reader along. They also demand more of a reader's memory and so are more difficult to read.

Suppose the main subject–verb pair comes early in a sentence and the rest of the sentence trails out behind it. This pattern, often called "loose," dominates most writing.

LOOSE SENTENCE: Suppose an ice age comes.

In this case, you, the reader, is the subject, or person who will "suppose." The main subject–verb pairing could not occur any earlier than this. But subject–verb pairs can be interrupted, and still completed, before the sentence is half over.

LOOSE SENTENCE: The water subtracted from the ocean to feed the glaciers was, even at the height of glaciation, only 4 percent of the total.

The extreme of this pattern of sentence is to pile detail after detail, and phrase after phrase, following the main subject and verb. Since the phrases pile up, or accumulate, this type of sentence is often called "cumulative."

CUMULATIVE SENTENCE: This debris can spiral out from the sun and smack the earth with a tidal wave of radiation, electric and magnetic fields, and high-energy particles, causing radio blackouts, electrical damage, and beautiful displays of Northern lights, or aurora borealis.

In this sentence, the subject, "debris," and the compound verbs, "spiral" and "smack," are followed by two lists—the contents of solar debris and their effects on earth.

These sentence patterns—periodic, loose, and cumulative—apply to all clauses. The following sentence is an example of a compound sentence containing two "loose" clauses:

LOOSE CLAUSES: They seem more studious than boisterous and, despite their devotion to the sun, some of them look rather pale.

In the first clause, "they seem" is not followed by a pile of phrases; also, "some look," is the basis for a quite ordinary clause. The loose pattern, then, is the ordinary pattern. It is neither highly suspenseful, nor does it trail off into mounds of detail.

So the subject–verb pairing determines the shape of the sentence. But so does one other factor: symmetry. Does the sentence have structures that repeat, or echo each other? Such sentences are called "parallel."

PARALLEL SENTENCE: That is why the polar waters are
        far richer in life
    than the tropic waters
    and
why the polar waters can
        support giant mammals
    that live on sea animals—
        such as great whales,
          polar bears,
        elephant seals,
    and so on.

This sample sentence is spread out so that you can see the parallel elements. The two "why" clauses present a contrast—the polar with the tropic waters. The concluding list shows parallels of animals within the category "giant mammals."

Throughout history, famous orators have used the parallel style to make their sentences more memorable; Cicero, Abraham Lincoln, John F. Kennedy, and Martin Luther King, Jr., were masters of the parallel structure, and not just within sentences, but between sentences and from one paragraph to the next. You may have noticed that this sort of repetition is used very effectively in Figure 1-9. The third paragraph lists freedoms of the weekend parent; the fourth paragraph lists things denied the weekend parent. Yet in both paragraphs "he does not . . ." is repeated as the dominant sentence pattern.

4d. Sentence Shapes in the Sample Passages

You may have noticed that the samples of periodic and cumulative sentences were taken from the Overbye passage. You also may have noticed that the samples of loose and parallel sentences came from the Asimov passage. In fact, Asimov's sentences are generally so short that they could not clearly be considered anything but loose sentences (the parallel sentence is the longest in his passage). Although the parallel sentence strings out from the subject–verb pair, these details are not merely piled on, or accumulated. In short, most of Asimov's sentences are designed for ease of reading; most of the Overbye sentences pile detail on detail, either before or after the main subject and verb. Many of Overbye's details are compressed into a small space; each sentence is packed.

4e. A Summary on Style: Readability or Compression?

For whom is Asimov writing? His passage was excerpted from *Science Digest*. Like *Reader's Digest*, this magazine is aimed at readers who want clear writing—laypeople who want to read about scientific topics. To appeal to these readers, Asimov uses short sentences, short words, and plenty of subordinators. If he uses introductory elements at all, they are generally short transitions, such as "right now" or "to be sure." If he writes a long sentence, he uses parallel structure to help make it easier to read. Isaac Asimov has written in a highly readable style suitable for a general audience.

For whom is Dennis Overbye writing? His passage is excerpted from *Discover*, a glossy science news magazine that contains reports on the frontiers of science for the educated layperson. Readers of this magazine expect to use their imaginations while reading the articles, not just as a result of reading the articles. They will usually have patience when a writer opens by setting the scene as Overbye does. They also generally do not expect a simple vocabulary. Overbye's sentences, then, accumulate details for a scene, add details in passing, and pile up details at the end. To pack his sentences with details, Overbye relies on *-ing* and *-ed* words, rather than the *that* and *than* subordinators that Asimov uses to include details. Although Asimov relies on numbers more than Overbye does, both writers depict scenes and describe events. Yet Overbye's style tends to paint pictures, whereas Asimov's gives facts and draws conclusions from those facts. In short, Overbye's style compresses much detail into sentences designed to make sensory appeals to his readers' imaginations.

Both styles are suitable for the readers each author intends to reach. And both the compressed style and the very readable style suit the topics the writers take on. Each style fits the approach taken by each writer—picturesque description or facts and figures with inferences. As a writer, you need to have both styles at your command, as well as a range of styles in between the very compressed and the very readable.

4f. The Uses of Style

Suppose you were to take an essay exam in, let's say, history or sociology. What sort of style would earn you the highest grade? You're writing for the teacher who led you to the information in the first place, so you don't need to simplify. You have a short time in which to show what you know, so you have to pack your essay with as much information as you can. A very compressed but factual style would suit you best—generally long sentences, probably with *-ing* and *-ed* words more than subordinators (or at least more complex sentences than short *and* simple sentences), and as many of the subject's technical and factual terms as you can use. How can you achieve such a style? One way is by practicing on review notes and writing practice essays for study.

Now suppose you have an English paper to do. You're writing to an educated readership in a class where style and imagination are high priorities. You may have a length requirement, such as 500 or 1,000 words. Which style suits your task? You can answer the question for yourself: Suppose two students write on the same topic, even using the same subject–verb pairs in their papers. But one emphasizes readability and shortness, whereas the other stresses imaginative and picturesque details. When style (in the sense of "grace" or "class" or "sophistication") matters, which student will get the higher grade? Probably not the student whose style stresses "just the facts."

Finally, suppose you have a business letter or report to write. Which style would serve better? The style that makes things quick and easy for the reader saves time and money. Here, clarity and simplicity are more important than compression and accumulation of detail.

In much academic writing, it is to your advantage to have a compressed style at your disposal so that you can get the edge on time or length limits and, most importantly, write for an educated readership. At other times, factual, readable, clear writing serves best, particularly when you write in a set form, as you must when doing, say, lab reports or business letters.

It takes experience to develop a range of styles from the very readable to the very condensed and even graceful. The exercises that follow show you several ways to work on style. You can learn quite a lot by reading a variety of styles and by trying to use varied sentence structures and lengths when you write.

For more information on the technicalities of the styles we have examined, look at "Conjunctions," "Verbals," and "Relationships" in the alphabetical listings.

EXERCISE 10. SENTENCE COMBINING

The passages below are from student writings that have been adapted by rewriting in very short sentences. Each passage demonstrates a different organizing principle or a different type of writing. As you work through these passages, you will be able to practice a variety of organization techniques as well as a range of styles.

You will quickly see that there are many ways to rewrite. For instance, the following passage could be rewritten many ways without altering the meaning. Correctness is not the issue; style is.

The fog felt strange. The fog was in the morning. The morning was early. The fog made me feel conspicuous. I stood on the pier. There seemed to be millions. The millions were people. The millions were well wishers. I felt anticipation. I felt overwhelmed.

Revision 1: The fog felt strange in the early morning; it made me feel conspicuous as I stood on the pier among well wishers. There seemed to be millions of them. I felt overwhelming anticipation.

Revision 2: As I stood on the pier in the early morning fog, I felt conspicuous, even though there seemed to be millions of people, all well wishers. Anticipation overwhelmed me.

Revision 3: Standing on the pier among millions of well wishing people (or so it seemed), I felt strangely conspicuous because of my overwhelming anticipation despite the early morning fog.

Revision 4: The early morning fog made me feel strange and conspicuous. As I stood on the pier among what seemed to me to be millions of people—well wishers—my feeling of anticipation was overwhelming.

Still other revisions are possible, of course. But the variety present in just these four revisions shows many possibilities. Words are added, repetition is avoided, words change form. Originally, the student wrote what is labeled Revision 4 here. Her sentences use the conjunctions *and* and *as*, the prepositions *among* and *of*, as well as the adjectives *early* and *morning*, before the subject, *fog*. Revision 3 shows, however, that the passage can be written as one sentence without too much strain. At first you may feel that sentences are "run ons" if they extend beyond two lines, but you have seen long "simple" sentences in this section on style. Length alone does not determine correctness. Besides, these are practice writings. Now is the time to take some risks to let your style expand so you can write a wider range of styles.

For each of the passages that follow, rewrite the passage so that it sounds better. Then rewrite the passage in as few sentences as possible to practice a more compressed style.

Passage A: From "Country Dawn" (space: far to nearer)

The night was black. The black is over. Morning arrives again. There is mist. The sun peeps through. The sun displays itself. The display is bright. The display is orange. The display is red. The display is yellow. The display fills the sky with color. The display changes darkness to day. Mountains are in the background. The mountains rise. The mountains are luminous. The mountains are rugged. The mountains are wondrous. The mountains are quiet. The mountains reach. The reaching is for the clouds.

Passage B: From "Structure of a Conventional Coal Mine" (space and process)(opening comparison: conventional and shaft mines)

A process is the same. The process is mining. The process is for mines. The mines are conventional. Another process is the same. The process is supporting. The supporting is of a roof. The sameness is for conventional mines. The sameness is for shaft mines. Each has a section. A section has six cuts. The cuts are in the seam. The cuts are wide. The width is 90 feet. The cuts are 150 feet apart. Cross-cuts are made. The cross-cuts connect the six seam cuts. The connecting cuts are made every 150 feet. The cuts leave blocks. The blocks are 150-foot squares. The blocks are called *pillars*. Pillars support the roof. Timbers support the roof. Roof bolts support the roof.

Passage C: From "Montana Bearhunt" (time and space)

There was a path. The path was made by animals. The path was south of camp. I started down. I walked. The walk was less than a hundred yards. I saw tracks. The tracks were made by a grizzly. The tracks were in the snow. The tracks were big. I had rarely seen bigger tracks. The tracks were fresh. I saw this. My heart broke into a run. I felt sick. I felt sweaty. Something was inside. It said go on. It said follow the tracks. The tracks led down the mountain. The tracks led into the forest.

My senses were turned up. My senses were at 150 percent. I stalked deeper. I stalked into the forest. The forest was like a jungle. The woods are large. The woods are dark. A calmness filled the forest. The calmness was strange. Everything got very still. Everything got very quiet. An intruder was somewhere. An intruder somehow managed. An intruder penetrated the forest. Everything knew. Everything was around me. The intruder was capable of destruction. The destruction would be great.

Passage D: From "Anatomy of a Phone Call" (process and space)

You speak into the handset. Your voice makes waves. The waves are sound. The *transmitter* changes the waves. The change is to other waves. These waves are electrical.

The transmitter has two parts. The *diaphragm* is small. It is thin. It is metal. It is a sheet. It covers a cup. The cup is small. The cup holds granules. The granules are carbon. The cup is the *carbon chamber*.

Waves strike the diaphragm. The waves are sound. The waves are from your voice. The granules are pressed. The pressing is together. The strength varies. The strength is in the current. The current is electrical. The current is from the transmitter. The waves change. The waves are sound.

Passage E: From "Demand Deposit Account" (definition)

"DDA" stands for Demand Deposit Account. It is the term. The term is official. The term is in banking. The term is for an account. The account is regular. The account is checking. The term means something. The funds are on deposit. The funds are available. The funds are on demand. Here's an example. The account is presented with a check. The check is for $50. The account must yield. The yielding is of that amount. At least $50 is available. At least $50 is in the account.

Passage F: From "Advertising Counts" (process: "how-to")

The garage sale will not be a success. The garage sale is the best ever. It is not advertised. The advertising is not proper. Be sure of something. Start advertising. The advertising is yours. The start is early. It is before the day. The day is planned. The day is of the sale. The sale is yours. One week is in advance. Two weeks are in advance. The advance should be sufficient. Your start is best. Your start is posting notices. The notices are free. Notices can be placed. The placing is on boards. The boards are for bulletins. Notices can be placed. The placing is on telephone poles. The notices can be placed. The placing is on light poles. You post notices. The posting is in these places. You check ordinances. The ordinances are local. The checking is for restrictions.

Passage G: From "Knowing a Little Can Save a Lot of Pain" (classification and examples)

The supervisor must explain something. The process is important. The process is labeling. The labeling is for containers. The supervisor must explain something. Each label stands for something. Here's an example. A label indicates something. The label says "flammable." The label is on a product. The product has a point. The point is a "flash point." The flash point is under 100°F. The product will ignite. The ignition will be easy.

A product has a label. The label says "corrosive." A corrosive is soda. The soda is liquid. The soda is caustic. The soda is used in plants. The plants are for treatment. The treatment is of water. A corrosive will cause pain. A corrosive will cause burns. The burns will be serious. The burns will be to skin. The burns will be to eyes.

A product has a label. The label says "oxidizer." An oxidizer is peroxide. The peroxide is with hydrogen. The peroxide is used in plants. The plants are for treatment. The treatment is of sewage. An oxidizer will burn. The burning is of skin. The burning is of eyes. The burning is with pain. The pain is little. The employee realizes something. The burn has occurred.

Passage H: From "The Edge of Irrelevance" (contrast)

A writer writes a script. The script is for a soap opera. The writer has an objective. The objective seems to be intermixing. The intermixing is of lives. The lives are of characters. The intermixing is as much as possible. Soap operas are a conglomeration. The conglomeration is of occurrences. The occurrences are irrelevant. There is no "moral." The moral is "to the story." A soap opera may be confusing. A soap opera may be unrealistic. These do not matter. There is a number. The number is massive. The number is of people. The people thrive. The thriving is on lives. The lives are of people. The people are fictitious.

Passage I: From "The Pressure to Poison Ourselves" (causes)

Why would one eat candy? One is told something. There is arsenic. The arsenic is in the candy. Smokers can't disbelieve. The disbelieving is of facts. The facts are shoved. The shoving is into faces. The faces are theirs. The shoving is at every turn. A smoker cannot quit perhaps. The not quitting is not because of addiction. The addiction is lifelong. The not quitting is because of something else. One person encourages the smoker. The encouragement is to quit. Ten faces reassure the smoker. The faces are smiling. The reassurance is about smoking. Smoking is dangerous. The danger is a bit. The bit is teeny. (An average is spent. The average is two inches. The spending is in space. The space is in ads. The ads are in magazines. The spending is on the warning.) Smoking is sexy. Smoking is wholesome. Smoking is romantic. Smoking is sophisticated. It's magic. A man becomes more manly. A woman becomes more independent. Men have the right. Women have the right. The having is equal. The right is to smoke. Women have the right. The right is now. The right is to contract cancer. The cancer is of the lung. The right is to die. The dying is from the cancer.

EXERCISE 11. Passage A and Passage B

Find a magazine article that you think is well written. Copy about five or six inches from one column in your own handwriting. Write a passage of about equal length (250 to 350 words) on another sheet. You may use a passage that you've already done, but it should not be easily recognized as yours. Label one passage "Passage A" and the other "Passage B." Give both to at least one other person and ask them to guess which one is yours and which is professional. (To make this a challenging comparison, you may wish to write your passage on the same subject as the magazine passage and even in a similar style.) When your readers explain their guesses, try to get them to give reasons other than "I saw you writing this in the library" or "I remember that incident—were you there, too?"

Look at the passages yourself. Summarize the differences between your style and the style you admired.

EXERCISE 12. Questions on Readability, Length, and Purpose

Use the passages from Exercise 11 to make the following specific comparisons.
1. How many words are in each passage?
2. How many sentences are in each passage?
3. What is the average number of words per sentence?
4. What organizing principle seems to dominate each passage? (your first impression or your best guess) How can you tell?
5. Which passage has more detail?
6. Which passage is easier to read?
7. Find the longest sentence in each passage. What makes it long? Is there a list, one or more semicolons, a quotation?
8. Find the shortest sentence in each passage. Does it occur in a place of emphasis, such as first or last in a paragraph? Does it perform an important function—such as summarize, paint a striking picture, make a joke, state a prediction, or some other important function? (Take your best guess—but see how it relates to the main idea of the whole article or of the specific paragraph.)
9. Which sentence do you consider to be the best written sentence of each passage? What makes it the best? Does it use, for example, a parallel, periodic, or cumulative structure, or is it sudden and blunt? Does it present the best information or does it paint the best picture?
10. Choose what you think is the easiest or simplest sentence to read in each passage. Try to tell why it is so readable.

Summarize your findings in a brief report; quote sentences to demonstrate your judgments and the reasoning behind them, especially for items 7, 8, 9, and 10.

EXERCISE 13. Sentence Imitation

Use the sentences you chose for items 7, 8, 9, and 10 in Exercise 12. Write down each one—certainly use the four magazine sentences, but feel free to use your own four as well. Leave enough space for two more sentences under each one you copy. For each copied sentence, do the following:

First, read the sentence several times to get the "feel" of how it is structured.

Second, write a sentence *on another subject* that follows this structure as closely as possible.

Third, without looking at either of the first two sentences you've got— the copied sentence and the imitation—write a new sentence on any subject that follows the original structure as closely as possible. (Don't concentrate on looking for the "right" pattern; just let the original sentence influence how you write this last, unaided sentence.)

EXERCISE 14. Professional and Popular Styles in Your Field

Find a journal in your major field (or a field you're interested in). Select an article that seems well written and photocopy the first page of the article. Using the *Readers' Guide*, find a popular article on the same topic as the journal article you selected. Photocopy the first two pages of the magazine article.

Using passages of at least 300 words (at least five inches of print in a column), follow the directions for Exercise 12. (You do not need to copy the passages by hand.) (How can you tell if a periodical is a journal? Look to see if there are "Notes" or "References" at the end of the articles; journal articles, of course, are written to professionals in a field. Articles in journals often begin with an "abstract," or summary, especially if they report original research or experiments. For a run-down on reading entries in the *Readers' Guide*, see Figure 2-2.)

EXERCISE 15. Sentence Collecting

Over the next month, find at least twenty sentences from your readings that are written exceptionally well (or just sentences with interesting structures). Then do the following:

First, copy each sentence as it appears in your reading. Note who wrote it and where you found it.

Second, write the sentence in a way that reveals its structure.

EXAMPLE:
"Pain physiologists have long debated whether specific pain sensors exist or whether pain results from the excessive stimulation of sensory cells that respond to touch, temperature, and pressure." (Jonathan B. Tucker, "An End to Pain," *Omni*, February 1979, p. 87.)

Clause Structure Pain physiologists have long debated
whether specific pain sensors exist
or
whether pain results from the excessive
stimulation of sensory cells
that respond to touch, temperature, and
pressure.

EXAMPLE:

"Long the butt of ridicule for their stolid ways and the ready object of oppression because of their desperate poverty and defensive clannishness, refugees from Eastern Europe's despotism by and large proved to be American workingmen of high conscientiousness, notable for loyalty, bravery, and endurance." (Richard Kluger, "An Act of Homage," rev. of *The Guns of Lattimer*, by Michael Novak, *New York Times Book Review*, 28 Jan. 1979, p. 12.)

Phrase Structure Long the butt of ridicule for their stolid ways
and
the ready object of oppression
because of their desperate poverty
and
defensive clannishness,
refugees from Eastern Europe's despotism by and
large proved to be American workingmen of high conscientiousness,
notable for loyalty,
bravery,
and
endurance.

Chart the structure as you see it—don't worry about having the "right" answers. Concentrate on what you can learn about how the sentences move.

For additional practice, use the directions for Exercise 13 for each sentence.

2 | research writing

A reporter follows up a lead for a story. Two parents-to-be read books on having babies and on child development. A mother asks neighbors and friends what they are giving their children for Christmas in order to get ideas about safe toys and durable clothing. A college freshman talks to a few sophomores to find out what an instructor is like. All these people are doing research— trying to find information to guide their judgment.

College research writing assignments give you an opportunity to become informed on a significant topic. Research writing displays your informed judgment.

College research writing assignments also train you in sharing ideas with others. This ability can mean many things. To share information formally, you need to know how to find it, how to judge its value and accuracy, and how to report it in ways that readers expect. Sensible judgments take time to develop, and typical research procedures take practice. So give yourself time to do your research project and be patient with yourself.

This chapter suggests the kinds of topics you might research. It also shows ways of doing and reporting research. Reading it carefully is your first research task—you need information before you can judge your own research process.

5. DECIDING ON A TOPIC

College research writing assignments require three things: judgment, focus, and slant.

5a. Judgment

Remember, your major task is to present your informed judgment about a topic. This requirement eliminates how-to topics, such as how to build a terrarium, how to use scuba diving gear, how to find more income-tax deductions, and other advice topics. What you must do is to identify which aspects of your topic call for judgments. For instance, someone who knows how to build a terrarium probably believes that plants are essential to a healthy indoor environment. It would take research to find out what indoor plants do for people physiologically and psychologically. A beginning research question might be: Do plants have enough physical and mental benefits to make them part of indoor environments such as schools and offices?

Someone who knows how to use scuba diving gear can conduct a similar search for a researchable topic that takes their interest and experience into account. People probably don't need to be convinced that scuba diving is fun and can be relatively inexpensive. But people who spend time in or on the water probably believe that undamaged water areas are necessary for our survival. It would take research to find out, for example, how much damage has been done recently to fresh-water environments. A possible research question might be: Is the space program helping to protect America's fresh water environments? Another research question might be: Should stricter laws or tougher enforcement methods be set up to protect our fresh-water environments?

Not everyone has such hobbies as indoor gardening or scuba diving. But you're probably interested in something that can lead to a researchable topic. You may want to find out if a straight 10 percent income tax would be better than the current regressive system of federal income taxation. You may want to argue that local agencies can do more to help victims of rape, robbery, or bunko schemes. You may want to advocate cheaper medical care, an end to nuclear arms, or more federal aid to education. Only you know your interests and beliefs, but you need a topic that you can live with for several weeks. You need a topic that you know something about, but want to find out more about. Your hobbies, your major, your interests and beliefs all hold research potential.

5b. Focus

Once you decide on a potential topic or two, you need to select a portion of the topic that you can report on in a few pages. Of course, you may not find a focus until you do some research (see the next section on doing research). But you need to look for a portion of your general topic area. For instance, you may feel that the current tax structure takes too much out of the ordinary worker's paycheck. But advocating reform of the federal, state, and local tax structures is way too large a topic for one research project. In fact, focusing on any one of the three levels may be too much. A student who wants to advocate a straight 10 percent federal tax for all incomes still has a huge task. Informed estimates on how much federal revenue would be gained or lost would be hard to find, and it would certainly take judgment to make sense of the data that sources would present. The ramifications of such a plan would be complex, and would take some research; for example, who would be the likely exceptions to such a plan, maybe people on welfare? Answering these questions would take judgment. One possible focus might be something like this: What groups would be reasonable exceptions to an across-the-board 10 percent federal income tax?

There are some topics that concern almost everyone. Topics like abortion, mercy-killing, child abuse, nuclear war, and divorce touch people deeply. They deal with issues central to human life; they deal with survival. Such topics can make fine research projects, but they require a narrow focus. For instance, divorce is a huge topic. Even focusing on children of divorced parents could fill a book. In a few pages, you might be able to provide a sensible informed judgment on a subtopic such as one of the following:

What can a classroom teacher do to ease the pain of children whose parents are getting divorced?

Should marriage and family courses be required for all high-school students?

Should marriage counseling be required before parents of small children can get divorced?

Such topics will not simply occur to you instantly. You may be a few weeks into your research before you find a focus on your topic. You may consult several articles, a few books, some newspaper articles; and you may talk to quite a few people before one or more possible subtopics emerges from your research. Your final research question and your final thesis statement may very well depend on what you find out from your sources. Remember, one reason for doing research is to form a sensible, educated opinion based on information.

5c. Slant

Slant means your approach to your readers. The research writing you do in your freshman year will train you to share research later in your academic career, so you should imagine the rest of the class as your readers. This image will help you decide how technical and persuasive to be.

Depending on your topic, you may have done some research that includes very technical information. Although your readers might be able to understand many technical terms, there's a mercy factor involved in reporting your research. If you want readers to keep reading, don't subject them to too much technical information. Of course, you have to look like you know what you're writing about. But this doesn't mean overloading your readers or being obscure.

When you pick a topic, then, you have to consider the mercy factor. You're not writing a dissertation or a professional journal article—yet. The topic you choose should have wide appeal, or at least your method of presenting your informed judgment on the topic should be easily understandable. For instance, you may want to do research on the best method for stocking a fish pond. Your answer might involve some complicated considerations of biology, chemistry, and pond ecology. To present your informed judgment in an interesting way will take quite a bit of rewriting. You'll have to have people read your drafts to see if your explanations are clear and your judgment seems sound. Some teachers may discourage you from choosing such technical topics; others may encourage them. If you do write on a technical topic, be sure you know what level of training your teacher assumes your readers have. Fair use of source material and your own purpose for writing will cause you to paraphrase your source material—that is, to report what your sources say in your own wording. But it is doubly difficult to translate technical material into understandable terms. If you decide on a technical topic, schedule plenty of time for rewriting.

Slant means considering not only how well trained on your topic your readers are but also how skeptical they might be about the stand you take. Assume that your readers do not necessarily see things your way, but that they have relatively open minds on your topic. Decide on your topic, and find a focus. But along the way, consider what your readers are apt to believe. For instance, if you advocate doubling the current military pay scale in order to keep more people in the armed forces, be ready to handle some immediate resentment from tax-minded readers. You'll need figures to show that your proposal could be cheaper than the present method of constantly training new recruits. You'll need some sort of testimony that pay is the major factor people consider in deciding whether to stay in the service.

In other words, as you focus on your topic, you'll need to figure out not just what subtopics to include but also to what depth to conduct your research, and, as you continue your research, what kind of information you will need to present. As you form your own judgment on your topic, your focus may shift or narrow. As you find out what information you can obtain, your focus may shift again. In the early stages of your research, then, be flexible—don't decide on topics too soon but don't be too ready to abandon a topic or a focus.

EXERCISE 1. Focusing Topics

The following is a list of topics followed by more focused topics. Your task is to suggest other focused topics.

EXAMPLE:
General:	Should the United States develop nuclear energy?
Focused:	How safe are nuclear reactors?
Focused:	Should the United States increase its budget for fusion development?
Focused:	Is our nuclear fuel secure?

1.
General:	Should laws against drunken driving be stricter?
Focused:	Should the drinking age be raised to 21?
Focused:	
Focused:	

2. General: Should government and industry hire more handi-
                          capped persons?
    Focused: Being blind doesn't mean being incapable.
    Focused:
    Focused:

3. General: Should mercy-killing be legal?
    Focused: Should a terminal cancer patient have the right to de-
                          cide when to die?
    Focused:
    Focused:

4. General: Should the United States spend more on the space
                          program?
    Focused: Is the shuttle program paying off?
    Focused:
    Focused:

5. General: Is the family dying out?
    Focused: What is the relationship between early marriage and
                          divorce?
    Focused:
    Focused:

EXERCISE 2. Judgment

For the topics listed below, put a J in the space next to the ones that call for
a judgment. Cross out the others.

EXAMPLE:

_____J_____   Do unborn babies have a right to life?

_____   ~~What is "natural childbirth"?~~

_____   1.   Is television killing our children's imaginations?
_____   2.   How can parents effectively regulate their children's
                         television viewing?
_____   3.   Does cable TV really offer alternative programming?
_____   4.   How does television comedy get us to laugh?
_____   5.   What is the image of Black Americans on television?
_____   6.   How do you set up an effective training program for
                         improving cardiovascular fitness?
_____   7.   Should the United States develop an effective anti-
                         ballistic missile program?

_____   8. Have Americans forgotten the true meaning of patri-
                    otism?
_____   9. Alternative financing can get you your dream house.
_____   10. Drugs are infecting our preteens and teenagers.

Follow-up to Exercise 2: If you crossed out any topics, can you rewrite them in a way that calls for judgment? Which makes a more effective research problem—a question or a statement? Notice that each item requires research, but not every item fosters open-minded research.

EXERCISE 3. Slant: Technicality

Rate the following topics as "highly technical" (HT), as "general interest" (G), or as "either" (E).

EXAMPLE:

___E___   The United States should develop laser weaponry as
                soon as possible.

___HT___   The United States can develop laser weaponry by the
                end of the century.

_____   1. Diamond-cutting is becoming a lost art.
_____   2. The federal government should guarantee free med-
                   ical care to all U.S. citizens.
_____   3. Over-drainage of the water table threatens the life of
                   every American.
_____   4. Every American high-school graduate should know
                   how to "talk" to a computer.
_____   5. Playing video games sharpens the imagination.

Follow-up to Exercise 3: For each item you marked E, write a brief technical explanation and an explanation for general interest. (Is each of these topics focused well enough for a brief research report?)

EXERCISE 4. Slant: Skepticism

Rate each of the statements below as "likely" (L) or "unlikely" (U) to be accepted by your readers. Note what questions each statement raises.

EXAMPLE:

_____U_____	Women should be drafted for combat. (Should anybody be drafted for combat? Doesn't it depend on how critical the situation is? Doesn't killing a woman decrease the chance of a nation's survival more than killing a man?)
_____	1. Every American should have at least two years of college.
_____	2. Public tax dollars should not be used to support school athletic programs.
_____	3. Parents, not schools, should educate children about sex.
_____	4. Prayer should be allowed in public schools.
_____	5. Gender should not affect auto insurance rates.

Follow-up to Exercise 4: Would your answers change if you imagined your readers to be a group of teachers rather than a group of fellow students? (It's not too soon to start imagining what kind of information you would need to support statements like those above.)

EXERCISE 5. Your Tentative Topics

List three topics that you would consider researching. You may use topics mentioned in this section, but make sure you choose something that strikes your interest. For each topic, do the following:

1. State your topic in the form of a question. Make sure the question calls for a judgment.
2. List one or two possible focuses within your general topic.
3. Label your topic focuses as technical or general interest.
4. Label your topic focuses as likely or unlikely to be accepted by your readers.
5. List what kind of information you think might help present your stand on your topic focus as a sensible, informed opinion.
6. Read the next section, keeping in mind that your topic choice and topic focus probably _should_ change as you find more information on your topic.

6. USING A WORKING BIBLIOGRAPHY TO FOCUS YOUR TOPIC

A _bibliography_, as you will probably recall, is a list of sources (not just books). A _working_ bibliography lists the sources that you plan to consult as you work on your research project. Following a general search strategy like the one informally detailed on the following pages can help you get library information efficiently.

To assemble a working bibliography, you may want to do some background reading on your topic, perhaps in the encyclopedia. But one of the purposes of doing a working bibliography is to start by doing background reading and then more focused reading. And you may consult sources besides those you read. Sometimes you will talk to people who know something about your topic; you may also run across a television, radio, or film documentary on your topic, or even a computer simulation. But most often research starts in the library.

To assemble a working bibliography, you should plan to spend an hour or two in the reference room or section of the largest library convenient to you, usually the main library on campus. Your standard tools will be the card catalog for books and the periodical indexes for magazines and journals. Plan to look at as many as a hundred titles to find between twenty and thirty sources worth seeking out in your library. Remember, a working bibliography starts as a list of sources you *plan* to find.

The title of the source will tell you immediately whether to write down the source's catalog or index information. If you see a likely connection between a title and your tentative topic focus, you'll probably write it down. Expect to start learning the key words and the names of major writers on your topic as soon as you start working in the reference area.

Before we look at a detailed example of how to form a working bibliography, here are some background tips on using the standard reference room tools.

6a. Card Catalog

The card catalog is a file on the bound materials held by your library. It always lists books, but it may include periodicals and even government documents. Some catalogs are on microfiche (pronounced MY-crow-feesh), small plastic cards that you look at with the aid of a projection screen. Other card catalogs are on 3″ × 5″ cards in alphabetically arranged drawers. Catalog cards can tell you a great deal about a book, but first you will need to find the titles of works on your topic. Look in the "Subject" section of the card catalog for your topic. Be ready to think of other names for your topic; also be ready to jot down other names for your topic from "cross-reference" cards planted where you look for your topic. For instance, your library might list books on child abuse under "child abuse" or "battered children" or under some other name. (The plate on the front of the drawers lists the first few letters of topic headings that can be found in the drawer. For instance, you would look for "battered children" in a drawer that might be marked "BA–BIC.")

Once you find a few cards listing books on your topic, look for each book title and decide whether it matches with your tentative topic focus. If it does, jot down the author's name, an abbreviated title, and the set of numbers and letters in the top left corner of the card—that's your local library's stock number for that book (librarians call it the "call number" because you need it to call for, or request, a book). Most campus libraries use the Library of Congress system of stock numbers; some public libraries use the Dewey Decimal System. Each uses two, three, or even four or five lines for stock numbers, so copy the entire set of numbers. The top line in the stock number is always a clue to the general section for housing books on a topic. Each of the other lines narrows down the shelf areas to the exact inch where the book you want is housed. (In libraries with closed stacks, a library staff member will find the books for you after you fill out a "call slip" for each one.) To get the books that look promising, you need to find the chart showing your library's floor plan and the stock numbers of books (first lines) kept on each floor. You also need to know which areas are open to you and which are not. Any cards stamped REFERENCE indicate books that are probably kept in a separate run of stock numbers right in the reference room. A card stamped RESERVE indicates a book that is kept in the reserve book room and that you'll have to ask for. If a book you want is not on the shelf, double-check the stock number to make sure you're in the right place. Look near the place the book should be to see if it's just been moved slightly out of position; glance at unshelved books nearby to see if someone else might have used it recently. Check at the main or check-out desk to see if the book has been checked out, or is on reserve or in a special collection. If the book has been checked out, you can ask to be the next user of the book by putting a "hold" on the book, usually by filling in your name, telephone number, and address on a form the staff member can give you at the main desk.

Sometimes books won't be hard to find at all. If you find a lot of cards on your topic in a drawer, you have an opportunity to narrow your topic focus. Look quickly through the cards to see

Figure 2-1.   A Catalog Card and Its Standard Uses

A CARD FROM THE SUBJECT SECTION OF THE CARD CATALOG

```
                    ①                    ②
  REFERENCE    SOLAR  ENERGY—HANDBOOKS,  MANUALS,  ETC.
                         ③
  TJ  ⑤         Solar  energy  handbook  /  Jan  F.
  810           ④Kreider,  editor-in-chief,  with
  .H35            Frank  Kreith.  —  New  York:  McGraw-
                  Hill,  c1981.⑧  ⑥                    ⑦
                  ⑨1092  p.  in  various  pagings:  ill.⑩ —
               ⑪(McGraw-Hill  series  in  modern
                  structures)

               ⑫ 1.  Solar  energy—Handbooks,
               manuals,  etc.
               I.  Kreider,  Jan F.,  1942-  II.  Kreith,
               Frank.
```

1. Subject heading	5. "Call" number	9. Book's length
2. Subhead	6. City of publication	10. Book has
3. Book title	7. Publisher	illustrations
4. Editors	8. Copyright date	11. Other information
		12. Other listings of
stamp: "REFERENCE"		this book

A BIBLIOGRAPHY CARD FOR A WORKING BIBLIOGRAPHY DONE ON
3″ × 5″ CARDS

```
①Solar energy                                    ②Kreider

   ③ Jan F. Kreider, editor-in-chief, with
   Frank Kreith. Solar Energy Handbook
   N.Y.: McGraw Hill, 1981.

   ④(can't check out) big, has illustrations
   probably a standard in field - probably how to but
   also costs
        ⑤
                                            ⑥ T J
                                               810
                                              .H35
```

1. Topic heading
2. Name for alphabetizing
3. Source note information
4. Expectations of contents and other notes on book's use
5. Space for use notes after book is in hand
6. Local call number

STANDARD BIBLIOGRAPHY ENTRY FORMAT APPLIED TO THIS BOOK (MLA)

Kreider, Jan F., with Frank Kreith, eds. *Solar Energy Handbook.* New York: McGraw-Hill, 1981.

STANDARD REFERENCE LISTING FORMAT APPLIED TO THIS BOOK (APA)

Kreider, J.F., with Kreith, F. (Eds.). *Solar energy handbook.* New York: McGraw-Hill, 1981.

what subject subheadings there are and what kind of books there are. Notice what main words seem to recur in titles and which author's names keep turning up. Recurring main words in titles may suggest a topic focus to you. For a few books worth looking for, jot down the author's name, an abbreviated title, and the call number.

6b. Periodical Indexes

The alphabet is all you need to know in order to use the variety of indexes for magazines, professional and trade journals, and newspapers that your library has. Periodical indexes are prepared from a selected group of magazines and journals as soon as they come out. These indexes list the titles of articles and other publication data under common headings. You can probably guess what heading will be used to list articles on your topic. The heading you need may not be the first one you think of. Also, headings will be different from one index to another. Some library reference rooms will contain a copy of the *Library of Congress Subject Headings* to help you find alternative listings for your topic. Be patient, think of other ways to list the articles on your topic, and expect to find cross-references—other headings given by the index makers that you can look under.

Figure 2-2. Periodical Index Entry Format, a Sample, and Its Standard Uses

FORMAT

1

2	3	4

5	6

1. title of article
2. author (if article is signed)
3. graphics abbreviation (see list in front of every index volume)
4. name of magazine or journal (abbreviated)
5. volume number: pages
6. date of magazine issue

Note: If no author is listed on a magazine article, the author slot will not be used. If the article is all print with no graphic aids, the content note abbreviation slot will not be used.

SAMPLE (from the *Business Periodicals Index*)

subject heading: **SOVIET UNION**
subject subheading: **Commerce**
subject sub-subhead: *Europe, Western*
Embracing the bear [Soviet-western Europe pipeline] L. Minard. map Forbes 129: 120–5 Je 7 '82

A BIBLIOGRAPHY CARD FOR A WORKING BIBLIOGRAPHY DONE ON 3″ × 5″ CARDS

① pipeline   ② Minard

③ Lawrence Minard, "Embracing the Bear," Forbes, June 7, '82, pp 120-125.

④ map-proposed pipeline route? Check how northern; check what countries hooked up
⑤

1. Topic heading
2. Name for alphabetizing
3. Sourcenote information
4. Expectations of contents and other notes on article's use
5. Space for use notes after article is found

STANDARD BIBLIOGRAPHY ENTRY FORMAT APPLIED TO THIS ARTICLE (MLA)

Minard, Lawrence. "Embracing the Bear." *Forbes*, 7 June 1982, pp. 120–125.

STANDARD REFERENCE LISTING FORMAT APPLIED TO THIS ARTICLE (APA)

Minard, L. "Embracing the bear." *Forbes*, June 7, 1982, pp. 120–125.

Most periodical indexes follow a standard format, and it doesn't take long to catch on to the code. Figure 2-2 shows this typical format, along with examples of a typical bibliography card and typical bibliography entry formats.

To compile a working bibliography, you need to look at the titles of the articles listed under your topic focus heading. To find the most recent information, start with the most recent issue of the index. It's bound in paper and dated on the front and maybe the spine. Plan to look in more than one issue of each index and more than one kind of index. Plan to spend at least an hour just looking in indexes for promising titles, titles that seem to match with your topic. When you find these titles, you should list all the information given on that title. But there's a catch. Indexes, to save ink and time, use abbreviated titles and other abbreviations to describe the contents of articles. Every issue of every index has a listing of titles in the front and a separate listing of abbreviations to describe contents. You will quickly learn the most common abbreviations from practice, but the first time you use an index you should read the "Prefatory Note" in the front and locate the two listings of abbreviations.

Sometimes you will find many articles listed on your topic in a single index issue. In this case, skim through the list of sub-headings and titles to see what topic focuses you can detect. Also, watch for authors' names that are listed again and again.

When you actually go to find the articles you choose as promising titles, you'll need to check in the reference room to make sure your library stocks the magazines you want for the dates you want. In some cases your library will have the actual magazine ("hard copy"); in other cases it will have the magazine or journal you want, but you'll have to use microfilm to read the article. Don't panic; anyone who knows the shape of the letter U can thread a microfilm projector.

There may be a time when your library will not have the magazine for the date you want. You may want to list plenty of articles at first in case your library does not have most of those listed in the indexes. Or you might want to compile a short list of promising articles, then check your library's "periodical holdings list" to see which you can get in your library.

Periodicals may or may not be kept in one general area of the library, so plan to make location notes from the periodical holdings list for your library. Plan to make changes in your working bibliography and in your topic focus and slant as you find out what kinds of articles are available in your library.

6c. Other Library Information Services

In some libraries, you can pay for computerized searches of data banks to which the library may subscribe. Many libraries subscribe to some sort of microfiche service. The most common is probably the ERIC service for articles and speeches on educational topics. But there are other services, such as STAR, which prints NASA documents and articles on aeronautics on microfiche. You may wish to ask your reference librarian about microfiche services.

Some libraries also subscribe to one or more collections of abstracts in various disciplines. These abstract collections index and summarize by topic journal articles in, for example, psychology, sociology, chemistry, and biology, and the results are bound once a year. To find the most current research results by professional researchers in your topic area (or field of study), check with your reference librarian to see what abstract collections, if any, your library stocks.

Newspaper indexes and collections of articles are growing in popularity. A few libraries stock *The Times* of London on microfilm and subscribe to its index; most libraries subscribe to *The New York Times Index* and stock the newspaper itself on microfilm. Newer newspaper indexes, such as *Newsbank*, give a few listings for articles in other city newspapers, so you may wish to ask your reference librarian which newspaper indexes your library has and which newspapers the library subscribes to.

6d. A Detailed Example: Starting a Working Bibliography

To demonstrate how to use library resources and what sorts of initial judgments you can expect to make, let's take one example and get it started. Figures 2-3 and 2-4 display extensive information you will need to use periodical indexes and to follow this example.

Sample Topic:	Solar energy
Sample Topic Question:	Should the United States spend more to develop solar energy faster?
Sample Topic Focuses:	Is a passive solar energy system as effective at heating as a conventional (oil, gas, electric) heating system?
	Is a solar cell system effective enough to substitute for a conventional heating system?
	Should the solar energy industry be a centralized or decentralized utility?

Although you may not be terribly interested in solar energy at the moment, this lengthy example can be very valuable as a demonstration of how to make crucial decisions in the early stages of your research. You may have to do some preliminary reading in an encyclopedia, handbook, or guide, or magazine article that surveys your topic to make up topic focuses. But your early questions should only be proposals to yourself about possible directions you could go with your topic.

Once you decide on two or three possible focuses for your topic, you'll need to list possible headings to look under for information on your topic in the card catalog and periodical indexes.

Sample Topic Headings:	energy, solar *or* solar energy
	heating, solar *or* solar heating
	solar heating, passive
	solar cells (photovoltaic cells)
	homes, solar designs *or* solar homes
	energy conservation

The *Library of Congress Subject Headings* may be useful at this point. You probably remember that catalog cards and notes in periodical indexes also "cross-reference" other names for topics.

Since solar energy is a relatively new topic, you need the most current information. So use the periodical indexes—but which ones? That depends on your slant. Figure 2-3 lists the common periodical indexes and the kinds of articles they list. Which ones would give you the best information? The *Readers' Guide* and *The New York Times Index* contain listings of articles for the lay reader on almost any subject. Once you start looking up

Figure 2-3.	General Contents of Common Periodical Indexes			
ACCESS	APPLIED SCIENCE AND TECHNOLOGY INDEX	BIOLOGICAL AND AGRICULTURAL INDEX	BUSINESS PERIODICALS INDEX	EDUCATION INDEX
General interest listings for new and regional and city magazines and special interest periodicals not in the *Readers' Guide*	Articles on: aeronautics chemistry computers construction electricity energy engineering environment fire science food science geology machinery mathematics mineralogy metallurgy oceanography petroleum physics plastics space science telecommunications textiles transportation	Articles on: agrichemicals agricultural economics agricultural engineering animal husbandry biochemistry biology botany ecology entomology environmental science food science forestry genetics horticulture marine biology microbiology nutrition physiology plant pathology soil science veterinary medicine zoology	Articles on: accounting advertising and public relations banking building chemicals communications computers cosmetics drugs economics electronics finance and investments industrial relations insurance internationals management marketing occupational health and safety paper and pulp personnel petroleum printing and publishing real estate transportation	Articles on: adult education arts audiovisual ed. comparative and international ed. counseling ed. administration elementary ed. English language arts health and physical ed. higher ed. languages and linguistics library science multiethnic ed. personnel services preschool ed. psychology and mental health religious ed. science and math secondary ed. social studies special ed. and rehabilitation teacher ed. teaching methods and curriculum vocational ed.

			READERS'	
ESSAY AND GENERAL LITERATURE INDEX	HUMAN- ITIES INDEX	THE NEW YORK TIMES INDEX	GUIDE TO PERIODICAL LITERATURE	SOCIAL SCI- ENCES INDEX
Essays from col- lections on areas including: anthropology art history history literary criti- cism musicology philosophy political sci- ence	Articles on: archeology area studies classical studies folklore history language and literature literary criti- cism performing arts philosophy political criti- cism religion	Summaries of articles that ap- pear in *The New York Times*	General inter- est listings, in- cluding news articles, reviews, and literature	Articles on: anthropology economics environmental science geography law and crimi- nology medicine political sci- ence psychology public admin- istration sociology urban and community planning

Figure 2-3. (Continued)

Figure 2-4. Selected Titles for Solar Energy Articles in Some Late 1982 Periodical Indexes

READERS' GUIDE (27 under 6 "solar" headings)

"How to Use Solar Energy to Recharge Your Batteries" il *Pop Electron*

"Concentrating Collector Yields High Heat without Tracking the Sun" il *Pop Sci*

"Downspout and Dryer Hose Combine in a Low-Cost Solar System" il *Pop Sci*

"Solar Collectors and Japanese Swords" [surface treatment for copper-gold alloys] *Sci News*

"Award-winning Solar Idea House" il *Better Homes Gard*

"Cancer from Beneath Your Home" [granite used for heat storage in solar homes releases radon; research by Robert Fleischer and others] il *Sci Dig*

"The Glass House Is Back" [passive solar dwelling in northern New Jersey] il *N Y Times Mag*

"Solar Home Secrets—Computer Data Reveal the Facts" il *Pop Sci*

"Total Sunpower" [214-unit solar community in Santa Fe, N. Mex.] il *Pop Mech*

APPLIED SCIENCE AND TECHNOLOGY INDEX (89 under 8 relevant "solar" headings)

"Contribution to the Theory of Drift-Field Solar Cells" bibl *App Phys*

"Solar Generators to Power French Satellite" il *Design N*

"Solar Leap: Grid-connected Solar Cells to Supply 1 Megawatt for California" *Eng N*

"On the Climatic Optimization of the Tilt and Azimuth of Flat-plate Solar Collectors" bibl *Solar Energy*

"Combined Gas and Steam Cycle for a Gas-cooled Solar Tower Power Plant" bibl flow diags *J Eng Power*

"Prototype Photovoltaic System Shows Promise, Could Succeed Despite Budget Cuts" il diags *EDN*

"Solar Energy Shows Promise But Costs Are High" *Power*

"Solar Total-energy Plant Comes on Line"   il   *Elect World*

"Solar Thermal Systems in Industry"   bibl   diags   *Am Oil Chem Soc J*

BUSINESS PERIODICALS INDEX (4 under 1 "solar" heading)

"Passive Solar Heat Has Active Wisconsin Fans"   *Chain Store Age Exec*

"Solar Risks: Few Seek Them But Most Companies Will Write Them" [insurance]   *Natl Underwrit (Prop Casualty Insur Ed)*

EDUCATION INDEX (2 under 1 "solar" heading)

"Pioneering with Solar Power"   il   *Com & Jr Coll J*

NEW YORK TIMES INDEX (7 under 1 "solar" heading)

"Article on Solarex Corp plan to build factory for production of power-generating solar cells in Frederick, Md., that will itself be powered by 224,640 solar cells on its south roof; Dr. Joseph Lindmayer comments; drawing . . ."

SOCIAL SCIENCE INDEX (2 under 2 "solar" headings)

"Solar Access Zoning Bonus"   *Pub Mgt*

BIOLOGICAL AND AGRICULTURAL INDEX (2 under 2 "solar" headings)

"The Original Blueprint for a Solar America"   bibl il   *Environment*

articles listed in the *Readers' Guide*, you will notice that some magazines and some writers are geared toward more educated readers. For example, an article in *Discover* or *Omni* might be harder to read than an article in *Reader's Digest* or *Science Digest*. Some periodicals print more "how-to" articles than essays or discussions on a topic. *Mother Earth News*, for example, is noted for its "how-to" explanations, as is *Popular Science*. On the other hand, news magazines, like *U.S. News and World Report* and *Time*, often present debates on topics. These magazines and *The New York Times* present useful background information, but your topic (or your instructor) may require primary sources. For a technological slant, you would of course look for listings in the *Applied Science and Technology Index* or the *Biological and Agricultural Index*.

In the *Business Periodicals Index*, you would find a list of articles on marketing or investment in the solar power industry. The *Education Index* would list articles on teaching the uses of solar energy as well as reports on academic research on solar energy. The *Social Sciences Index* would list articles on the economics or the politics of solar energy. In other words, each index supports a different slant on a topic, and, because of their slant, most cover certain subjects. (You will notice, by the way, that the subjects in Figure 2-3 are not headings.)

Figure 2-4 lists titles selected from late 1982 issues of some periodical indexes. The number in parentheses after the index name is the total number of articles listed in one issue of one index. (Remember, you often have to look through several issues of one index to find articles on your focus and slant; but start with the most recent you can find in the paperback issues of an index.) Also listed are the abbreviated name of the magazine that prints the article and content note abbreviations. Let's see how we would go about assembling a working bibliography on solar energy.

Some of the titles relate to the focuses we started with. For instance, the *Readers' Guide* and the *Business Periodicals Index* issues each list one article on passive solar heating. To pursue this focus, we'd need to look at other issues of these periodical indexes and the *Applied Science and Technology Index*, which lists articles on home design.

The *Applied Science and Technology Index* issue listed about a dozen technical articles on solar cells not shown in Figure 2-4. As we read, we'd need to see what distinction, if any, there is among solar cells, solar batteries, and solar collectors. Maybe just one of these would suit a focus on effectiveness. The two contrasting views of cost from the *Applied Science and Technology Index* might bear on effectiveness: "Prototype Photovoltaic System . . ." and "Solar Energy Shows Promise But . . . ."

The centralized/decentralized issue might include such articles as "Solar Leap: Grid-connected . . . California" and "Combined Gas and Steam Cycle . . . Plant" on the side of centralized solar utilities and maybe "Solar Total-Energy Plant Comes on Line." "Downspout and Dryer Hose . . . ," "Solar Home Secrets . . . ," and the articles on passive solar houses might support decentralization, as would the article on the Solarex Corporation factory for decentralized industrial energy.

So each of the focuses in the sample list could lead to a wealth of information, both technical and nontechnical.

Even this brief list of articles suggests still other leads. For instance, "Cancer from Beneath Your Home" suggests that some solar heating systems may be hazardous. The "Solar Risks" article on insuring solar structures might fit in here. Unfortunately, there may be very little information available on such hazards.

The title "Solar Collectors and Japanese Swords" suggests an industrial use of solar energy in making metal alloys; perhaps there are others that suggest a focus on a use of solar energy other than in heating. On the other hand, solar energy uses in space, as suggested by "Solar Generators to Power French Satellite," might make an interesting report supporting a call for solar power in space. For instance, the feasibility of solar powered satellites might be used to argue for funding research on space colonies, such as those proposed by Gerard O'Neill.

Finally, the title "The Original Blueprint for a Solar America" suggests a background article worth reading, perhaps an overview article to start with.

The point of working through this detailed example is simple. You have to start somewhere, but your first few hours in the library are only a start. As you read more on your topic, you'll get smarter about it. You'll see more connections between one focus and another. After a while, you'll begin to see enough related titles to choose a direction. In the solar energy sample, for instance, the most interesting topic might be the debate over having central solar energy facilities to send electricity to our homes and businesses or decentralized solar units to make energy-independent homes and businesses and schools. Working out a compromise between central and independent energy supplies would take a great deal of thought and research. On the other hand, there are hundreds of articles a year on solar cell development; research would be easy, but to draw comparisons with conventional heating systems, you might have to pick through piles of articles or look up other articles on conventional heating systems for contrasting figures on cost and capacity.

In short, you have to use your judgment during the entire research process. When is a working bibliography long enough? When is it time to leave the reference section to look for books and articles on the shelves? When is a topic focus specialized enough for you to look through collections of abstracts, government documents, or the library "vertical file" of pamphlets? It takes experience, patience, and common sense to make these initial judgments. And it takes time.

EXERCISE 6. ASSEMBLING A WORKING BIBLIOGRAPHY

Go to your library's reference section to consult the card catalog and the periodical indexes. Decide if your topic focus is recent enough to start with the indexes; if so, decide which index besides the *Readers' Guide* you should go to. (Start with the *Readers' Guide* for background articles and other possible topic focuses.)

Make a preliminary working bibliography of twenty to thirty items. Find out which ones are in your library by consulting the "periodical holdings list" in the reference section. Determine where each item is located (open stacks, closed stacks, reference section, reserve room, special collections, or periodicals section). (Are you using 3″ × 5″ cards for your working bibliography? Review Figures 2-1 and 2-2.) To use standard bibliography entry formats on your working bibliography, preview section 12 and refer to the models as you compile your working bibliography.

EXERCISE 7. ADJUSTING YOUR TOPIC FOCUS

After you have made a working bibliography, jot down three or four possible topic focuses and decide whether your earliest hunches about topic focuses could work out. (You may want to start making separate piles of bibliography cards to see which focus looks most promising.)

7. MAKING NOTES

Making notes from your research is relatively easy if you have written down your topic focus and if you keep track of your sources.

Your preliminary reading and early note-making should lead you to focus on a few subtopics. As you see what information goes with other information in your notes, you can begin to set your organization. For a project as complex as a research paper, you should use an outline from time to time to take stock of the topics and evidence you might want to include in your final paper. Your early outlines may be little more than lists of what you have and what you need. But as you gain more insight into your topic and as you begin to form a thesis, focus, and slant on your topic, you'll need to plan in some detail. At some point, you should set out your main ideas and your major support in order to see what you've got and judge how convincing it is. Outlining in sentence

or paragraph form with lists of sources for each part could help
you chart your course to a final draft. (See the section on outlining
in the alphabetical listings of the handbook.)

To keep track of your sources, you will need a system. For
your list of sources, you will probably find a card system most
convenient. Figures 2-1 and 2-2 show sample source cards, called
"bibliography cards" because they contain information that you
would need to do a bibliography at the end of your research
report. By filling out a card for every item you read and every
person you talk to, you will need to do very little source identification on your notes.

When you come across informtion that might help you to
form and support your judgment on a topic, you need to decide
how to record it. Your choices are photocopying, quoting, paraphrasing, and summarizing. Resist the urge to photocopy everything—doing so is only postponing your decision on what parts
to use and what to make notes on. Also resist the urge to check
out a pile of books and to quote and paraphrase right from their
pages. This approach makes you juggle information and organization and style and source notes all at the same time. It often
leads to poor use of sources (plagiarism, inaccurate footnoting,
omitting footnotes). You should plan to use plenty of cards for
notes. Most people use 3″ × 5″, 4″ × 6″, or 5″ × 8″ cards for
notes—pick the size that's convenient for you, but plan to put only
one idea or one set of data on a card. You may need several cards
for one source because you can't be sure about the order or the
extent of the information from that source that you will finally
use. Your notes will probably be a mix of summary, paraphrase,
and quotation.

Figure 2-5 shows bibliography and note cards for portions
of data taken from two sources used to prepare a research
presentation on the search for extraterrestrial intelligence. Notice
that *quotations are marked with quotation marks at both ends*. You must
mark quotations because after a day or two—or a week or two—
you won't remember which words are yours and which are your
sources', and you'll have to look up the information again (if it's
still available). But also notice the parts that are not quotations.
These notes don't sound much like the quoted parts, except,
perhaps, for the technical terms. You may wish to review uses of
quotation marks in the "Quotation Marks" section in the alphabetical listings.

Figure 2-5A. Sample Note Cards

Possible Topic Focus: Are there other (habitable) planets?

Shklovskiy   stellar rotation

summary

The spectroscopic discovery of stellar rotation in the 1930's by O.L. Struve and G.A. Shayn (Soviet) revealed that, although surface temperatures, mass, brightness, etc. vary regularly down the main sequence, there is a sharp drop-off of angular momentum between F5 stars and the smaller F, G, M, and K stars. "Most probably," the reason for the drop is that the stars, like the Sun, are orbited by planets that contain most of the angular momentum from the original nebula.

quotation

"But this implies that at least several billion stars in the galaxy must possess planetary systems. Let us recall that over 150 billion stars of all types are counted in the galaxy. As is known, our sun is located near the plane of the galactic equator, in the vicinity of one of the spiral branches. Nearly 10,000 stars are counted within a 100 light-year radius sphere, and a substantial part, if not all of them, are dwarfs of G, K, and M types." ((But, as Cameron notes later (p. 26), "about 80 percent of the stars in the solar neighborhood are in binary systems." So stars may have other stars with them, not necessarily planets and not necessarily habitable planets: see notes on planet distance and composition.))

judgment

Bracewell   habitable planets?

"Only about one in ten of the slowly rotating stars
would be likely to support life after we reject double
stars and planets whose atmospheres are too light or too
dense. Remaining would be a total of about 10 billion
suitable stars in our own galaxy. Of these, many
probably have a planet of the right size in the right
place. Although we do not know what this fraction might
be, a conservative estimate of the total number of such
planets in our galaxy would be around one billion." (p.
8)

judgment   (1% habitable? too optimistic? There doesn't <u>have</u> to
                  be a planet anywhere outside our solar system.)

question   (any evidence from radio astronomy for companions or
                  planets?)

reminder of   (See notes on Dole's book—odds of planet placement
related   from Bode's law—all far-fetched guesswork & fancy math?
evidence   or maybe substantial?)

71

angular momentum   Shklovskiy

Shklovskiy, Iosif S. "Is Communication Possible
  with Intelligent Beings on Other Planets?" Trans.
  from _Priroda_, 21, No. 7 (1960). In _Interstellar
  Communication_. Ed. Alastair Graham Walter
  Cameron. New York: W.A. Benjamin, 1963, pp. 5-16.

(Russian-once did a book with Carl Sagan on SETI)
(dated, but may have interesting ideas still applicable)

---

angular momentum   Bracewell

Bracewell, Ronald N. _The Galactic Club: Intelligent
  Life in Outer Space_. San Francisco: W.H. Freeman,
  1975.

(also good for chances of radio contact: chart)

            QB / 54 / .B69 / 1975

Figure 2-5B.   Sample Bibliography Cards

7a. Guidelines for Using Source Material

The following guidelines describe in detail the fair and legal
use of sources in student research writing. The final guideline
defines plagiarism.

1. *Quoting* means placing quotation marks around someone's *exact
   words*, word by word, without making any changes to the quoted
   words. You do not have to quote full sentences from your source,
   and you can leave out irrelevant words by using an ellipsis at the
   point where the words are left out.
2. When you are not quoting someone's statements, put quotation

marks around only unique words or technical terms from a given source.

3. When you are not quoting, you should be either paraphrasing or summarizing. It is neither quoting nor adequate paraphrasing to add words and leave out words here and there as you copy.

4. *Paraphrasing* means writing someone else's *idea* in your writing style. This means changing all the sentence structures and as many as 90 percent of the original words—but keeping the meaning that the writer or speaker apparently intended.

5. *Summarizing* means condensing someone's *ideas* to roughly 10 to 25 percent of their original length. To summarize, pick out the main ideas and perhaps major details and put them in your own words.

6. Selective summarizing is to use someone else's ideas that relate only to your topic and to ignore the rest of what the source says.

7. Whether you are writing someone else's words verbatim (quoting word-for-word) or using your own writing style (paraphrasing or summarizing), you must document the source of your information to credit the source with the ideas and to establish the credibility of those ideas. Documentation means pinpointing the exact sentences in your paper that draw from source material. This is done by using either a number that refers the reader to a footnote or endnote or a parenthetical indication of the source. (See Figure 2-11 on documentation styles.)

8. *Plagiarizing* means to give the appearance that someone else's words or ideas are yours. If you copied someone else's words without quotation marks, you would be giving the impression that those words were yours—and that's plagiarism, even if you provide a footnote. The most serious form of plagiarism is to leave out the quotation marks when copying on a final draft *and* to leave out attribution and source note.

7b. Summarizing, Paraphrasing, Quoting, Attribution, and Footnoting

Figure 2-6 demonstrates summarizing, paraphrasing, quoting, attribution, and footnoting. (By the way, the words "footnote," "endnote," and "sourcenote" all mean telling exactly who your source is. Technically, footnotes use the bottom of the appropriate page for this information; endnotes list all such information in a numbered list just before the bibliography; and sourcenotes occur

POSSIBLE TOPIC FOCUS: Black efforts to achieve racial equality in the armed forces during World War II had more impact than many people realize.

Original Passage:
The spring of 1940 was crucial for the War Department in making decisions on black participation in the defense of the United States. As blacks continued to agitate for more equality, the ballot, coupled with patriotism and loyalty, became powerful forces in black strategy for gaining concessions from the military and from the federal government. Such pressure forced the War Department to appoint Judge [William] Hastie civilian aide to the Secretary of War. Hastie's role, however, would be different from that of Emmett J. Scott, black special assistant to Secretary of War Newton Baker during the First World War. He viewed Scott as an adjuster of racial ills rather than a leading voice for justice and social change. Throughout World War I, Hastie felt that Scott maintained a conservative approach on matters affecting black soldiers. He was determined that the black community would not view him as an appeaser of racial inequality. Rather than submit to War Department pressures, Hastie worked vigorously for total integration and equal opportunity within the military establishment.

Source: Phillip McGuire, "Judge Hastie, World War II, and Army Racism," *The Journal of Negro History*, 62 (1977), 351–52.

SUMMARY (emphasis on general pressures):
As a result of the loyalty, patriotism, and election-year (1940) pressures of blacks, the War Department appointed Judge William Hastie as special assistant on racial matters. Hastie resisted pressures within the War Department and worked actively for blacks' equal military service.

SUMMARY (emphasis on Hastie):
Appointed in 1940, Judge William Hastie worked actively to realize the desires of the black community for equal treatment in the military, despite counter-pressures from within the War Department, where he served as civilian assistant to the Secretary.

PARAPHRASE (emphasis on general pressures):
In early 1940, black Americans wanted more equality for their people in the armed forces. The country needed loyal, patriotic service

people, and blacks made themselves heard in this election year. As a result of these pressures, the War Department appointed Judge William Hastie to assist the Secretary of War with racial matters. Hastie planned to be more activist than his World War I predecessor, Emmett J. Scott. The activism in the black community encouraged him to resist the pressure within the War Department to minimize blacks' desires to serve equally with whites in the military.

PARAPHRASE (emphasis on Hastie):
When Judge William Hastie was appointed to a War Department post on racial matters in 1940, he saw as his responsibility being more activist than his World War I counterpart, Emmett J. Scott. He also saw greater opportunity for success, given the patriotic spirit of the times and the election-year pressures from the black community. Although there were War Department attitudes against racial equality in the military, Hastie argued from his position within the establishment to eliminate racial inequality in the armed forces.

QUOTATION (with attribution):
According to historian Phillip McGuire, Judge William Hastie "was determined that the black community would not view him as an appeaser of racial inequality" while he worked in the War Department, advising the Secretary on racial matters.

QUOTATION (of full sentence, with attribution):
"As blacks continued to agitate for more equality," reports historian Phillip McGuire, "the ballot, coupled with patriotism and loyalty, became powerful forces in black strategy for gaining concessions from the military and from the federal government."

FOOTNOTING:
Any of the above uses of McGuire's information in a formal research paper requires the following footnote (numbered in sequence with your other uses of information):

[3] Phillip McGuire, "Judge Hastie, World War II, and Army Racism," *The Journal of Negro History*, 62 (1977), 351–52.

(The page reference for the first quotation is *352* by itself. The second quotation comes from page 351, so *351* by itself is the accurate page reference for it.)

Attribution mentions the source's name just before, in the middle of, or just after a quotation, paraphrase, or summary. Using attribution clarifies where your source's ideas begin, so attributions help to signal support for your major ideas in a paper.

in charts compiled or adapted from one source. Some people just refer to "notes," but this term can be confused with notes on note cards. Don't be surprised to hear these four words used inter-changeably, but see Figures 2-11 and 2-12 for documentation styles.)

Some trial and error is usually involved in making notes accurately and in ways that are fair to the original writer. At first you may have to do quite a bit of double-checking to make sure your notes and final draft fit the guidelines listed in section 7a. Be patient and allow plenty of time to check your work because you must report your research accurately and in the standard format that your instructor requires you to follow.

Keeping track of your sources does much more than help you to avoid plagiarizing. Look back again to Figure 2-5 to notice what else is on the note cards besides notes. In the left-hand corner is the source identification (written in full on the bibliog-raphy card). In the top right-hand corner is a heading for the information noted; this heading characterizes the information and helps you to group related information—and to outline. (The heading might even be from an early outline used to narrow the focus of research.) Finally, page numbers for notes from printed materials pinpoint the information exactly. Footnotes and in-text references use single page numbers rather than listing all the pages for an article or the total pages for a book.

The notes in parentheses on the note cards in Figure 2-5 evaluate the credibility of the information on the card and give leads to other sets of notes. First-impression evaluations like these can help you decide later how believable your information is at first glance. You need to assess how much to explain so that your readers can understand. You need to decide whether you need more convincing information or whether you should alter your judgment in the face of weak support.

You also need every aid in grouping information. Cross-references and headings can always be scratched out or erased later, when you redesign your plans for presenting your research.

Finally, you need to bounce sources against each other, as shown in the notes in Figure 2-5. One source may contain information or expert reasoning that supports or casts doubt on what another source says. You'll find that clashes among sources set the battle lines in the debate on your topic. They may lead you to major arguments that oppose your judgment (which you may have to explain away in your paper) or cause you to adopt a pro and con format for presenting your judgment. This clash of information from sources gets easier to interpret as you read more on your topic and review your existing notes from time to time— by rereading or by re-organizing your working outlines. The next section contains more details for evaluating your sources.

EXERCISE 8. A PASSAGE FOR PRACTICING USES OF SOURCE MATERIAL

To practice the skills presented in this section, work with the passage below, which is adapted from an article in a Paris newspaper. Do the following tasks.

1. Make a bibliography card from the source note. Use the "possible topic focus" as a topic heading for your card.
2. Summarize the passage twice. The first time, emphasize how the collective farm at Doney was organized. In your second summary, emphasize the hardships the Cambodian families faced at Doney.
3. Quote an important idea from the passage twice. First, begin with an attribution to the writer of the article (the last four words of the passage are those of Pin Yatay). Second, quote the most important sentence in the passage (your judgment) with a different kind of attribution. (See Figure 2-6 to review "attribution.")
4. Paraphrase the first paragraph of the passage.
5. Using a combination of summary, paraphrase, and quotation, make a note card appropriate to the topic. Use headings, the page number, and your own comments in addition to your notes. Use quotation marks around exact wordings taken from the passage.

***

Possible Topic Focus: Was the reorganization of Cambodia worth the suffering it caused?
Possible Topic Focus: Does forming a Communist government destroy individuality in a society?
Original Passage:

On this collective farm—organized and run almost as a military camp with strictly defined production divisions, companies, and battalions—every member was integrated into a specialized plowing, land-improvement, or fertilizer-production unit (*angpheap*). Children were divided by age and supervised by specialists who made it clear that "Angkar," not their parents, supplied their food and saw to their upbringing. Thus the family gradually began to lose its importance and the individual—essentially reduced to his producing properties—was placed in service of the collective. In January of last year the people of Doney began taking their meals not with their families but at canteens in their places of work.

For Pin Yatay, Doney was a nightmare. Facing privation, the total absence of health care, back-breaking daily labor, and epidemics of dysentery and malaria, entire families were wiped out. Yatay lost thirteen of his kin, among them his second son, age six, who died of an infected foot wound. All were buried, he says, in a "collective grave" near the hospital. He, his wife, his elder son, and his cousin—sole survivors of the original family group—were "completely bloated for months."

Source: Roland-Pierre Paringaux, "Cambodia's Closed Society: The Swift, Relentless Pursuit of Collectivization," *Atlas World Press Review*, Dec. 1977, p. 19.

8. EVALUATING YOUR SOURCES

Critical judgment is needed to evaluate your sources fairly. This judgment develops over a lifetime of reading in a variety of fields, but critical reading can be as simple as thinking.

First, be realistic. As you begin doing research in a field, you're probably not going to "prove" a new truth or establish a new "fact." Although initially they may not be apparent to you, there are some assumptions to research, and what passes as "proof" is often an agreement among professionals about how to interpret the observations and data of researchers. In your own research writing, the best you can do is to present your judgment as reasonable. To establish reasonableness, you need to have done enough research to present diverse information and professional views on your subject. But the amount of research is not as important as the quality of your sources and how well you interpret your sources' information.

Second, figure out what to expect. If you are presenting your research in a formal research paper or term paper, you should expect to write seven to fifteen typed pages, according to a recent survey of college English practices.*

In a paper of that length, you should expect to use an appropriate blend of source information along with your own topic sentences, transitions, explanations of your source's data, and evaluations of your source's opinions. Figure 2-7 presents one

* See James E. Ford and Dennis R. Perry, "Research Paper Instruction in the Undergraduate Writing Program," *College English*, 44 (1982), 828.

Figure 2-7. Blending Information from Different Sources

THESIS
Because of their particular circumstances and needs, dolphin communication is so different from human communication that we may not talk with dolphins very soon.

Excerpt:

Somewhat sophisticated communication among dolphins has been observed. Being extremely social animals, they need some type of information system to assure unity, protection, and cooperation among the group.[6] An example of an information network of sorts can be seen in an episode observed in 1962 by a group of scientists. A group of five bottlenosed dolphins sent out a scout to investigate an artificial barrier. The dolphin used his sonar clicks to examine the barrier and then swam back to the group whistling. All five then swam through together.[7] Their communication was used as a means of protection and unity.

What are the chances of dolphin communication techniques being used for more than orientation, safety, or a minimum of relationships between dolphins?

Scientists that have addressed the question responded with a number of hypotheses. The answers range from the unbelieving to the very active imagination of one particular scientist. Melba and David Caldwell are members of the unbelieving group. "Whatever the reason," they claim, "all other animals [besides man] exchange information nonverbally. Although their communications are limited largely to the 'here and now,' this is obviously all that is needed for them to get along beautifully. . . ."[8] The Caldwells seem to believe that the dolphins' communication is only for survival. On the opposite end of the spectrum is John C. Lilly, M.D., who believes that dolphins have their own language, "delphinese," which is based on sending and receiving "acoustic pictures." In supporting his opinion, he notes that dolphins use sonar for identification and that "dolphins use sonic communication to modify one another's behavior."[9]

[6] Melba C. Caldwell and David K. Caldwell, "Communication in Atlantic Bottlenosed Dolphins," *Sea Frontiers*, May/June 1979, p. 130.
[7] Michael Parfit, "Are Dolphins Trying to Say Something, Or Is It All Much Ado About Nothing?" *Smithsonian*, Oct. 1980, p. 77.
[8] Caldwell and Caldwell, p. 133.
[9] John C. Lilly, M.D., *Communication Between Man and Dolphins: The Possibilities of Talking with Other Species*, (New York: Crown Publishers, 1978), p. 156.

Source: Ronda Jones, "Dolphin Talk," Research paper, J. Sargeant Reynolds Community College, 1982, pp. 3–4, 7.

student's evaluation of the debate over dolphin communication. She was on her way to developing a rather skeptical thesis (judgment) when she wrote the passage excerpted here. You'll notice that she gives footnote numbers after she gives a summary of the Parfit report of the incident and after her paraphrase of the Caldwells' opinion, not just after the quotations of the Caldwells and Dr. Lilly. (Some students get confused about where to put footnote numbers in their paragraphs.) She has footnoted every fact and professional opinion—every bit of source information— that she used in this section of her paper. But you should notice something more subtle. She has gone beyond the point where she is impressed by the big names in dolphin communication research.

Later on, this student rejects the two extremes she mentions here and cites as the most promising research path attempts to teach dolphins an artificial language. You don't always have to steer a middle or alternate course to seem reasonable, but you do need a healthy skepticism about your sources' claims and their conclusions. You need to do some smart research.

To do smart research (critical reading and listening), it helps to be systematic. The rest of this section lists the kinds of things you need to consider about your sources. Smart research doesn't mean you should either reject or accept everything your sources say. Smart research means finding where your sources agree, where they disagree, and why. Study this listing of considerations as a kind of checklist. All these points may not apply to every book, article, pamphlet, TV news report, and person you consult. Be flexible; take advantage of the considerations that do apply to one of your sources. Also, be ready to make comparative judgments like "This source uses statistics more believably than that source" or "The quotations from eyewitnesses in this source seem more convincing than those in that source." Considerations like the ones listed below will help you decide when to take notes and how much note-taking to do. They will also help you decide which notes to include when you present your research and when to go hunting for more information or better information.

8a. Recency

Is your source's information up to date? For instance, what was true of religious cults in the 1960s and 1970s may not be true of cult activities and influence in the 1980s. A 1975 article on "deprogramming" may be historical background now.

8b. Authority

What credibility does your source have? Magazines like *Time*, *U.S. News and World Report*, *Omni*, *Ebony*, *The Nation*, *Psychology Today*, and other news magazines are noted for checking their facts and presenting more than one side of an issue. Not all publications or publishers have this reputation. [Consult Bill Katz and Linda Sternberg Katz, *Magazines for Libraries*, (New York: R. R. Bowker), for evaluations of 6,500 periodicals.]

With regard to individual writers, is there information about the source's educational credentials or experience? What else has your source written on this topic? Is your source famous as a spokesperson on this topic? (Where can you find information on this person—*Who's Who*? Does the source's name recur in the card catalog or *Reader's Guide*?) Does your source have an economic motive for the opinions in the article, such as Lee Iacocca speaking on the quality of Chrysler automobiles? Is your source writing in a field in which he or she is known? For instance, a Nobel Prize-winning physicist speaking on health matters or chemistry may not be as convincing as a health researcher or chemist.

8c. Research

How does your source get information? Is your source an original researcher in the field? For instance, Carl Sagan works in his experimental lab at Cornell testing theories related to the possible existence of extraterrestrials. He also keeps track of the research his Cornell colleague, Frank Drake, does in radioastronomy at the Arecibo observatory in Puerto Rico. Most people are apt to know Sagan as a popularizer of scientific ideas or as a guest on talk shows, but he has impressive scientific credentials and research experience. Nevertheless, the data of an original researcher in solar astronomy, for instance, might be more valuable than Sagan's clear summary of data in astronomy. (In other words, is your source a primary source, such as an original researcher or eyewitness, or a secondary source who is reporting somebody else's research or observations?)

How recent and reliable are your source's sources? Does your source clearly credit information and expert opinion either in the paragraphs or in footnotes or endnotes? Writers for professional journals sometimes must credit information in rather elaborate ways; writers for popular magazines may mention their sources in passing and maybe not at all. Neither method guarantees valid information, but clear crediting of reputable sources helps make the information more believable.

8d. Factuality

Does the source reason from facts and support judgments with hard data? To what extent does the source rely on expert opinion, guesswork, or even hearsay (rumor) to make a case? Facts are not enough for an effective research presentation, but arguments without facts have no substance. One recent theorist, for instance, spent most of her article reinterpreting information that was already accepted in her field; she cited sources mainly to refute them, but her inferences (about the impact of the printing press) were very persuasive. Another author in the same journal used statistics to interpret the history of literacy in America as a succession of clashes—of social classes, of races, and then of the sexes. His use of the facts was often questionable and unconvincing. For instance, he argued that "research shows" that males experience more failure with reading and writing than females. The facts he used to support his claim were from a study involving students in kindergarten through second grade who took a "battery of tests," which he did not name. Unfortunately, he ignored other studies that show males as "catching up" by the end of high school; instead, from this study of elementary school children he drew conclusions about men entering the work force. Facts are important, but they have to be interpreted fairly.

8e. Types of Evidence

As you read your sources' evidence and listen to people talk about your topic, look to see what types of evidence you find most persuasive.

Does your source rely on numbers—that is, statistics? If so, are the statistics used fairly and precisely, or are they one-sided, sloppy, or too packed together to be understandable?

Figure 2-8 shows numbers used in three different ways. In

Figure 2-8.   Some Uses of Numbers to Support
Conclusions

EXAMPLE 1

The fact is clear that inbreeding in modern populations gives rise to a much higher transmission of undesirable genetic traits. Probably the most detailed study of the effects of inbreeding has been made in Japan, where first-cousin marriage is encouraged. Not only did the researchers find a higher frequency of infant death and malformations, but they also discovered that children born of related parents suffered from numerous handicaps. These included smaller stature and lower weight, a delay in the age at which children walked, a weaker hand grip, and lower performance in verbal tests and in virtually every subject taught in school.

Source: Peter Farb, *Humankind* (Boston: Houghton Mifflin, 1978), p. 413.

EXAMPLE 2

Genetic screening laws . . . have been proliferating in this country with essentially no public debate. Some of these laws can indeed help to anticipate and prevent serious diseases. However, they can also provide the opening wedge for a eugenics program. Already, 46 states have some type of genetic-screening program, most of them mandatory. Massachusetts hospitals routinely screen newborns for nearly 30 genetic defects on a voluntary basis. A bill already passed by the N.Y. State Senate would require mandatory testing for seven specific genetic defects, with others to be designated by the State Health Department without additional legislative authorization.

Source: Frederick Ausubel, Jon Beckwith, and Kaaren Janssen, "The Politics of Genetic Engineering: Who Decides Who's Defective?" *Psychology Today*, June 1974, pp. 30–32.

EXAMPLE 3

With tax revenues from gambling adding millions of dollars to state coffers, it would be hard for legislators to turn away from it. Last year alone, lotteries brought in 2 billion dollars in 15 states, according to a Public Gaming Research Institute report. The Michigan Lottery, which is the biggest in the nation, increased ticket sales from 83 million dollars in 1972 to 410 million dollars in 1980. According to Stanley N. Welborne, in an article for *U.S. News and World Report*, the "tax take" of states "has increased an average of 12.5 percent a year since 1968."

Source: Karen Blanton Cohen, "An Analytical Report on the Pros and Cons of Gambling," Research Paper, J. Sargeant Reynolds Community College, 1981, pp. 1–2.

the first example, values are compared; no actual numbers appear. In the second example, the authors use numbers to depict the size of a growing problem. The third example presents figures on the growth of an industry, the legalized gambling industry. Although the third example uses numbers most densely, it does not strain the reader's patience or ability to understand. More important than the density of numbers, though, is the support the numerical information gives to the writers' judgments. In the first example, the writer summarizes expected and unexpected information to show the dangers of inbreeding. In the second example, the writers use numbers to show how widespread genetic screening had become by 1974 and the volume of screenings that were ordered, sometimes without review by the elected officials who ordinarily make state laws. The numbers reinforce their worried tone. The student writer of the third example summarized data from a newsmagazine to support her suggestion that legalized lotteries tempt states with big revenues; her later conclusion is that, like any form of gambling, state-supported gambling rarely benefits the gamblers.

Does your source list examples or single cases to support a point? Are the examples typical, or do they represent extremes or one-time occurrences? The list at the end of Peter Farb's paragraph in Figure 2-8 gives examples of genetic-based problems that can result from inbreeding. The examples from Massachusetts and New York, noted in the paragraph from *Psychology Today* in Figure 2-8, amplify what two of the forty-six states involved do that worries the writers. The authors may well have used these states to represent the extreme rather than the average because their point is to express their shock at the spread of genetic screening programs. The student writer of the third sample in Figure 2-8 later informally reviews the case of a reformed gambler in order to show the effects of "being hooked" on gambling.

Figure 2-9 shows two special kinds of examples: an anecdote, a story about the past told briefly to make a point, and a scenario, a brief story about the future told to show how life would be if present trends continue. Bill Russell's anecdote probably represents an extreme case, but it could support a variety of topic focuses (thesis statements) about growing up black and poor in America or about the surprising ways in which mother love shows itself or about the hardships of childhood. Like any autobiographer, Russell is a primary source when he writes about his own experiences and observations.

Figure 2-9. Specialized Examples—Anecdote and Scenario

ANECDOTE

Once, when I was nine—just after we moved to West Oakland—a bigger kid walked by our project and slapped me across the face, then kept right on going. The local kids wanted to let me know that whatever I'd brought inside me from Louisiana didn't swing much weight with them. My mother saw me get slapped and came running out. She grabbed me and took off running until we caught the guy. There wasn't any doubt about what was going to happen: she made me fight him right there in front of her. I closed my eyes and went in swinging. While the little blows were flying, one of my opponent's friends cheered him on. In the heat of the fight this friend said something about me that offended my mother. So when the fight was over and I rushed to her for comfort, she just pointed at the friend and told me what he had said, so I had to fight him, too. I won the first fight and lost the second, but I didn't care. The scrapes and bruises were nothing compared with my mother's proud approval.

Source: Bill Russell and Taylor Branch, *Second Wind: The Memoirs of an Opinionated Man* (New York: Random House, 1979), p. 10.

SCENARIO

It's 7:30 in the morning and you're sitting down having a cup of coffee, but you're at work not at home. The work day started at six and you're thinking of the roast beef sandwich in the bag on your desk. Lunch isn't until ten and you're hungry now, but you decide to wait anyway.

At lunch you're thinking of what you have to do when you get off work at two. You noticed the lawn needs mowing, but you have to sharpen the blades on the push mower. You have to stop by the bike shop for a new tire for your spouse's bike. Then there's always the firewood that needs to be chopped.

After a late supper at five, you sit down to read the evening newspaper. While you're reading the paper, the sun goes down and darkness sets in. You strike a match and light a couple of candles. They don't really provide adequate lighting, but you try to finish the paper anyway before getting ready for bed at 8:00. The day starts around sunrise and ends around sunset.

This may be the typical day for a person if we run out of oil.

(David Pangburn, student)

David Pangburn selected a few effects of oil depletion to play up in his opening scenario. By projecting the reader into the future as an inconvenienced office worker, he sets up his optimistic conclusion—how we would manage without oil and without environmentally threatening alternative energy sources.

Does your source quote, paraphrase, or summarize expert or eyewitness statements? If so, are the statements clearly attributed? Do you sense that the writer may be quoting someone out of context or leaving out words so that the quoted person's views become distorted? Does the writer try to set any context for the views attributed to the speaker? (See Figures 2-6 and 2-7.)

8f. Logic

Do the conclusions your source draws from the evidence he or she presents make sense? Are they too optimistic? Are they too negative? Are they too easy for complex issues?

Many things can go awry when writers attempt to draw conclusions on the basis of the evidence they present. Here are a few of the things you may find yourself saying as you read and talk to people about your topic:

1. "He can't tell that from one example." (hasty generalization) Few researchers try to base very broad conclusions on only one example or one case study. A writer who points to one black general as an example of minority opportunity in the armed forces would not be as convincing as the writer who tallies the number of black Army officers, finds a percentage, and places that percentage against the figures for ten and twenty years ago.

2. "Shouldn't this writer be looking for more examples like this one?" (generalizing from a small sample) The writer who cited the elementary-school test results to support a claim that males fail more than females in reading and writing needs to look further, perhaps to a review of research on the topic or to nationwide testing samples like the college boards.

3. "Her judgment doesn't seem to match her evidence." (irrelevance) The same writer was citing elementary-school test results to support conclusions about males entering the workforce. He mistakenly implied that the pattern he saw in second grade held throughout school.

4. "Is it really that simple?" (either/or thinking) The writer who suggests that integration should be achieved through busing or abandoned as a goal sets up an either/or choice. Such a choice overlooks efforts to integrate neighborhoods and probably overlooks the common goals that break down by income level rather than by race.

5. "Just because these two things happen together doesn't mean that they cause each other." (cause and effect, or *post hoc*) The fact that the murder rate in the 1960s and 1970s rose after a moratorium was placed on capital punishment does not necessarily mean that "murderers" thought they could "get off scot free." A writer who suggests this might be overlooking figures on the number of murders prosecuted in an era of "plea bargaining" as well as the most common motives for murder. Are most murders as premeditated and carefully planned as they so often are presented in television crime dramas? Are most murders contract killings? Do murderers consider the death penalty before they kill?

6. "Doesn't this idea contradict what this writer said earlier?" (inconsistent argument) Occasionally, you may notice that a writer seems to be trying "to have it both ways." A writer who argues for abortion in certain cases but considers abortion to be murder may be caught in a contradiction—or perhaps a moral dilemma. Contradictions tend to show up when you interview someone on a complicated issue—there's no time during an interview to revise, but revision occurs very often before publication.

There are some logical considerations you will have to watch out for in evaluating your sources. You may not even be conscious of attitudes such as these:

7. "She's cute" or "She's famous," so I'll read this source first; or "He's a jerk—I don't care much what he said about this." (reputation) Cute and famous people have no monopoly on wisdom or knowledge. True, fame in a field may be well earned; in consumerism, for instance, Ralph Nader and Betty Furness both have reputations for checking their facts and for alerting people to the possible dangers of products on the market. But they are not the only people aware of hazardous products.

The opposite consideration applies to sources you may react to negatively. You should try to be aware of possible ulterior motives because some people argue in self-interest—an example would be the writer who advocates rezoning of a residential area for business and who owns land in the affected area, thus standing to profit from the rezoning. But generally you should try to evaluate ideas on their merits—not because of the personality or reputation of the one suggesting the idea. Famous and attractive people can be dead wrong, even corrupt; and even someone you don't like can have a good idea. If you tend to be "conservative" on an issue, don't reject an idea just because it is proposed by someone you regard as a "liberal." Consider the idea and its factual support—even if you have to change your thinking a little bit, or more than a little bit.

As you read your sources, beware of labels. An editorial writer may brand someone an "appeaser" or a "snob" in order to undermine the person's proposal. But labels tend to be snap judgments, not reasoned evaluations.

8. "Darn right!" or "That's nonsense!" (emotional responses) Emotional responses are human; there's some evidence that people respond to everything emotionally before making any other kind of response. But you should be aware of the basis of your agreement or disagreement with a source. If you agree for emotional reasons, you may simply be responding out of your own bias. The same is true for emotion-based disagreements. Some issues, like abortion or religion, get to people emotionally because they affect people's self-images; but even such "hot" issues require carefully reasoned judgments.

You should also be aware of how your sources can work on your emotions. A picture of a starving child can be a fact as well as an emotional appeal. Emotional appeals can be very persuasive, but emotion should not be the sole basis for deciding an issue. Emotion can, however, get people involved with an issue.

9. "That settles that!" (snap judgments) The sooner you find a topic focus, the easier your research will be. It is vital that you find a good question. The answer, however, takes time—maybe even years. The research paper or report you present during the term represents your current thinking on a topic. For controversial issues, especially those that are new to you, expect to change your mind— or, better, expect not to make up your mind until you find out as much as you can. We change as we learn from information and experience. As you do research on your topic, then, try to withhold a "final" judgment as long as you can, and don't be too impressed by your first few sources. Most controversial issues—like abortion, capital punishment, and arguments over spending on defense vs. social needs—are never really "settled" once and for all without

change. Instead, the prevailing opinion on such issues changes as circumstances in societies change. Your research should help you to reason out your opinion, for the moment.

10. "All my sources are saying the same thing." If you find yourself making a judgment like this, be careful. You may be looking only at the facts your sources mention and not at their judgments. For instance, two sources may both state that Japan attacked Pearl Harbor on December 7, 1941; but one source may claim the American Pacific Fleet could have been moved because American authorities knew of the attack in advance. The other source may claim that American authorities in Washington, D.C., suspected an attack was coming but that word did not reach Hawaii in time. The wording here is crucial—"knowing" and "suspecting" are two different things. The implications are also subtle—delays in delivering messages do not constitute a conspiracy to get America involved in World War II. Facts are only facts; in your sources and in your own research presentations, they must be arranged and interpreted to support a reasoned judgment (a thesis).

Sometimes sources do say the same thing. Sources may simply be passing on the "received view," or the prevailing opinion on a topic and the support that commonly goes with it. If you find your sources echoing each other, dig deeper. You may be using outdated books or only current newsmagazines; go to the primary sources, the professional journals. Or go to the underground press or the new journals in a field. Or work your way back to the first person you can find who said this "same thing." For most topics, though, you will find plenty of disagreement if you look hard enough. Feel free to provide your own disagreements with your sources, but then try to find support, too.

8g. Clarity

Is your source readable? If something is hard to read, it could be that you aren't familiar with the words and phrases common to the field—yet. It could also be that a writer is being obscure, perhaps hiding one side of an issue or hoping to impress readers with "big" words. When you're new to a field, it's tough to separate technical jargon from bombast ("snow jobs"). Be patient—try to find a simpler reading, perhaps a secondary source, and then go back to the reading that was too hard and see if it makes more sense. If it's still tough, look at the opening, the abstract (for a professional journal), and the ending or "conclusions" section. You may find articles in *Science News* easier to read than those in *Astronomy Today* and *Psychology Today* easier than *Cognitive Psychology*, but the price you pay is timeliness. The "tough" professional journals are primary sources; the "easy" popular magazines may not cover some primary research until two or three years later (until it's a "big" topic in the field), and they are one step removed from the actual research. Primary journals are aimed at the most experienced readers, demand the most critical judgment, and require the most careful paraphrasing (and the least quoting) in your notes, but they deliver the most current information in a field.

For any of your sources, then, "clarity" is a relative term. A professional source may or may not define the most important terms used in the article, give extensive examples, provide transition sentences and clues to main ideas. But if you use a variety of sources, you should be able to translate most of what you find into terms that your readers can understand.

EXERCISE 9. COMPARING TWO SOURCES

Evaluate two articles that you have read and that you plan to use in your research presentation. Make notes on the *quality* of those sources based on the ten considerations in this section. Organize your notes to support a comparative judgment, such as "A is generally better than B as a source on this topic" or "A is better for these qualities: a, b, c, and d; but B is better for these qualities: e, f, g." Your task is *not to summarize* the content, but to weigh the merits and faults of each article as a source.

Some ground rules: Pick articles of about the same length. Both should be either primary sources (such as from journals) or both secondary sources (such as from popular magazines). The sources do not have to agree (present the same view), but they should be on the same topic. Use footnotes.

EXAMPLE:
Here's what one student did with this assignment.

Time vs. *Eagle* on Arms Sales to the Third World

The selling of weapons made by countries such as the United States, the Soviet Union, Great Britain, France, Italy, Brazil, Israel—the major arms makers—to the Third World countries has been going on for some time.

Should these sales continue? Should they be stopped or limited? The benefits and the problems of arms sales are discussed in articles that appeared in *Time* magazine and in *Eagle* magazine in 1981.

The *Time* article was compiled from reports of several *Time* correspondents. It was researched by Betty Satterwhite Sutter, whose specialty is armament stories, and written by Associate Editor Walter Isaacson as his assessment based on the correspondents' reports. Isaacson concluded that the arms trade has created a global powder keg.[1]

The *Eagle* article was written by Yoran Hamizrachi, who usually writes articles on NATO and the Middle East. Hamizrachi concluded that Third World countries need more arms to quell internal violence and stop outside aggressions that disrupt their governments' political and economic leanings toward the United States.

The authors' approaches to the arms sales problem are quite different. The *Time* article presents two sides; it lists the pros and cons of selling weapons to Third World countries and benefits to both the seller governments and the buyer governments in weapons deals. "Selling weapons," Isaacson writes, "has proved an effective way for developing nations as well as superpowers to gain influence. Arms sales can make friendly countries stronger and stronger countries friendlier. It has a greater immediate impact than building dams or sending economic aid and is certainly more lucrative."[2] But Isaacson also states drawbacks. "The limits of weapons to win friends and influence is less than lasting; many long term weapons are sold to what may be short-term friends."[3] Even worse, "many nations continually get weapons and want to try them out."[4]

Isaacson also gives disastrous results that can, and do, occur. "The most vivid example of the limitations of weapons to win friends and influence countries is Iran: after $10 billion of arms deliveries, the Shah was deposed and replaced by Ayatullah Ruhollah Khomeini's violently anti-American regime."[5] Isaacson's article is full of information, including examples like Iran, and even graphs to show the increase of arms exported to Third World countries, as well as shocking photos of weapons in the hands of children in some of these nations.

The *Eagle* magazine article has no graphs or photos. The writing style of this article is mostly opinionated. It is very one-sided and only shows a right-wing view of the situation. It constantly blames much of the trouble in Third World countries on left-wing Communist groups attempting to bring down right-wing governments who are friendly to the United States. "The increasing terror wave in the Philippines is the result of an agreement reached between various Liberation and terrorist organizations—mainly the Moslem rebels of the National Liberation Front and the communists of the Popular Army."[6] Hamizrachi constantly claims these governments need more weapons to suppress the unrest that these terrorist groups (all Communist in some form) cause. Hamizrachi also quotes unnamed "Pentagon sources."

The *Time* article, in contrast, uses many references for different material and lists sources of information clearly, as in this sample sentence: "According to the Bureau of Labor Statistics, every $1 billion in arms exports directly supports about 50,000 jobs."[7] Because of its objectivity and clarity, Isaacson's article is much more convincing than Hamizrachi's. Hamizrachi gives information, but he never informs the reader where his information was taken from. His article is far less persuasive because it is so one-sided; as a consequence, it could only "convince" those who already believe as he does.

Notes
[1] Walter Isaacson, "Arming the World," *Time*, 26 Oct. 1981, p. 38.

[2] Isaacson, p. 33.

[3] Isaacson, p. 36.

[4] Isaacson, p. 38.

[5] Isaacson, p. 36.

[6] Yoran Hamizrachi, "A Hotline of the Secrets Behind Tomorrow's Headlines," *Eagle*, April 1981, p. 61.

[7] Isaacson, p. 36.

(Victor Ripley, student)

9. SAMPLES: TWO CHRONICLES OF RESEARCH

The weekly reports shown in Figure 2-10 demonstrate two procedures used to complete research papers. Although both reports are composites of experiences, you should view them as demonstrating two levels of the experience of writing a research paper. Neither is a demonstration of "perfect" research, but one report clearly displays more wisdom, more efficiency, and possibly more effort than the other. Which process do you think might produce the higher grade? As you read through the weekly reports, check off the things you consider "smart research." The items you check might serve as a general plan, or calendar of things to do, as you complete your research project.

Depending on how much experience you have in doing research and how much you know about your subject, you should plan to spend between 25 and 100 hours to complete a full-length research paper (seven to fifteen typed pages). Some students do their writing in "clumps" of several hours over one or more weekends, but you should try to spread your research over a few

Figure 2-10. Two Reports of Research Experiences

	REPORT 1	REPORT 2
week 1	thought about a topic; checked list in text, browsed through magazines I had, read encyclopedia articles on a couple of topics; tried to make topic questions.	did a free writing on one or two topics to see what I knew or could think of; circled main words in my free writings and wrote one-sentence summaries, then turned these into topic questions; tried listing possible topic focus questions; went to library to start working bibliography for each topic: used card catalog, *Reader's Guide* (2 most recent issues), & *N.Y. Times Index* for background and easier readings—picked 10 for each topic that looked promising; added and crossed out from topic focus questions.
week 2	looked in card catalog; didn't find much, thought about changing topic; read my high school research paper, thought about just updating it; looked through local newspaper for ideas.	chose the more interesting of the two topics; picked two possible focus questions, concentrated on one; read three articles from the working bibliography (they suggested best topic focus); tried a phrase outline based on the three articles; listed two local "experts" I could talk to; made tentative questions for polling a few students (never did interviews or poll, but the question list helped me change my working outline); called a county agency for pamphlets (turned out to be propaganda and how-to stuff, but gave one side of local picture).
week 3	checked *Reader's Guide*; found cross reference to my topic, found six articles	checked *Applied Science and Technology Index* for state-of-the-art information: found a

listed—our library only had 2; read them, made some notes.

couple articles our library has; checked *Business Periodicals Index* for marketing & investment angles: not too promising a subtopic but found one interesting article.

week 4   made a tentative thesis based on the articles I read; looked in card catalog under cross-reference (heading I had found in *Readers' Guide*,) didn't find much.

made tentative changes in topic outline, wrote a few summary notes based on my reading so far to see what I had learned & what I remembered best; tried an opening paragraph and formal thesis.

week 5   asked the reference librarian for help: found pamphlet in the vertical file and got five more headings to look under; checked new headings in card catalog: found 3 books (one book on shelf—photocopied one chapter); checked *Readers' Guide*, found 8 articles that our library had, photocopied 2.

revised working bibliography from revised topic outline: checked out 2 books from library, kept notes from original 3 articles from *Rs' G*, 2 from *Ap. Sci. & Tech. In.*; drafted major section of paper, found holes in support—went back to library to find statistics to pin down statement of problem, found a couple of usable tables I'll have to summarize.

week 6   made notes from 2 articles in library, photocopied 1 other; returned book (not as good as I thought it would be).

completed first draft; ending was weak, wanted to find better solutions—went to library to find costs of best "solution" I had found so far; called local person with "know-how" for interview—refused interview but was polite; called second person—no interview but she suggested a couple of sources (one I'd already run across & found not especially useful; the other was new to me & I found it on reserve in our library).

week 7   sources all saying pretty much the same thing; re-

new source from reserve had a suggested solution that

vised my tentative thesis to agree (match) with sources; started first draft, made tentative outline (topic list); finished first draft, got 2 people to read it.

seemed more cost-effective than others, but still had bugs; did second draft: refined the problem-solution thesis, ended with "no ideal solution but" couple that work in human & in financial costs; got three people to read draft; did detailed sentence outline to check flow of argument & completeness of support.

week 8

did final hand draft; found typist; had to redo source notes for correct form & add bibliography; typist took two days extra; proofread typed copy; handed in paper: 6 pages with 15 notes and 6-item bibliography.

changed a couple sections after readers mentioned getting confused (I hadn't paraphrased enough & so was still too technical in problem statement); switched a good example to opening after two readers praised it; used local info. from pamphlets for a "call to action" ending after solutions reviewed; typed final copy, including diagram in appendix; proofread typed draft before handing it in: 9 pages with 30 notes from 7 different sources, 10-item bibliography.

weeks, if possible. You'll need time to read, react to, and write about your research—in addition to the time you'll need just to do the reading. You'll need extra time if you choose to take a poll, a formal survey, or conduct interviews; and you'll need extra time for proofreading even if you use a typist to type your final draft.

You may have noticed as you read the two weekly reports in Figure 2-10 that Report 1 mentions having trouble finding information on the topic and some delay in settling on a topic; Report 2 shows an earlier topic choice but after some shopping around—and after having an earlier focus on a topic. The trouble with getting a topic, as shown in Report 1, stems from not knowing how to label the information needed for the topic—how to find the right headings to use for the topic. Report 2 shows how to use various kinds of discovery writing—a free writing to get started, a summary to take stock, and partial and complete drafts. Report 2 also shows how to use various outline forms to get organized and to check organization after the bulk of the writing is done. Finally, Report 2 shows broader and deeper research—using more indexes, reading more articles, and working back and forth from writing to research and back to writing. This cycle allows ideas to grow and judgments to form. It also allows the writer to develop a way to organize, start, and stop the presentation.

10. SAMPLE: EVALUATING A FORMAL RESEARCH PAPER

This section offers you a chance to evaluate a student's formal research paper. The criteria you use should be those that are established in this chapter. Your major criterion should be whether the paper presents a well-reasoned judgment based on facts—your evaluation should not be based on whether you agree or disagree, but on your assessment of the quality of the presentation. And, as with any research source, the presentation should be as up-to-date as possible, establish the writer's authority, demonstrate sufficient research and factuality, use a variety of types of evidence, use logic and emotion fairly, and be clearly written. Keep these criteria in mind as you read through the sample research paper. Then follow the instructions in the exercises following the sample. The questions at the end of the paper (keyed to the marginal letters found throughout the paper) are provided to help you judge its quality. (For a sample cover page, see "Manuscript Form" in the alphabetical listings.)

Military Pay: A Need for Change

[a]
One of the most controversial issues within the military services is the inequity of the current pay system. Inadequate pay has been identified as a major reason for low retention rates of trained personnel in all branches of the military. There has been considerable discussion in the recent past about the military pay system. Numerous articles have expounded upon the inadequacy of the current compensation package. Conversely, proponents of the current system claim that the inadequacies in pay are merely perceptual. This shortfall causes severe hardships for both single and married active duty servicemen, which effects retention and recruiting, as well as having an adverse impact on the readiness capabilities of our armed forces. Based upon all available information, I believe the compensation package is, in fact, inadequate by civilian [b] standards and it is time for government leaders to take positive steps to correct the military pay and benefit package.

[c]

With the institution of the All Volunteer Armed
Force in 1972 came the promise from the Government
to keep military pay comparable with the civilian
sector of our society. However, since the government made this promise, military pay and benefits
have been lagging behind the inflation rate of our
country. The cost of living rose by 59.9% between
December 1972 and October 1978 while military pay
rose by only 40.8% over the same period of time.[1]
Only once out of those seven years has a military
pay increase been close to the inflation rate. In
1980, actual purchasing power of service personnel

[d]

has been reduced as much as 20%, compared to their
civilian counterparts.[2]

[e]

Moreover, military pay is not only falling behind
the inflation rate, but is one of the lowest pay
systems in the United States. A new recruit's pay
is currently below minimum wage. In fact, the
$448.80 per month basic pay a new recruit receives
is only about 83% of what the government has set as
the monthly minimum wage.[3] Skilled military professionals with years of valuable experience find
themselves being paid a wage comparable to that of
a civilian apprentice. As examples, a toll collector on the Coronado Bridge in San Diego makes more
money than a skilled Navy electronics technician

with six to eight years of service. The starting
salary of a California State Highway Patrolman is
higher than that of a Navy Lieutenant with four
years in service and who is qualified as an Under-
way Officer of the Deck on his ship.[4] Add ten to

[f] twenty hours per week of required overtime to the
above examples and the salary comparability shows
an even broader expanse.

> The crews now on station in the Indian Ocean
> commonly work 100 hours and seven days a week
> to keep their ships functioning smoothly. It
> is unreasonable to expect sailors—or sol-
> diers or airmen—to make such an effort for
> pay that puts their families close to the
> poverty level.[5]

Even in view of all the comparable statistics,
many congressional leaders still argue that with
the extra benefits military personnel receive, the
pay is not as bad as it appears. Extra benefits
such as free medical care, incentive pay and bonuses are constantly used as reasons for not increasing or for capping military pay to lower percentage rates than originally proposed.

[g] While it is true that extra benefits do add an
extra margin to military salaries, they also are

inadequate. For example, incentive pay and bonuses, such as hazardous duty pay, have not increased in over ten years.[6] Taking the one time $2,000 re-enlistment bonus many military personnel receive, averaging it over a twenty year plus career, it comes to only $100.00 of additional taxable income per year.

The "free medical care" authorized by the government is only totally free for active duty personnel. For lack of trained medical specialists such as orthopedists, many dependents are referred to civilian specialists. Additionally, shortages of trained physicians in many areas has caused the closure of some military hospitals, resulting in curtailment of medical care for retired personnel and dependents of both active duty and retired personnel. When military hospitals lack these trained personnel or are closed, retirees and dependents must use a program called the Civilian Health and Medical Program of the Uniformed Services (CHAM-

[h]   PUS).

Under the CHAMPUS program, dependents of active duty personnel must pay a $50.00 per year deducti-ble charge for one dependent or $100.00 deductible per year per family for outpatient care. In addition, 20% of all outpatient charges must be paid by the recipient. Inpatient care costs are $25.00 or $4.80 per day, whichever is greater. Retired personnel and their dependents must also pay the $50.00 or $100.00 deductible per year depending on family size, plus 25% of outpatient charges. For inpatient care, 25% of the charges must be paid.[7]

[i] Should extensive periods of treatment be required, medical care could become very costly, further eroding individual military salaries.

With both the inflationary lag and the erosion of

[j] benefits working against military pay, single and especially married military personnel are finding it increasingly difficult to make ends meet. The average military salary, including all pay and allowances, for all enlisted personnel is $9,900 per year. The Bureau of Labor Statistics says the min-

[k] imum income necessary for a lower standard of living for a family of four is $11,546 per year.[8]

Further compounding the difficulties encountered by military personnel and their families are housing costs. Military personnel receive a housing allowance, but the high costs of housing near military installations are sometimes double this allowance. The average housing allowance for the San

Diego area is $279.00 per month, while the average housing cost is $492.00. In Washington, D.C. the average housing allowance is $299.00 per month, while the average cost is $623.00.[9]

Average figures, unfortunately, do not carry the full impact of the difficulties currently being encountered. Low ranked military personnel and many higher ranked personnel with large families do not even make enough money to cover the cost of housing and food in some areas, which forces them to resort to the use of welfare and food stamps. It has been estimated by the Third Quadrennial Review of Military Compensation that 100,000 military servicemen and women are eligible for food stamps.[10] In a <u>Baltimore Sun</u> interview with twenty-five petty officers at the Moffett Naval Air Station, ten indicated that they considered themselves eligible for

[l] welfare, and half said they were eligible for food stamps. Many others said they resorted to taking part-time jobs, or had working wives in an effort to avoid using welfare or food stamps.[11] At Langley Air Force Base, Virginia, it has been estimated that 35% to 40% of the 5,000 officers and enlisted people have part time jobs.[12]

Inadequate pay scales, erosion of fringe bene-
[m] fits, and difficult living conditions military per-

sonnel must face have resulted in serious manpower
shortages. These shortages have an adverse impact
on military readiness. As we enter a new decade, we
currently find our military forces at their lowest
levels since 1950. Last year all branches of the
military failed to meet their recruiting goals.[13]
To further compound this matter, thousands of
highly skilled professionals leave military service
each year, and their reason, more often than not,
is "the pay."

> If we are to attract and retain young Ameri-
> cans to the military, we must act positively
> to reverse both the reality and the percep-
> tion of the past decade. We must make the
> compensation systems for military service
> such that our people perceive them as, at
> least, not a financial burden and, better
> still, competitive with the civilian soci-
> ety.[14]

[n] Shortages of personnel in all branches of the
military is sighted as one of the major deterrents
to the military readiness capability of our armed
forces. The Navy currently lacks 20,000 skilled
petty officers, the Army 46,000 noncommissioned officers and the Air Force more than 3,000 noncommissioned officers.[15]

This massive shortage is indeed a grim situation.
Without trained personnel, the military is finding
it increasingly difficult to function. Until recently, the USS Canisteo, a Navy supply ship, was
one of the most efficient auxiliary ships the Navy
has, but now it is unable to join the fleet because
of severe manpower shortages [16] At Langley Air
Force Base, Virginia, the training is poor because
of personnel turnover; flight crews are having to
work double shifts and aircraft maintenance is running behind schedule. In a letter to the Secretary
of the Navy, Admiral Hayward, Chief of Naval Operations, recently wrote, "The number of ships that
reported themselves not ready because of personnel
shortages in November 1979, was more than three
times that of the previous November. The number of
ships reporting themselves only partially ready due
to undermanning was up 150 percent during the same
year." He also stated that he would be willing to
sacrifice some new ships if the money would be used
to raise Navy pay.[17]

Meanwhile, as personnel shortages increase at
alarming rates, Congress still does not realize
that pay is the major cause. Congress says a pay
increase will be too costly. However, they fail to
realize the cost of training new personnel. The

following Navy training costs are indicative of the costs incurred by all services. The cost of training an aviation fire-control technician is approximately $50,000. Last year over 300 in this classification left the navy. The cost to retrain new personnel to fill those positions will run $15 million. $7,000 is spent to train a boiler technician, and last year over 1,000 left the navy. The cost to retrain new personnel to fill those positions will run $7 million. The most extensive expenditures, however, are generated by the $345,000 per person cost of training Navy pilots and naval flight officers. Last year 1,600 pilots and flight officers left the Navy, which generated replacement training costs of over 600 million dollars.[18] Add up the

[o] cost of retraining thousands of other personnel for the more than 60 ratings the Navy alone has, and it is difficult to imagine how Congress can overlook these exorbitant expenditures.

Currently, there are several military pay increase bills in various stages before the House and Senate, but the future looks grim for all of them. After the bureaucracy finishes appending, amending,

[p] cutting and capping, the percentage of increase is likely to end up as a token portion of the original proposal. The Armstrong Amendment, which proposed a

3.4% pay increase, has already been scrapped. The Office of Management and Budget package deals mainly with extra benefit pay. The Ron Paul bill would give military personnel an immediate 10% raise and twice yearly raises equal to the Consumer Price Index, but it has little backing and little chance of enactment.

Two bills that still remain are the Nunn–Warner Amendment and the Hollings–Domenici plan. They are being introduced concurrently in Congress and they are the strongest of all the bills thus far. The Nunn–Warner Amendment proposes increases in all allowance areas such as housing, sea pay, and re-enlistment bonuses. The Hollins–Domenici plan proposes an 11.7% increase for all military personnel. Both bills have strong support and there is a good chance for enactment of these concurrent bills.

[q]

It is evident that the current military pay system is inadequate. Military pay must be increased in an effort to bring military pay to competitive levels with the civilian economy. Increases in basic pay, housing allowance, food allowance and travel expense are necessary to reverse the increasing number of personnel leaving military service. Additional bonuses for personnel in key ratings such as pilots, electronics technicians, and

others in highly technical and professional fields
must be authorized in an effort to close the gap
between military and civilian pay. Plans such as
the re-institution of the draft, in my opinion,
will not work. The draft will only temporarily
solve the personnel shortages. Without a pay increase, the exodus of skilled personnel will continue as more and more of them find it impossible
to live on military pay. The end result will be a
fully staffed, but untrained, unready military organization. The United States will then be left in
a far worse position, with respect to military
readiness, than originally.

Congress must now make the final decision. The
inadequacy of the military pay system has been ex-
plicitly pointed out, and the wrong decision at
this time could be irreversable. It is time for the
President, Congress, and the people of this country
[r] to face reality. Unless the military pay system is
corrected, the alternatives to be faced are an un-
dermanned, undertrained military force to meet the
threats of our society.

Endnotes

[1] Senator William L. Armstrong (R–CO), "The All Volunteer Armed Force Is in Trouble," Naval Affairs, January 80, p. 11.

[2] John J. Spittler, "People Power," Sea Power, February 1980, p. 4.

[s]

[3] Armstrong, p. 11.

[4] "Is Anyone Listening?," Navy Times, 19 May 1980, p. 11, col. 2.

[5] "For Want of a Boilerman," Chicago Tribune, 24 April 1980, p. 37, col. 2.

[6] John J. Spittler, "People Power," Sea Power, February 1980, p. 4.

[7] Interview with Lieutenant Commander Richard B. Kurtich, Navy Recruiting District, Richmond, Va., 22 May 1980.

[8] Armstrong, p. 11.

[9] Spittler, p. 4.

[10] "Families Urged to Use Food Stamps," Navy Times, 7 April 1980, p. 20, col. 1.

[11] "Navy Petty Officers Say They Can't Live Near California Base," Baltimore Sun, 24 April 1980, p. 14, col. 2.

[12] Charles W. Corddry, "Over Half of Base's F-15s Cannot Fight Immediately," Baltimore Sun, 24 April 1980, p. 3, col. 2.

[13] Armstrong, p. 11.

[14] "No Hope Now For Better Pay, Defense Says," Navy Times, 24 March 1980, p. 3, col. 3.

[15] Armstrong, p. 11.

[16] "For Want of a Boilerman," p. 37.

[17] Paul Smith, "CNO Says He Would Sacrifice Ship Money to Increase Pay," Navy Times, 7 January 1980, p. 1, col. 1 & 2.

[18] Spittler, p. 4.

[s]

Bibliography

[t] Armstrong, William L., Senator (R-CO.), "The All
Volunteer Armed Force is in Trouble," <u>Naval
Affairs</u>, Jan. 80, p. 11.

Corddry, Charles W., "Over Half of Base's F-15s
Cannot Fight Immediately," <u>Baltimore Sun</u>, 24
April 1980, p. 3, col. 2.

"Families Urged to Use Food Stamps," <u>Navy Times</u>, 7
April 1980, p. 20, col. 1.

"For Want of a Boilerman," <u>Chicago Tribune</u>, 24
April 1980, p. 37, col. 2.

Interview with Lieutenant Commander Richard B. Kurtich; Navy Recruiting District, Richmond, VA.,
22 May 1980.

"Is Anyone Listening?," <u>Navy Times</u>, 19 May 1980, p.
11, col. 2.

"Navy Petty Officers Say They Can't Live near California Base," <u>Baltimore Sun</u>, 24 April 1980, p.
14, col. 2.

"No Hope Now For Better Pay, Defense Says," <u>Navy
Times</u>, 24 March 1980, p. 3, col. 3.

Smith, Paul, "CNO Says He Would Sacrifice Ship
    Money to Increase Pay," <u>Navy Times</u>, 7 January
    1980, p. 1; col. 1 & 2.

[u] Spittler, John J., "People Power," <u>Sea Power</u>, Feb-
    ruary 1980, p. 4.

Questions and Exercises for Evaluating the Sample Research Paper

[a]   Does this background paragraph give equal weight to both sides of the pay debate?

[b]   This thesis states the basis of comparison and implies a call to action.

[c]   This paper is printed with its flaws intact. How much does inconsistent capitalizing of "government" affect the credibility of this paper?

[d]   Spittler's original sentence ended with ". . . caused the actual purchasing power of service personnel to be reduced as much as 20%, compared to their civilian counterparts." Has the student plagiarized? How would you advise the student to change this sentence?

[e]   This transition links the topics of the two paragraphs.

[f]   The first four notes blend data from three sources.

[g]   This transition announces an attempt to refute the above opposing argument.

[h]   Why is there no endnote to verify the facts in this paragraph? How should writers verify what they know from personal experience?

[i]   The endnote verifies the source of the facts. The student's conclusion from the facts follows.

[j]   This transition summarizes the two major issues treated so far.

[k]   Is the writer indicating the "poverty line" or an average lower class income? What credibility is lost with this unclear phrase?

[l]   How do you think the petty officers made their consideration?

[m]   This transition summarizes the three major issues treated so far.

[n]   This sentence makes a transition between subtopics.

[o]   The Spittler article has furnished most of the cost figures used in the paper, but the writer used an organization independent of the Spittler article.

[p]   What does the writer seem to assume here about the reader's attitude toward Congress?

[q]   Where would you expect endnote numbers on this page? What is lost here in credibility if the review of Congressional measures is not verified?

[r]   Do you agree with the writer that military pay should be increased?

[s]   Second and later notes for a source already listed in full once use only the author's last name and the page. (If no author is given, the title is repeated with the page.)

[t]   This bibliography lists only sources actually used in the paper: 9 articles from 5 periodicals and 1 interview. What other sources might the writer have used? What kind of information would you need to be convinced of the writer's viewpoint?

[u]   Did this writer use the correct formats for notes and bibliography? (Compare these with the prescribed formats for interview, magazine, and newspaper near the end of this chapter.)

EXERCISE 10. OUTLINING A FORMAL RESEARCH PAPER

Do a "paragraph outline" of the sample paper. The transitional sentences will help you. (See "Outlining.")

EXERCISE 11. SUMMARIZE THE SAMPLE

Write a detailed summary of the sample paper. In other words, paraphrase the sentences from Exercise 10—the thesis and topic sentences. The "details" in a detailed summary should be the major support for topic sentences. Unless you are quoting, you should use your own words and sentence structures.

Do not simply list topics but give full statements. That is, do not simply say things like "Harvey Author tells about A. Subject's married life, then goes on to say certain things about his work." Instead, use statements like "Harvey Author claims that A. Subject's married life helped his career because his wife, Betty Subject, stood by him when he fought his way off the bottle and because she acts as a supportive critic of all his new songs."

EXERCISE 12. EVALUATE THE SAMPLE USING THE GIVEN CRITERIA

Write your evaluation of this sample paper. Use the criteria summarized just before the sample and questions in the margin of the sample, but support your evaluation. That is, do not simply state "The writer cites reputable sources" but rather "The writer cites such scientists as Carl Sagan, the noted Cornell and NASA exobiologist, and Frank Drake, director of the observatory with the world's largest single-dish radio telescope. Both are primary searchers for signs of extraterrestrial intelligence."

The next section concerns the format of a research paper. For now, you should make notes on anything in this sample paper that you would like your paper to have—such as clear transition statements. You may also want to note practices to avoid. (By the way, you should not be too hard on this student writer for using "outdated" information. The student wrote on a current events topic using research that was up-to-the-minute at the time of writing.)

11. FORMAT OF A FORMAL RESEARCH PAPER

The sample paper in the last section demonstrates many features of format, but there are rules and variations you need to know about. Finalizing a formal research paper is a training exercise. You don't need to be creative; you simply need to follow instructions and models of common practices. Even if you have done a research paper before, you may not be aware of the current conventions. For instance, it is now customary to:

1. Double-space everything. (Variations: quadruple space under your title on the first page, and under your headings on the "Notes" page and "Bibliography" page.)
2. Use English rather than Latin in the endnotes. (After the first full endnote for a source, use the writer's last name and a page number instead of "*Ibid.*," "*Op. Cit.*," etc.) (Look at the "Notes" page in the sample research paper.)
3. Use one-inch margins in each of the four margins on a page. (Variations: Leave two inches at the top of your "Notes" page and your "Bibliography" page above these headings.)
4. Set up a long quotation (longer than four lines of your paper) by triple-spacing above it and below it, double-spacing within it, and *not* using quotation marks at the beginning and the end. Indent each line 10 spaces at the left. (Look at the long quotations in the sample paper.)

Some decisions about format come from formal organizations in a field. These common practices, or "conventions," are written down in handbooks for people who wish to publish in a field. The rules and styles for notes and bibliography in this book and most English textbooks come from the handbook published by the Modern Language Association:

Joseph Gibaldi and Walter S. Achtert, *MLA Handbook for Writers of Research Papers, Theses, and Dissertations*, Student Edition (New York: Modern Language Association, 1977).*

(But see the insert about the new MLA guidelines in the back of this text.)

---

* New MLA guidelines are being developed to coincide with the author name and author–title styles shown in Figure 2-11.

You should also know that there are such manuals for several disciplines, including biology and psychology, that there are separate manuals for business reports, and that companies large enough to have their own technical writing staffs may also have their own style manuals for format conventions. In other words, be flexible—don't be surprised if the conventions you see demonstrated and described in the following instructions differ slightly from what you have been trained to use.

11a. Documentation

Before we take a very detailed look at the style for notes and bibliography prescribed by the Modern Language Association, let's briefly examine the way that writers in some academic fields and in business writing document sources, using styles different from the MLA style. One style that some research journals commonly use is the style prescribed by the American Psychological Association, known as the APA style, described in a manual sponsored by the association:

Publication Manual of the American Psychological Association, 2nd ed. (Washington, D.C.: American Psychological Association, 1974).

Figure 2-11 lists the various styles of documentation commonly used in different fields. What style you use is *not* up to you; rather, the style you use depends on the type of research presentation you are making and the conventions for that type in the field. Remember, the MLA style shown in detail later in this section is customary for research papers done for college English classes.

One rare variation of the MLA style puts references in the text by using parentheses around much of the information that would go into an endnote. Here's one example:

Dr. Vincent J. Fontana (*Somewhere a Child Is Crying* [New York: Macmillan, 1973], p. 56) reminds parents that they need to provide more than food, shelter, and medical care to children.

A review of research done on a topic by various researchers or a paper requiring only one or two references might use this form.

Figure 2-11. Documentation Conventions Other Than Footnote/Endnote Style

AUTHOR NAME STYLE

Parents should remember that not only do they need to provide a child with nutrition, shelter, and doctor visits, but also they must extend of themselves their "parental affection touch" (Fontana, 56). Again, the foster parents are not always the best solution for neglected children, for they may see foster parents the same way they saw their natural parents, neither parent being able to love them (Anderson, 480).

AUTHOR–DATE STYLE

Parents should remember that not only do they need to provide a child with nutrition, shelter, and doctor visits, but also they must extend of themselves their "parental affection touch" (Fontana, 1973, 56). Again, foster parents are not always the best solution for neglected children, for they may see foster parents the same way they saw their natural parents, neither parent being able to love them (Anderson, 1977, 480).

AUTHOR–TITLE STYLE (if more than one work by same author used)

Parents should remember that not only do they need to provide a child with nutrition, shelter, and doctor visits, but also they must extend of themselves their "parental affection touch" (Fontana, *Somewhere*, 56).

References

Anderson, George M. "Child Abuse." *America*, 136 (1977), 478–482.

Fontana, Vincent J., M.D. *Somewhere a Child Is Crying*. New York: Macmillan, 1973.

NUMBER STYLE

Parents should remember that not only do they need to provide a child with nutrition, shelter, and doctor visits, but also they must extend of themselves their "parental affection touch" (1:56). Again, foster parents are not always the best solution for neglected children, for they may see foster parents the same way they saw their natural parents, neither parent being able to love them (2:480).

References

1. Vincent J. Fontana, M.D. *Somewhere a Child Is Crying.* New York: Macmillan, 1973.
2. George M. Anderson. "Child Abuse." *America,* 136 (1977), 478–482.

Source of Example: Student, "Child Abuse," Research Paper, J. Sargeant Reynolds Community College, 1979, pp. 5, 12.

N.B. Each style includes the exact page number for the information used.

11b. Why Documentation Is Needed

As a freshman, you may not be required to give copies of your research papers to your classmates. When you take upper-level courses in your major or graduate work, however, you may often have to share your research. Anyone interested in your topic may want a copy, or your research presentation may introduce your classmates to one aspect of your major field. Whether you work in the field, teach, or do professional research—or all three—you may write for publication in the journals in your field. All of this information sharing requires a system for recording sources so that your readers can follow your leads, and even use parts of your sources for their own research.

At the freshman level—at any level, for that matter—you need to establish the reliability and authority of your research writing. In matters of judgment, as you know from experience, people do not simply take your word for fact. They need assurance that your judgment is informed. Thus, in order to share information and establish credibility, you need to document your work.

11c. When to Document

For credibility, you must provide a note for every opinion, judgment, or speculation you use in your paper that comes from any of your sources. If you turn back to Figure 2-7, you will see how this excerpt from a student's paper shows one way to acknowledge the opinions of professionals from written works. Not only does Ronda provide endnotes, but she also sorts out the professional opinions in a controversy—whether dolphins have their own highly developed language. The sources you read and talk to will influence how you think on a subject, even if you sometimes reject their opinions. You owe it to your readers to show those influences; not showing the sources that influenced you is dishonest research writing.

You must also give a note for every fact your readers might dispute. That is, you must document every fact that is not "common knowledge" to the general public. Yes, different people know different things, but you must use your judgment to establish your credibility. For example, you can expect most people to know that leukemia is a form of cancer, but not how many Americans die of leukemia in a given year. You can expect most readers to remember that Skylab fell out of orbit, and maybe even that parts of it landed on Australia, but you can't expect readers to remember the exact date—and they don't expect you to remember it, either. Especially if the exact date is important (such as to calculate whether the U.S. and the U.S.S.R. had space stations in orbit at the same time), use it and tell where you found it by using a note.

What if several of your sources give the same opinion or the same fact? You still have to document what your readers don't know as facts. The documentation will be most useful if you cite the source that best presents the opinion or the information. To cite your source that is best on a given subtopic, you need to keep track of your sources carefully (or recheck your sources).

11d. How to Document

As you draft your research paper, you must make notes for yourself keeping track of which sources you are using as you go along. If you do not want to slow down the flow of your writing, just put the author's last name and the page number from your notecard into your draft in parentheses at the point where you stop using the source. Check number placement in Figure 2-7. Parenthetical notes in drafts become regular note numbers in the final draft or they become in-text references.

Some people—those who can stand the interruption—put the note numbers in the draft as they write and keep a list along side that translates the note number into the exact note form required. Such a list serves as a rough draft for typing the "Notes" page.

How do you know what number to use? That's easy. Just start with [1] after you first cite anything from your sources. The second time you use a fact or opinion from your sources, label it [2] in your draft at the point where your source data stops. Figure 2-7 shows a part from the middle of a student's research paper, but you can tell from her endnotes list that the order of numbers is the order in which Ronda has used the various opinions and reports from her sources.

But putting in the numbers is the easy part. The part that takes practice comes next. You have to choose which type of note form to use as a model for your notes for each source. There are slightly different types for books, periodicals, interviews, government documents, and media sources, but they all follow the same basic structure. For notes and for bibliography listings, you have to tell *who* your source is, *what title* your source used, and *where* and *when* your source gave the information. For printed materials, notes also give the exact *page* on which the exact information or opinion is located. The sample note forms later in this section can serve as models for you to follow as you set up your "Notes" page in your research presentation (or your footnotes, if you are required to put your notes at the bottom of the page on which you use the source data). The slightly different forms for your "Bibliography" page are modeled in a parallel list. It takes practice to remember even the most common forms, so it is important that you use the lists of note and bibliography models to set up your "Notes" and "Bibliography" pages, as well as your bibliography cards.

11e. Basic Form for Notes and Bibliography

All documentation is based on one form for reporting who, what, where, and when for your sources. Figure 2-12 shows the basic form as a kind of grid or template, or set order of slots. It may help you to think of documentation forms as ways to fill this same set of slots for a given type of source. The models in Figure 2-12 show the most common forms of documentation. The "who"

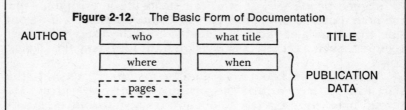

Figure 2-12.   The Basic Form of Documentation

The Basic Form Applied to a Book with One Author

FOOTNOTE or ENDNOTE
     * Peter Farb, *Word Play: What Happens When People Talk.* (New York: Knopf, 1973), p. 85.

BIBLIOGRAPHY ENTRY
Farb, Peter. *Word Play: What Happens When People Talk.* New York: Knopf, 1973.

The Basic Form Applied to a Weekly Magazine

FOOTNOTE or ENDNOTE
     * Stanley N. Welborne, "Compulsive Gambling, A Spreading Epidemic," *U.S. News and World Report*, 28 Jan. 1980, p. 73.

BIBLIOGRAPHY ENTRY
Welborne, Stanley N. "Compulsive Gambling, A Spreading Epidemic." *U.S. News and World Report*, 28 Jan. 1980, pp. 73–75.

slot is usually filled by the writer's name, but it can be empty and it can be filled by the name of an editor, corporation, agency, or group. The "what" or "title" slot usually has an underlined title of a book, magazine, pamphlet, or even a title of a television or radio program—any separate publication. The title slot can also include titles of parts of publications and titles of unpublished works in quotation marks. For a review of how to use quotation marks and underlining in titles, consult "Quotation Marks" and "Underlining" in the alphabetical part of this handbook.

Based on the samples in Figure 2-12 and the models later in this section, here are some general statements about the forms you must use for documentation in the MLA style.

1. Notes for printed matter always end with page numbers, but a bibliography entry often ends before the page number slot.
2. Notes are punctuated as if they were sentences, by using commas between parts and a period at the end, and indenting only the first line five spaces.
3. Notes always start with a raised number and a space after it.
4. Bibliographic entries are punctuated like paragraphs, by using periods between major parts and at the end—but indenting each line after the first line five spaces.
5. Notes are listed in numerical order.
6. Bibliographic entries are listed alphabetically. If there's nothing for the "who" slot, the item is placed in the alphabetized bibliography by the first word in the title slot (except for "a," "an," or "the," of course). Usually the author's last name serves to place an item in the alphabetized bibliography (indenting later lines sets it off).
7. Trained readers expect to see information accurately documented in the right slots with the right punctuation and indenting.
8. Using documentation forms precisely is close work that takes practice and concentration, especially if you are not used to the forms.

The last two statements above are not exactly "rules," as the other six seem to be. But you should regard them as rules. Even experienced writers need to check their documentation for accuracy and for whether they have followed the prescribed forms in their field. So expect to spend some time using the models below and checking your documentation procedures and forms. (You may learn this lesson from hindsight, but you must keep track of your sources from the very beginning in order to document accurately. Review Figures 2-1, 2-2, and 2-5.)

12. MODEL DOCUMENTATION FORMS—MLA STYLE

"Documentation" means using in-text references, footnotes, or endnotes *and* using bibliographic entries. Your "Notes" page and your "Bibliography" page at the end of a formal research paper may or may not list identical sources in different formats. But your notes will lead your readers to exact pages to find the information and opinions you have taken from sources. Your bibliography lists recommended reading, so it might include a source or two that you did not cite in your notes but found worth sharing.

The models below follow the basic form in Figure 2-12. The models demonstrate only those types you are likely to need most. If no model fits your source exactly, check the *MLA Handbook* in your library. You may have to use your judgment to supply the information a reader would need in order to get hold of your source (remember the sharing function of research presentations).

Don't try to invent your own forms or rely on your memory. Just find the model that fits your source and substitute the information for your source into the form. For books, you will find this information on the title page and the copyright page. For periodicals, you will find the information on the contents page. Of course, you also can use the information from the catalog card for books and the periodical indexes for magazines, journals, and newspapers—but you have to put the information in the MLA form. (Here's where your bibliography cards come in.) (Numbers in notes below can serve as numbers of models.)

Model Forms for Books

BOOK: ONE AUTHOR

Footnote/Endnote

[1] Ronald N. Bracewell, *The Galactic Club: Intelligent Life in Outer Space* (San Francisco: W.H. Freeman, 1975), p. 5.

Bibliography Entry

Bracewell, Ronald N. *The Galactic Club: Intelligent Life in Outer Space.* San Francisco: W.H. Freeman, 1975.

BOOK: TWO AUTHORS

Footnote/Endnote

[2] Bill Russell and Taylor Branch, *Second Wind: The Memoirs of an Opinionated Man* (New York: Random House, 1979), p. 10.

Bibliography Entry

Russell, Bill, and Taylor Branch. *Second Wind: The Memoirs of an Opinionated Man.* New York: Random House, 1979.

[In MLA style, only the first author's name is given with the last name first.]

BOOK: THREE OR MORE AUTHORS

Footnote/Endnote

[3] Merlin C. Wittrock, and others, *The Human Brain* (Englewood Cliffs, N.J.: Prentice-Hall, 1977), p. 65.

Bibliography Entry

Wittrock, Merlin C., and others. *The Human Brain.* Englewood Cliffs, N.J.: Prentice-Hall, 1977.

[This book lists eight authors, although Wittrock is the primary author. Wittrock chose not to have his first name used on the title page or in the preface, but it is listed on the catalog card and on the book's copyright page under "Library of Congress Cataloging in Publication Data."]

BOOK: EDITOR OR EDITORS

Footnote/Endnote

[4] Jan F. Kreider with Frank Kreith. *Solar Energy Handbook* (New York: McGraw-Hill, 1981), pp. ix–x.

Bibliography Entry

Kreider, Jan F., with Frank Kreith. *Solar Energy Handbook.* New York: McGraw-Hill, 1981.

BOOK: ARTICLE IN A COLLECTION—AUTHOR AND EDITOR

Footnote/Endnote

[5] Pauline Bart, "Why Women See the Future Differently from Men," in *Learning for Tomorrow: The Role of the Future in Education,* ed. Alvin Toffler (New York: Vintage/Random House, 1974), p. 35.

Bibliography Entry

Bart, Pauline. "Why Women See the Future Differently from Men." In *Learning for Tomorrow: The Role of the Future in Education.* Ed. Alvin Toffler. New York: Vintage/Random House, 1974, pp. 33–55.

[The editor's name is associated with the title of the entire book just before the publication data. This book is a paperback under Vintage, a special Random House imprint.]

BOOK: SECOND OR LATER EDITION

Footnote/Endnote

[6] Frank Smith, *Understanding Reading: A Psycholinguistic Analysis of Reading and Learning to Read,* 2nd ed. (New York: Holt, Rinehart and Winston, 1978), pp. 108–109.

Bibliography Entry

Smith, Frank. *Understanding Reading: A Psycholinguistic Analysis of Reading and Learning to Read.* 2nd ed. New York: Holt, Rinehart and Winston, 1978.

[The number of the current edition will be printed on the title page, but first editions are not marked. The copyright page will list the most recent publication date—list the copyright date, marked by a ©, not a printing date.]

BOOK: ONE VOLUME IN A MULTI-VOLUME WORK

Footnote/Endnote

[7] John Canaday, *Baroque,* Vol. II of *The Lives of the Painters* (New York: Norton, 1969), pp. 409–410.

Bibliography Entry

Canaday, John. *Baroque.* Vol. II of *The Lives of the Painters.* New York: Norton, 1969.

BOOK: A TRANSLATION

Footnote/Endnote

[8] Franz Kafka, *The Castle,* Definitive Edition, trans. Willa and Edwin Muir (New York: Schocken Books, 1974), p. 161.

Bibliography Entry

Kafka, Franz. *The Castle.* Definitive Edition. Trans. Willa and Edwin Muir. New York: Schocken Books, 1974.

[An edition number or label comes before the translator's name, but an editor's name would follow the translator's name.]

Model Forms for Periodicals

MAGAZINE: WEEKLY (MONTHLY)—WITH or WITHOUT WRITER'S NAME

Footnote/Endnote

[9] Walter Isaacson, "Arming the World," *Time,* 26 Oct. 1981, p. 38.

Bibliography Entry

Isaacson, Walter. "Arming the World." *Time,* 26 Oct. 1981, pp. 28–38.

*[Articles from **monthly** magazines use the same listing but without the day's date before the month. Articles might not have an author listed; in that case, you start with the next item— the article's title—next to the note number or the bibliography margin.]*

NEWSPAPER: DAILY

Footnote/Endnote

[10] Charles Cox, "Education Officials Explore Japan," *Richmond Times-Dispatch,* 28 Nov., 1982, Sec. C, p. 16, col. 1.

Bibliography Entry

Cox, Charles. "Education Officials Explore Japan." *Richmond Times-Dispatch,* 28 Nov. 1982, Sec. C, p. 16, col. 1.

[A weekly newspaper, such as The New York Times Book Review, *should be listed in the same form as a weekly magazine. If a paper issues more than one issue per day, the issue should be listed just after the paper's name:* New York Times, *Late City Ed.]*

JOURNAL: CONTINUOUS PAGE COUNT THROUGHOUT THE ANNUAL VOLUME

Footnote/Endnote

[11] James E. Ford and Dennis R. Perry, "Research Paper Instruction in the Undergraduate Writing Program," *College English,* 44 (1982), 828.

Bibliography Entry

Ford, James E., and Dennis R. Perry. "Research Paper Instruction in the Undergraduate Writing Program." *College English,* 44 (1982), 825–831.

[The p. *abbreviation for* **page** *is not shown when the volume number is shown; magazine forms don't use volume numbers, journal forms often do. Some journals do not number volumes, only issues; others count pages in each issue separately. To tell the difference, you often have to look at consecutive issues. For these journals, include the issue number:* 14, No. 3 (1948), 17–22 *or (if no volume number is given on the journal)* No. 3 (1948), pp. 17–22.]*

REVIEW

Footnote/Endnote

[12] S. Michael Halloran, rev. of *Reinventing the Rhetorical Tradition,* ed. Aviva Freedman and Ian Pringle, *College Composition and Communication,* 33 (1982), 94–96.

Bibliography Entry

Halloran, S. Michael. Rev. of *Reinventing the Rhetorical Tradition,* ed. Aviva Freeman and Ian Pringle. *College Composition and Communication,* 33 (1982), 94–96.

[Documentation follows the normal form for the journal, magazine, book, or newspaper in which the review appears. But it begins with the name of the reviewer and cites the author or editor after the title of the item reviewed.]

GOVERNMENT, CORPORATE, AND GROUP DOCUMENTS

Footnote/Endnote

[13] Bernard M. Oliver, *Project Cyclops: A Design Study of a System for Detecting Extraterrestrial Intelligent Life* (Moffett Field, Calif.: Stanford/NASA/Ames Research Center, 1971), pp. 7–8.

Bibliography Entry

Oliver, Bernard M. *Project Cyclops: A Design Study of a System for Detecting Extraterrestrial Intelligent Life.* Moffett Field, Calif.: Stanford/NASA/Ames Research Center, 1971.

[Often a single author will not be listed, but a commission, agency, or group will be listed on the cover or a title page for a book or pamphlet. Similarly, as in the example above, the publisher is not listed; instead, the sponsoring agency, company, or group is listed in the publisher's position. United States government documents are usually printed by the U.S. Government Printing Office: Washington, D.C.: U.S. Government Printing Office, 1983.*]*

INTERVIEW

Footnote/Endnote

[14] Personal interview with Betty Jane Olmstead, Occupational Therapist Aide, Medical College of Virginia, Richmond, Virginia, 16 May 1983.

Bibliography Entry

Olmstead, Betty Jane. Personal interview. 16 May 1983.

TELEVISION or RADIO PROGRAM

Footnote/Endnote

[15] *Reagan at Midterm,* narr. Roger Mudd, prod. Anthony Potter, NBC White Paper, 28 Dec. 1982.

Bibliography Entry

Reagan at Midterm. Narr. Roger Mudd. Prod. Anthony Potter. NBC White Paper. 28 Dec. 1982.

[For local programs, list the local station and city. The names of the narrator, producer, writer, director, or other responsible people help to establish the authority behind the program, so include these if possible.]

UNPUBLISHED MANUSCRIPTS

Footnote/Endnote

[16] Ronda Jones, "Dolphin Talk," Research paper J. Sargeant Reynolds Community College, 1982, pp. 3–4, 7.

Bibliography Entry

Jones, Ronda. "Dolphin Talk." Research paper J. Sargeant Reynolds Community College 1982.

[Titles of unpublished dissertations, research papers, and other manuscripts are put in quotation marks rather than underlined. No comma separates the name of the institution from the type of manuscript or from the date.]

If essential information is not printed on your source, you may have to estimate or use an abbreviation, as follows:

> **no place of publication given—**
> > **[United States]**   **OR** **[n.p.]**
>
> **no publisher given—**
> > **n.p.**
>
> **no date given—**
> > **[1981?]**   **OR** **n.d.**
>
> **no page number can be calculated—**
> > **[n.p.]**

These estimates or abbreviations go in the appropriate slots in the documentation form you have chosen. They most frequently occur with pamphlets that follow the form for government, corporate, or group documents, a variation on the basic form for books.

EXERCISE 13. CHOOSING MODELS TO CORRECT FORMS

Below are incorrectly done documentation forms. Answer the multiple-choice question to pick the correct model, and then rewrite each as a correct footnote/endnote and as a correct bibliographic entry. (Use the first page number listed to make your footnote/endnote.)

EXAMPLE: incorrect form:
(10)   Isaacson, Walter, Arming the world, Time Oct. 26, 1981: 28–38.
The above data is probably for
(a)   a book with one author
(b)   an article in a collection
√ (c)   an article in a weekly magazine
(d)   an article in a monthly magazine

corrected footnote/endnote form:

[10] Walter Isaacson, "Arming the World," *Time*, 26 Oct. 1981, p. 28.

corrected bibliography entry form:

Isaacson, Walter. "Arming the World." *Time*, 26 Oct. 1981, pp. 28–38.

When you write the correct forms, you must include periods, spacing, commas, quotation marks, and underlining in the proper places.

1.   26.   Song of Solomon by Toni Morrison, (Signet/New American Library, New
York, 1977), p. 163–173.
The above data is probably for
(a)   a book with one author
(b)   a book with an editor
(c)   a book with no author listed
(d)   an article in a collection
Write out the correct note and bibliography forms.

2.   27.) Richardson, Steven M. and Willson, Lee Anne; *"Cosmic Contamination:
Elemental Clues to the Sun's Birth" Astronomy*, vol. 8, no. 6, June 1980, pp.
6–22.
The above data is probably for
(a)   an article in a collection
(b)   an article in a monthly magazine
(c)   an article in a weekly magazine
(d)   an article in a newspaper (daily)
Write out the corrected note and bibliography forms.

3.   28 Susan Carey, The Child as Word Learner; *Linguistic Theory and Psychological Reality*, edited by Morris Halle, Joan Bresnan, and George A.
Miller—Cambridge, Massachusetts, MIT Press, 1978, 264–293.
The above data is probably for
(a)   an article in a weekly newspaper
(b)   an article in a collection
(c)   an article in a monthly magazine
(d)   a book with more than three authors

EXERCISE 14. AN ADVANCED FORM PROBLEM

The answer to the following problem *cannot* be found in the list of sixteen models above, at least not in any one place. The task is to write a correct bibliographic entry for an essay in a two-volume anthology. The information is given in jumbled order.

NAME OF THE ENTIRE ANTHOLOGY: *Writing: The Nature, Development, and Teaching of Written Communication.*
NAME OF THE AUTHOR OF THE ARTICLE: Ellen W. Nold
PLACE OF PUBLICATION: Hillsdale, New Jersey
NAME OF THE VOLUME CONTAINING THE ARTICLE: Volume II, *Writing: Process, Development, and Communication*
NAME OF THE ARTICLE: "Revising"
PUBLISHER: Lawrence Erlbaum Associates
EDITORS OF THE ENTIRE ANTHOLOGY: Carl H. Frederiksen, Marcia Farr Whiteman, and Joseph F. Dominic
DATE OF PUBLICATION: 1981
PAGES: 67–79

13. SUGGESTED TOPICS

Research projects take a long time, and they can be frustrating work. To bear the strain, you should design a topic that interests you. To choose your topic, look to your long-standing interests, your curriculum (major), your career interests for topics that call for your judgment. You may prefer to look to the topics listed below, but any topic you choose will need your own focusing and slant. This list is simply an informal collection of ideas that might provoke your thinking.

1. Should women (juveniles) suffer the same punishment as adult men if they commit the same crimes, such as murder or armed robbery?
2. There's still a gap in the fossil record at about the time modern man emerged. In your opinion, where did modern humans come from?
3. Should the office of Vice-President (should the Electoral College) be abandoned (or replaced with something else)?

4. Should the United States (together with Russia?) try to colonize space? (See work by Gerard K. O'Neill of Princeton and considerations of Skylab and Russian long-term operations in space stations.)

5. What should (local, state, national governments, or agencies or volunteer groups) do to help older Americans resist crime? (Has direct deposit of Social Security checks reduced muggings of retired citizens, for instance?)

6. What should be done to help victims of child abuse, rape, wife beating, or alcoholism?

7. What should be done to help child abusers, relatives of alcoholics, or victims of incest?

8. What should be done to help divorced parents, widowed parents, children of divorce, children of a recently deceased parent?

9. Should adopted children be able to find out legally who their natural parents are? (open birth records)

10. Who is responsible for children's sex education, religious education, civic education?

11. Who killed the people of Cambodia, Uganda, the Jews of Europe and Russia, and their political prisoners? (There are obvious answers, like Idi Amin or Stalin; but there are also less obvious answers.)

12. Does television (or schooling, arcade games, or studying only "practical" subjects) kill the imaginations of America's children?

13. Who really controls the U.S. economy? (Beware of easy answers.)

14. Should the U.S. spend more (less) on the space program, defense, social programs (Social Security, health care, welfare, school aid)?

15. What should be done to save America's fresh water supply, air, wildlife, oil supplies, national (or state) parks, bridges, roads, public utilities?

16. What should be done to save America's construction industry, steel industry, potato industry, auto industry?

17. (Why) should America develop mass transportation systems, geothermal energy, fusion power, laser energy, solar energy, coal energy?

18. Should the U.S. develop laser weaponry, an international agricultural effort to feed the world, satellite weapons, an international economic effort to reduce trade barriers?

19. What should be done to develop America's (South America's, Africa's, Asia's) human resources?

20. What should be done to reduce teenage pregnancy, drug abuse, traffic deaths/accidents, venereal disease, birth defects?

Here are some less common topics, which may require more analysis and focus:

21. the Jim Jones Guiana massacre versus the American dream
22. Indian (black, women's) literature of the 1960s (1970s): pride and identity reasserted
23. beyond the microchip: the next generation of computers
24. forbidden sciences: vivisection, eugenics, chemical warfare
25. the year 2050: how X has changed (X = religion, ecology, energy, any nation, Antarctica's resource value, the city, etc.)

3 an alphabetized handbook

14. COMMON USES OF A HANDBOOK

14a. A Handbook as an Editing Guide

Part of finishing a writing involves checking it to see that everything conforms to the practices that readers expect, such as conventional grammar, spelling, punctuation, and acceptable wording. To signal that a portion of your writing does not conform to the current conventions of writing, your instructor may mark individual items and write an abbreviation called a "correction symbol," or an "editing symbol." You then must translate the symbol into a page reference so that you can look up an explanation of the conventional practice. Figure 3-1 shows a paragraph of writing marked with some of the correction symbols used in this text. Some instructors use section numbers rather than correction symbols. The symbol chart inside the back cover will help you translate symbols into brief explanations of the convention as well as lead you to the proper page numbers.

How to Use Editing Symbols. Reread your paper with your book open to the symbol chart at the back. As you read through, take each editing symbol and find it on the symbol chart. Then turn to the page or pages listed for that symbol and scan the examples given. Look at your sentence marked for correction and try to find a comparable example. Read the general advice at the beginning of the section and the numbered bits of advice throughout the section. As you read, note anything that is new to you. Also, try to apply the advice to the line marked on your paper.

Figure 3-1. A Paragraph Marked with Correction Symbols

We can't win if we keep poisoning our water, land, and air. Look at the last 20 years. We dumped atomic waste into the ground along geologic faults and caused earthquakes. They build atomic reactors on geologic faults. We shipped nerve gas across the country on rickety railroad tracks to dump them into the ocean. Encased in concrete and lead, but some old ones are breaking open. Our river catch fire. Our oil spill onto our beaches and our land, our grain elevators explodes. Dumping zinc, mercury, and kepone, even poorly treated sewage gets into the rivers of North America.

ps   *t*   *p agr*   *frag*   *p ref*   *s-v*   *d mod*

ps	=	person shift
t	=	tense shift
p agr	=	pronoun agreement
frag	=	sentence fragment
p ref	=	pronoun reference
s-v	=	subject–verb agreement
d mod	=	dangling modifier

A CORRECTED COPY

We can't win if we keep poisoning our water, land, and air. Look at the last 20 years. We dumped atomic waste into the ground along geologic faults and caused earthquakes. We built atomic reactors on geologic faults. We shipped nerve gas across the country on rickety railroad tracks to dump it into the ocean. The gas was encased in concrete and lead containers, but some of these are breaking open. Our rivers have caught fire at times. Oil has spilled onto our beaches and our land. Our grain elevators sometimes explode. We have even dumped zinc, mercury, kepone, and poorly treated sewage into the rivers of North America.

For instance, look at the "t" symbol connecting two circled verbs in the Figure 3-1 sample. One verb is past; the other is present tense. Which is correct? It depends. Since the passage talks about the past two decades, the verbs should probably be past tense throughout the paragraph, especially since the writer seems to have in mind isolated cases. The verbs could be put in the present tense if the writer decided to discuss the examples as ongoing or constant practices. If, according to the evidence presented in other parts of the writing, some examples are isolated cases and others are constant occurrences, then the examples should be sorted into two groups and presented in separate paragraphs.

In short, to use editing symbols best, you need to apply them in the context of your writing. An editing symbol may or may not single out an instance of unconventional wording. For instance, the issue marked by the "t" was the mismatch between two verbs. But changing a single verb does not settle the issue in this case. The verbs would have to be made consistent throughout the essay.

How to Take Editing Symbols.   You should probably consider the editing symbols on your papers as simply part of the training your college tuition pays for. Your teachers assume that you will want your writing to have that finished look of good writing. Some instructors mark most of the items they notice; others mark only the items that need the most work. In either case, your job is to know what the editing symbols mean and to apply what you learn from studying the handbook to your writing.

Often, editing symbols show up only on graded writings. Don't be misled into thinking that the symbols somehow add up to your grade. Look at the writing in Figure 3-1. The corrected copy contains all the changes, but it still gives few facts and figures. As a summary paragraph, it may work as is. But as an informative paragraph intended to give evidence, it falls short—it mixes examples, omits cases of air pollution, and leaves out details of where and when the incidents happened and who reported them. It even omits the issue of landfills. In other words, correct writing is not necessarily good writing. The example in Figure 3-1 is a journal entry, written in outrage. It suggests several essay topics, even a research project. But the paragraph isn't finished, even though the corrected copy is letter perfect.

If you feel your papers have too many editing symbols, or if you receive a low grade because you haven't written according to the conventions, you need to examine your writing process. Consider the choices you make continually as you write. Who can keep track of everything? As the journal excerpt in Figure 3-1 demonstrates, sometimes emotion is more important than presenting all the evidence. But for graded work you need extra time. You need time to study the corrections your instructor has listed on your work. In later drafts and writings, you will need extra time, once your ideas and organization are fairly well set, to proofread your writing for corrections. Don't expect miracles; you may see the same correction symbol on several of your writings. Do expect improvement over time as you practice writing.

14b. A Handbook as a Reference Tool

Especially if you are not very experienced with writing, you may need to know about some of the things in this handbook. Don't wait for your teacher to point them out; do your own research. Anybody in college can use the card catalog, the periodical indexes, and other library resources. As you can see from the table of contents, information on these resources is waiting in Part II for anyone who needs it. Perhaps you would like to spell better than you do. The section on spelling in this alphabetical handbook contains especially useful suggestions about this troublesome skill. If English is not your native language, you may often need to turn to "Irregular Verbs" or to the "Verb Form Chart" in the "Passive Verbs" section. Even native speakers will find these sections handy. If your use of dictionaries has been limited to looking up definitions or synonyms in pocket dictionaries, you may be surprised to learn what the "Dictionary" section says about using words in writing.

Generally, you should not try to study points of grammar that you do not need to know because you risk studying incorrect patterns you did not use. Also, overstudying grammar can give you writer's block, a paralyzing fear of being less than perfect in anything you write. As Part I suggests, you have to think on paper to get your ideas together. Rough notes to yourself are supposed to give you ideas, not a fear of writing. Nevertheless, you may appreciate some advance warning about proofreading skills that your college teachers expect (and not just in English). So here's a troubleshooting list. The sections of the handbook that discuss typical breakdowns in sentence structure are these:

cs, d mod, frag, mis mod, ro.

The sections that discuss typical confusions that occur within sentences and between sentences are these:

ms, p agr, p ref, ps, s-v, t.

Use the editing symbol chart as suggested above, to study these sections of the handbook.

Finally, remember that a handbook for English is not like the multiplication tables or logarithmic scales. A handbook can explain certain patterns, but the variety of English is infinite. You have to use your judgment and apply handbook advice to the particular context of your writing. Your growth as a writer depends more on your ingenuity and willingness to take risks than on writing safe, uncomplicated sentences. Good writing is much more than rules and basics. Your growth as a writer does not have to wait until you "master" basic grammar; the quality and accuracy of your writing can develop together.

The Format of Handbook Entries.   Each section of the alphabetized handbook begins with a general explanation of a conventional pattern, though not always a "rule" to follow in all situations. Examples of particular patterns are then given. One or more exercises will give you practice on the pattern shown in the section. Finally, a section called "Special Hints" mentions particular points of caution, summarizes, or gives information that is especially helpful in using a pattern in your writing. At first, the symbols and numbers of a handbook can seem confusing and put people off. But with some practice, you will begin to see the regular structure of entries and will be able to read quickly through an entry to find the information and examples you need.

A Special Hint.   If you have trouble finding something by name or if you run across a term you don't know, go straight to the index at the back of the book to find the best pages for the term. Don't be surprised when you see terms in the handbook entries; use the examples to make sense of them. These terms are often jargon words that are handier for instructors than for students; don't worry about memorizing terms and their definitions—concentrate on following the revision patterns shown in the examples.

abst | 15. ABSTRACT AND GENERAL WORDING

Use words that specify single things rather than using words that name categories.

Abstract, general words are names of categories. Words like *transportation, equality, sports, logarithm, systematic, interfacing,* and *healthy* are too general and don't help readers see the pictures you have in mind. Concrete, specific words like *apple, piano, running, Washington Monument, Mustang, Donald Duck,* and others refer to particular things. So if a general word is a key word in a passage of your writing, you can make your meaning clearer by using particulars.

EXAMPLE:

general: Although these rugs are terribly expensive, the initial outlay is well worth it.

REVISED: Although these *Oriental* rugs are terribly expensive, *costing about $3,500 for a 5' by 7' rug,* this initial outlay is well worth it.

Words that are always capitalized specify particular places, original compositions, organizations, belief systems, or people. So names like Mississippi River, *A Farewell to Arms,* NASA, Hinduism, and Martin Luther King specify individual things or people. Titles are always *specific* and *concrete* because they name one composed work, although the things named in titles may not be very specific—such as "The Courts of Chaos," *The Amityville Horror.*

(s)   (g)   (s)   (g)

EXERCISE 1. GENERAL AND SPECIFIC WORDS

Write a *g* in the blank next to the general words and an *s* in the blank next to the following specific words.

_____	transportation	_____	automobile
_____	money	_____	Buick Skylark
_____	economics	_____	biology
_____	botany	_____	dollar
_____	oranges	_____	Beth's Volkswagen

You may have noticed right away that some words are more general than others. You may also have noticed that some specific words can indicate thousands of things. To identify one of the many Buick Skylarks manufactured over the years, a writer would have to give some particular details: *the blue, 1971 Skylark with a mashed left front fender and a customized license plate reading BROKE.*

EXERCISE 2. LEVELS OF GENERALITY

The words on the list above that concern biology could be ranked like this: *biology* (very general), *botany* (general), and *oranges* (specific). How would you rank the three words from Exercise 1 that concern money and the four words that concern transportation?

Although writers may use very general words in their thesis statements and somewhat general words in their topic sentences, the support sections of paragraphs are usually filled with specific, concrete words. For example, if a writer for a business magazine says that wages for union workers are increasing rapidly, the writer will also mention specific figures and unions, such as average salaries for members of the AFL-CIO or UAW for the last few years. The support for topic and thesis statements must be specific to be clear.

EXERCISE 3. GENERAL SENTENCES

Which of these two sentences contains mostly general, abstract words?

_____ 1. "We have begun to appreciate the awesome interconnectedness of the sea world that makes all marine life everywhere subject to our actions."

_____ 2. "We have learned, for example, that DDT used in Africa has appeared in the tissue of Antarctic penguins thousands of kilometers away." (Carl Roessler)

EXERCISE 4. RANKING LEVELS OF GENERALITY

Rank the following five items from most general (1) to least general (5).

_____	appreciate	_____	Antarctic
_____	sea world	_____	penguins
_____	marine life		

EXERCISE 5. A DEFINITION WITH SPECIFICS

Use specific terms to explain one general topic that you select. Use words in your practice writing that are as specific as those you ranked (4) and (5) in Exercise 4 above.

EXAMPLE:

Photosynthesis (2) is a process (1). Green plants (3), like apple trees (5), honeysuckles (5), roses (5), and other flowering plants (4) especially, use it to make carbohydrates (3).

SPECIAL HINTS

To help you think of specifics, you may wish to glance over "The Topic Grid" in section 1c or the question list of "Common Organizing Principles" in section 3.

adj ‖ 16. ADJECTIVES

Use words with adjective endings to create vivid images of people, places, things, or ideas. Adjectives make your writing more concrete and specific.

Adjectives often end with particular letters. Some common adjective indicators are the endings *-able, -al, -an, -ant, -ar, -ative, -ent, -ial, -ible, -ic, -ical, -ious, -ive, -ose,* and *ous.*

"Adjective," however, does not name a particular set of endings, but a particular job or function in a sentence. The job of an adjective is to specify more about persons, places, things, or ideas. As the example below shows, endings are only one way of signaling such specifics to your readers.

EXAMPLE:

"We are seated on *a crude wooden* bench in *the scanty* shade of *the overlapping* roof of *a dilapidated* and *malodorous* leprosarium *isolated some* distance to *the* north of *the* village. . . ." (Father Sebastian Englert)

Adjectives, then, can occur in three positions:

1. before nouns: *a crude wooden* bench
2. after nouns: leprosarium *isolated*
3. after verbs of being and linking: The leprosarium was *dilapidated* and *malodorous*.

EXERCISE. SUPPLYING ADJECTIVES

Add adjectives to the following paragraph. The first five sentences have slots where adjectives should go. Supply adjectives for the last three sentences on your own.

During _____ night _____ stars had shone. _____ frost fell on us. I shivered. My face felt _____ since my moustache and _____ hair were covered with _____ dew. Sleeping under _____ sky, especially near _____ timberline, was _____ experience. Even during summer, mountains of Colorado get at night. When sky began to pale toward east, I shifted inside bag to get for sun that would warm mountainside. Even light that did reach us during morning warmed us less than we had hoped.

SPECIAL HINTS: TYPES OF ADJECTIVES

As you work out problems of wording or clarity in your rough drafts, use this checklist of adjective types to see if there is a way to be more vivid or specific.

ARTICLES: *a, an, the*
Use *the* before nouns that specify unique things. Use *a* or *an* before nouns that indicate any one of a group. Use *an* before such general nouns that begin with the vowel *sounds* of *a, e, i, o,* and *u.* (It is customary, however, to write "*an his-*torical event.")

DEMONSTRATIVE ADJECTIVES: *this, that, these, those*
Use *this* and *these* to refer to near or recent things; use *that* and *those* to refer to topics more distant in time or space. Use the singular forms *this* and *that* only before singular nouns.

DESCRIPTIVE ADJECTIVES: Use descriptive adjectives to specify the dimensions of your subject and your impressions of it; descriptive adjectives include literary (*dilapidated, malodorous*) and technical (*metric* mile, *Vernier* caliper, *Neolithic* era) adjectives.

INDEFINITE ADJECTIVES: Use indefinite adjectives to assist nouns in generalizations: *Most* farms in the country are threatened by the drought.

INTERROGATIVE ADJECTIVES: *whose, which, what*
Use these before nouns in questions: *Whose* garden is this? *Which* horse won? *What* bill passed?

NUMERICAL ADJECTIVES: Use these to specify exact or approximate numbers before nouns: It takes *six* weeks to get the parts from Germany.

PROPER ADJECTIVES: Use these to specify names: *Vernier* caliper, *United* States, *African* violet

RELATIVE ADJECTIVES: *whose, which, what*
Use these words in indirect questions and to set up clauses that further identify nouns: He wondered *which* insecticide had been sprayed on the forest. The doctor *whose* training has been slipshod is a prime candidate for a malpractice suit.

adv ‖ 17. ADVERBS

Use adverbs, which often end with *-ly*, to specify where, when, why, or how some action happens. Use adverbs in front of verbs, adjectives,
and other adverbs to make them less abstract
or general.

EXAMPLE:
Finally pausing for breath, she gasped quickly but *softly* while
(when)   (how)   (how)

seeming to look *distrustfully* from one *grandly* smiling face to another.
(how)   (how)

SPECIFICS

(1) adverbs without the *-ly* ending: Adverbs like *very, too, so, down, well,
soon,* and others are used to add intensity, to indicate direction, or
indicate when or how something is done.

EXAMPLE:
Although she was *very* tired, she was not *too* tired to dance *so well*
that she brought the house *down*.

(2) Adjectives that end in *-ly*: A few *adjectives* end with *-ly*, such as *lonely,
homely,* and *comely*. Be sure to use them before nouns.

EXAMPLE:
A *lonely* traveller sometimes appreciates *homely* chores.

(3) Words that can be adjectives or adverbs: Some words, like *early* and
only, can be either adjectives or adverbs, depending on how they
are used.

EXAMPLE:

"The *early* bird catches the worm" was the *only* adage he seemed to know. (*both adjectives*) He got up *early* to run, but he *only* ran a mile. (*both adverbs*)

EXERCISE 1. SUPPLYING ADVERBS

Add adverbs to the following paragraph.

Before we wake _____, I look _____ly at her and I smile _____ly. I'm _____ _____ glad she's my wife. Although we stumbled through the first few months of marriage _____ly, we seem now to glide through our married days _____ly and _____ly and our married nights _____ly and _____ly.

EXERCISE 2. CONTINUING THE CONTEXT

Continue the writing from Exercise 1 using adverbs to vivify actions and intensify emotions. One approach would be to follow up the comparison that has been started between the early months of marriage and the current state of the marriage. Use your imagination to put yourself in the place of the man, or switch the point of view of the entire writing to that of the wife.

SPECIAL HINTS: ADVERBS AND DIALECT

Use the following usage guide to make sure that your adverbs fit the level of writing required by an assignment—usually the "standard" usage. (See "Dialect or Language Level" for an explanation of the labels used below.)

COLLOQUIAL:	She dances good.
STANDARD:	She dances *well*.
NONSTANDARD:	She glides angelic.
STANDARD:	She glides *angelically*.
NONSTANDARD:	She sings impossible well.
STANDARD:	She sings *impossibly well*.
COLLOQUIAL:	She has a right pretty house.

STANDARD:	She has a *beautifully* decorated home.
INFORMAL:	She has a beautiful furnished apartment.
STANDARD:	She has a *beautifully* furnished apartment.

apos/no apos | # 18. APOSTROPHES

Use an apostrophe to signal that letters or numbers have been left out; to form the plurals of letters and numbers; and to form the possessives of persons, places, things, and ideas (to make nouns and indefinite pronouns possessive).

EXAMPLES:

(1) omitted letters and numbers: *'82* model cars; *can't, won't, weren't (for contractions with not)*; *I'm, she's, they're (for contractions with am, is, and are)*

(2) plurals of letters and numbers: *5's, A's, 1990's, 1870's*

(3) possessives: *Jerry's, Edna's,* the *dog's* collar; *everybody's* responsibility, *anybody's* concern

According to one theory, the ' has replaced the *e* from the *-es* ending that was used to signal possessive forms in English hundreds of years ago.

To determine whether to use *'s* or the ' alone, use the *sound* of the noun according to these guidelines:

(a) Use *'s* to show the possessive form of singular and plural nouns that do *not* end in the *sound* of *s* or *z*. Also use the *'s* for singular nouns of one syllable that *do* end in the sound of *s* or *z*.

EXAMPLES:

Singular: person's, anybody's guess, the legislature's plan, my brother-in-law's car, the horse's gait

Plural: women's rights, sheep's wool, fathers-in-law's arrangements

(b) Use ' to show the possessive form of plural nouns that end in the sound of *s* or *z*. Also, generally use the ' for singular nouns of more than one syllable that end in the sound of *s* or *z*.

EXAMPLES:
Singular: *Aristophanes'* comedies, *Siemans'* furnace
Plural: the *Smiths'* house, those *scientists'* methods

SPECIFICS

(1) joint ownership: If two people own something together, show the possession signal after the last person listed.

EXAMPLES:
Jack and *Harvey's* car, the Smiths and *Joneses'* duplex

(2) similar ownership: If two people own the same kinds of things, show the possession signals separately by adding apostrophes to the name of each person and using plurals to tell what they own.

EXAMPLES:
Jack's and *Harvey's* hang gliders, the *Smiths'* and the *Joneses'* home computers

(3) things that "own": Possession, ownership, or belonging can be shown with an apostrophe, with an *of* phrase, or with a *for* phrase.

EXAMPLES:
last *year's* profits	the profits for last year
tomorrow's news	the news of tomorrow
the *course's* requirements	the requirements of the course

(4) personal pronouns: Personal pronouns never use an apostrophe to show possession (but personal pronouns can be used in contractions).

EXAMPLES:
possessive forms	*contractions*
my, mine, our, ours	I'm (*I am*), we're (*we are*)
your, yours	you're (*you are*)
his, her, hers, its	he's (*he is*), she's (*she is*), it's (*it is*)
their, theirs	they're (*they are*)

(The relative pronoun *whose* also shows possession, but the contraction *who's* means *who is*.)

(5) things: Most writers use adjective forms instead of possessive forms
     to signify that a thing belongs to a category

EXAMPLES:
scientific experiments   OR   *Dr. Rossiter's* experiments
                        (*rather than "science's experiments"*)

(6) gerunds: Possessive forms are often used before verbal nouns that
     end in *-ing.*

EXAMPLE:
We are excited about *Swenson's* running for office.

EXERCISE. PROOFREADING FOR APOSTROPHES

Insert or remove apostrophes to correct the paragraph below. Leave correct
uses alone. Use the *s* with the ' when necessary.

"Keeping up with the Jones'es" will mean something entirely different
in the 80s and 90s than it did in the 50s and 60s because the Joneses lifestyle
is changing. The fuel shortages of 73 and 79 indicate that we may soon be
"keeping *down* with the Jonese's." As the cost of everyone living soars, the
status of anyone gas guzzler or oil-heated sprawling ranch house plummet's.
Its going to be difficult to turn on an electric fan without feeling downright
unpatriotic. Instead of Americas worshipping cubic inches and horsepower,
America will define status by the number of miles per gallon. The "350s" are
giving way to the "30s-in-town-and-50s-on-the-highway." Being pragmatist's,
Americans wont tolerate a threatening dependence on foreign energy sources
for long; being accustomed to luxury, theyre not going to enjoy changing their
lifestyle's.

SPECIAL HINTS

- Use the apostrophe to show possession, not for ordinary plurals
  (never *two dog's* but *two dogs*).
- Use apostrophes to form contractions (never *wont* but *won't*, never
  shell when you mean *she'll* for *she will*).
- Do not use an apostrophe with a personal pronoun to show
  possession or belonging. Personal pronouns use a different spelling
  to show possession (never *her's* but *hers*, never *their's* but *theirs*).
  Distinguish especially between *it's* and *its*. Contrary to what you
  might expect, the possessive pronoun *its* takes no apostrophe.

awk ‖ ## 19. AWKWARD or MIXED SENTENCE STRUCTURES

Check your sentences for faulty subordination, duplication of prepositions, faulty equations, misuse of question word order, and mixed metaphors.

SPECIFICS

(1) faulty subordination: Do not try to use *which* clauses or prepositional phrases as subjects.

EXAMPLES:

faulty:	Which the band had played was what he wanted.
REVISED:	The *song, which he had been trying to learn,* was the tune the band was playing.
faulty:	In learning a new job skill takes hard work.
REVISED:	*Learning a new job skill* takes hard work.

(2) duplication of prepositions: When you use *which* with a preposition like *in, for, at,* and others, you only need to give the preposition once.

EXAMPLES:

faulty:	The city in which she was living in was Boston.
REVISED:	The city *in which she was living* was Boston.
REVISED:	She was living *in Boston.*

(3) faulty equations: Similar parts of speech should be used on both sides of *is* to express comparable ideas.

EXAMPLES:

faulty:	Television is commercial. (noun = adjective)
faulty:	Television is a commercial enterprise. (*Can "television" be classed as an "enterprise"?*)
REVISED:	*Producing* television programs is a commercial *enterprise.*

(4) misuse of question word order: In indirect questions, what you wonder about should be stated in normal word order.

EXAMPLES:

faulty: I wonder did he know who I was.

REVISED: I wonder *if he knew* who I was.

(5) mixed metaphors: Implied comparisons can enliven writing, but overlapping metaphors can sound strange and be unintentionally funny.

EXAMPLES:

mixed: She was outfoxed by a wolf in sheep's clothing.

REVISED: She was *outfoxed* by a *clever swindler*.

EXERCISE. REVISING A PASSAGE

Revise the following paragraph to fix the faulty sentences. Leave correct sentences alone.

The neighborhood in which I live in includes several interesting people. Mr. Keegle is a wise owl of a man with a croaking voice. In marrying Mrs. Keegle was a strange match because she is like a one-person garden party. She floats over the green carpet of her yard, talking to her flowers like a chatterbox. Mrs. Meyer is a fence over which she leans over and sometimes chatters with Mrs. Keegle. With neighbors like these, which I don't need birds and squirrels.

SPECIAL HINTS

Although there are plenty of ways to derail a sentence, there is one reliable way to keep a sentence on track—concentrate while you are writing and proofread after writing in order to check the word order of your sentences. (To review your options in structuring sentences, see sections 4a and 4c.)

Be especially careful with the word *which*, the prepositions *in, for,* and *at,* and implied comparisons (metaphors), especially those we may take for granted (like "outfox").

br/no br || 20. BRACKETS

Use brackets within quotations to enclose words needed to make your meaning clear.

EXAMPLE:

confusing: "A few scientists have speculated that some form of life may exist in its upper atmosphere."

CLARIFIED: "A few scientists have speculated that some form of life may exist in its *[Jupiter's]* upper atmosphere."

In this case, supplying the name of the planet makes the quotation sensible for the reader. If your meaning is not clear from your context, you need to add a clarifying word or phrase to the quotation.

BRACKETS NOT NEEDED: *As far as Jupiter is concerned,* Dr. Walker noted that only "a few scientists have speculated that some form of life may exist in its upper atmosphere."

Most readers would probably prefer that the context identify the subject of the quotation rather than have the quotation interrupted. Use either context or brackets to be clear, but never use both.

SPECIFICS

"sic": If you must quote a sentence that contains an error, use [*sic*] immediately after the error to signify that the original writer, whom you are quoting, made the error in grammar, punctuation, or spelling.

EXAMPLE:
"A few chinpanzees [*sic*] have been taught to communicate in sign or with lighted-symbol keys."

In this case, the misspelling for "chimpanzees" occurred in the original passage.

EXERCISE. SUPPLYING BRACKETED INFORMATION AND *SIC*

For the following sentence, decide where bracketed information and [*sic*] should go.
"When the reporter said elections for the rest of the century will be decided by the three E's, he seemed prophetic."
background information: The three E's were listed earlier in the reporter's comments as "Economics, Energy, and the Environment."

SPECIAL HINTS

If possible, arrange the context of your quotations so that you do not need to use brackets. But if you must, use brackets only inside of quotations—and then only to add clarifying words or [*sic*] to label a recognized error in a passage you are quoting. Do not confuse brackets with parentheses. (See "Parentheses.")

bus ‖ 21. BUSINESS LETTERS

Write business letters in a way that shows concern for your reader's convenience: Make them clear, concise, and correct.

EXAMPLE:
The following example shows the parts of a standard business letter. Modern letters commonly start everything on the left; letters should be typed.

PARTS OF A BUSINESS LETTER

(1) heading: your return address and the date of mailing; on company letterhead stationery, use only the date.

(2) inside address: name, position, and address of the person you are writing to.

If you write to a company, you should begin with the line for company name and request the attention of a person or department at the end of the inside address: "ATTN: Mr. Wilson" or "ATTN: Order Department".

(3) salutation: the name of the person you are writing to.

If you don't know the name, use a nonsexist salutation by turning the position or department name into a salutation: "Dear Order Department Staff." End the salutation with a colon.

(4) body: your message.

As soon as possible, tell what you want and give complete information, such as stock number, color, price, and quantity for order and complaint letters; include event name or mutual business contact for letters of congratulation, application, request, and other letter types. Mention anything enclosed besides the letter itself, such as payments, invoices, copies of previous letters. Mention anything being mailed separately, such as merchandise you are returning for refund or repair, and tell when and how it was shipped (such as fourth class or parcel post). Single-space within paragraphs; don't indent.

(5) complimentary close: a courtesy showing respect.

"Sincerely" should do. End with a comma.

(6) signature: your handwritten name and your typed name beneath it (leave four blank lines to write your name).

Other lines below the signature can be used to mention enclosed items ("Enclosure"), a carbon copy or photocopy sent to someone concerned with the letter ("cc: John Howard"); or the typist's initials, if you are not the person typing the letter, followed by a slash and your initials in capital letters (adh/EH).

The following letter and envelope show typical spacing for the standard letter parts and addresses, as well as the clear, brief, and simple ("cbs") style that is expected in business correspondence.

CONTINENTAL CABLEVISION OF VIRGINIA, INC.

February 7, 1983

Dear Subscriber:

In light of recent media coverage and some subscriber inquiries, we felt an explanation of our actions regarding Channel 20 might be helpful.

As you know, our programming has included three distant broadcast signals: WTTG Washington (Channel 5), WDCA Washington (Channel 20), and WTBS Atlanta (Channel 17). A recent ruling by the Copyright Royalty Tribunal, an obscure congressional bureaucracy, imposed a penalty tax for carrying more than two such stations. This tax of 3.75% of all revenues increased copyright charges by nearly $250,000 for 1983. We felt this increase was both unreasonable and unwarranted. The copyright fees for 1983 for providing the eight other broadcast channels (5, 6, 8, 12, 23, 57, 35 and 17) would be $86,000; if a third independent (WDCA, for example) was carried, copyright fees would be $333,000. Incidentally, these fees do not benefit the Federal Government but rather are distributed to the movie producers, broadcasters and sports interests.

We had four options: (1) absorb the costs; (2) increase subscriber charges; (3) reduce other programming to offset costs; or (4) drop one of the three independent stations.

Absorbing the cost of almost one-quarter of a million dollars a year was really not a viable business alternative because of the monies involved and because of the unreasonably high cost of carrying the extra channel. Channel 20 would cost each of our subscribers more than $8.00 per year, while such popular services as CNN, Nickelodeon, and USA Network only cost $1.80 each per year per subscriber.

Increasing monthly charges to cover this new tax would mean all subscribers would pay an additional monthly fee of $.70 simply to carry this "extra" signal. We did not believe then, and we do not believe now, that most of our subscribers would feel that one channel was worth such an increase.

3914 WISTAR ROAD   •   RICHMOND, VIRGINIA 23228   •   PH: (804) 262-4004

Reducing other programming to offset these costs was another alternative. We would have had to drop a number of popular services such as Nickelodeon (3), CNN (10), USA (15), ESPN (24), and others to cover these costs. Clearly, this was undesirable.

We decided to drop Channel 20 because a recent survey conducted for us showed it to be the least watched of the three distant channels. Further, its programming was duplicative of the new Richmond independent, Channel 35, and Atlanta's 17. Simultaneously, we substantially increased the USA Network (15) by adding non-sports programming previously not shown, and introduced the Cable Health Network.

For us this was a difficult decision and, as anticipated, not everyone has agreed. Because of the subscriber interest generated by this change, we have temporarily reinstated Channel 20 while we survey subscribers as to their preferences. We have agreed with the Board of Supervisors to be bound by the results of the survey. The Board has directed the Cable Television Advisory Committee to review and approve the survey questions and methodology, which they have already done. The telephone survey will be conducted by an independent professional research organization based here in Richmond and will consist of a number of telephone interviews with randomly selected subscribers.

The survey will determine subscriber preference for several options: (1) continuing carriage of WDCA with each subscriber paying the tax of $8.40 per year ($.70 per month); (2) replacing WDCA with either WOR New York or WGN Chicago with an increase in fees of $9.60 per year ($.80 monthly); or (3) dropping WDCA and maintaining present rates and services. We expect that the survey results will be available later this month.

We apologize for the confusion presented by our poor communications with you. Unfortunately the time between the issue of the full CRT order and its effective date was very short. Further, they issued conflicting interpretations of their order. This has been a pointed lesson to us as to the importance of keeping you, our subscribers, informed. This letter is an attempt to make up for our omission; please give it your full attention.

Sincerely,

Richard D. Turnamian

Richard D. Turnamian
System Manager

CONTINENTAL CABLEVISION

Mr. Eric P. Hibbison
8400 Penobscot Road
Richmond, VA 23227

3914 Wistar Road
Richmond, Virginia 23228

EXERCISE. WRITE A LETTER YOU CAN USE

Write one of the following in the form of a standard business letter.

a. Request a sample style sheet from a magazine or journal published in your field or on your interest. (A style sheet is a set of specifications for writers who plan to submit articles. You should know common specifications in your field. Look on the contents page of the magazine or journal, or the back of the contents page, to find the editor you should write to for a style sheet.)

b. Write a letter to the editor of a local newspaper in which you praise or disagree with a recent editorial.

c. Request a job description for a job you would want after you earn your degree. (Write to the personnel manager of a company you'd like to work for; especially if it's a local company, call the company's central number and ask for the correct name, job title, and mailing address for the personnel manager.)

SPECIAL HINTS

Place your business letter beside the model in this section to compare the way information is arranged within parts, punctuation, and spacing. Be sure to sign your name in ink. Try to keep the entire letter to one page, if possible.

cap/no cap ‖ 22. CAPITAL LETTERS

Use a capital letter at the beginning of every sentence. Always capitalize the words *I* and *O*. Begin the individual ("proper") names of people and things with capital letters.

EXAMPLE;

*A*ctress *J*oanna *C*ameron used to portray a high school chemistry teacher who could change into a goddess by saying '*O* Mighty *I*sis!"

SPECIFICS

(1) job titles: When someone's official title forms part of the person's name, capitalize the title. When the job is mentioned after the name, do not capitalize it. Official job titles are generally capitalized if they refer to unique jobs or top government jobs.

EXAMPLES:
Governor Weaver   *but*   Agnes Weaver, the governor
Bishop Johnson   *but*   James Johnson, the bishop
the President of the United States
Ralph Cramden, candidate for Grand Moose

(2) titles of composed works: Capitalize the first word in a title or subtitle and all other words except for those conjunctions, articles, and prepositions that are less than five letters long.

EXAMPLES:
The Mutiny on the Bounty   "Yesterday"
Winning Through Intimidation   "In the Penal Colony"

(3) place names: Capitalize words considered part of place names.

EXAMPLES:
Harding Community College   Mt. Everest
Yellowstone National Park   Crossroads Shopping Mall
(*but* a community college, a mountain, a park, a mall)

(4) individuals: Capitalize the names of individual organizations, events, movements, eras, days of the week, months, courses with numbers, brands, languages and nationalities, and names for inhabitants of a place—anything specified as a unique thing rather than as a general category.

EXAMPLES:
God	*but*	the gods of ancient Egypt
NATO	*but*	a treaty alliance
the Civil War	*but*	a civil war
Monday	*but*	tomorrow
January	*but*	the first of the month
Data Processing 1	*but*	a data-processing course
Packard	*but*	an automobile
Thanksgiving	*but*	a holiday
the Old West	*but*	going west for the summer
Interstate 70	*but*	the highway
McBurn County	*but*	the county courthouse

English, Japanese, Kenyan, etc.
Denverite, New Yorker, Arizonan, etc.

EXERCISE. PROOFREAD FOR CAPITALIZATION

Correct any errors in capitalization as you rewrite the following paragraph.

According to *fortune* magazine, 1975's five largest industrial corporations were exxon, general motors, ford, texaco, and mobil. The five largest retailers were sears, whose sales topped $13 billion, safeway, j.c. penney, great atlantic and pacific tea, and s.s. kresge. The top seven industries' sales all surpassed the sears figures. The $42 billion of business done by exxon surpassed the gross national products of most of the World's nations, except for those of canada, mexico, brazil, australia, japan, india, and eight European Countries, according to figures listed from the AID in the 1976 *cbs news almanac* table "gross national product: world regions and nations."

SPECIAL HINTS

Do not capitalize a word merely because it is important. Capitalize names of unique people and things, like names of countries and languages. And start each sentence with a capital letter.

case ‖ **23. CASE (GRAMMATICAL CASE)**

Make sure the forms of your pronouns fit the situation, the case.

In pronoun usage, *case* means the change in spelling to indicate whether a word is used as an object or a subject. For instance, the word *who* represents the subject—the person doing the action of the sentence. In another case, *whom* represents the object of discussion—the person being acted upon.

DOERS (SUBJECTS)	RECEIVERS (OBJECTS)
I, we	me, us
you	you
he, she, it	him, her, it
they	them
who	whom

We have problems deciding which pronoun forms to use because we customarily use pronouns formally with strangers, especially when we talk or write to people for business purposes. Contrast the way pronouns are used in the formal and the informal telephone conversations written below.

EXAMPLES:

formal:
JB: Mortinson Associates.
LC: To *whom* am *I* speaking? Is this Jane Bartlett? This is Lee Chu.

>   JB: Yes, this is *she*.
>   LC: Do *you* and *I* have an appointment for 10:00
>   a.m. tomorrow?
>   JB: Yes, *we* do. Meeting at your field site is
>   acceptable to *me*; is that still where *you* want
>   *me* to meet *you*?
> informal: Cindy: Hello?
>   Betsy: Hi, is that *you*, Cindy?
>   Cindy: Yeah, it's *me*. Betsy? How are *you*? *I*'m glad
>   to hear from *you* again. *Who* did you get my
>   number from?

In the formal conversation above, notice how often the word *to* determines the form of the pronoun used. In speaking and writing, similar prepositions require object pronouns after them, as do verbs and verbals. Because they switch around normal word order, questions make it difficult to select pronouns in formal situations.

In the informal conversation above, notice how often the pronouns are used in contractions. Notice, also, the use of *me* where a formal situation would require *I* and the use of *who* where a formal situation would require *whom* as an object after *from* ("From whom did you obtain my telephone number?").

EXERCISE. FORMAL PRONOUNS ON THE PHONE

Because of complaints about the informal way that some people at your company answer telephone calls, your boss asks you to draft a sample formal phone conversation. Draft your sample conversation so that it demonstrates the formal usage of pronouns. Go over the draft to check for correct pronoun case usage. Be sure the person answering the telephone mentions the company's name first and maintains a polite tone throughout the conversation.

SPECIAL HINTS

Especially for college writing and business writing, use pronouns formally, including *whom*. If the pronoun you use is an object of a preposition (whether it follows the preposition or not), be sure to use the object form. To decide which pronoun form to use in questions, you will sometimes need to turn questions into statements for yourself before selecting the correct pronoun.

cl ‖ 24. CLICHÉS

Avoid using worn-out images or phrases, called clichés, and instead use a fresh comparison or no comparison. Since a cliché (pronounced klee-SHAY) is a choice of words set by tradition, using clichés hides your individual style.

EXAMPLE:

cliche: I've known Clyde since he was *knee-high to a grasshopper*.

REVISION: I've known Clyde since he was a toddler. (*improved by using no comparison*)

REVISION: I've known Clyde since he was just a seedling. (*improved by use of a comparison that hasn't been used often by others*)

EXERCISE. REWRITE A TRITE PASSAGE

Rewrite the following paragraph to eliminate the clichés. (*Hint:* Many clichés, since they are comparisons, use *as* or *than.*)

    The tried and true game of baseball is as old as the hills. Being a baseball fan is in the blood of American boys. Many are the lads who started tossing a baseball even before they could walk. Baseball is as popular as the day is long.

SPECIAL HINTS

If you've heard a comparison or a phrase frequently, it may not fit your topic exactly. Avoid the trite, tired, "safe" approach to your topic because this approach usually oversimplifies the topic and underestimates the reader's expectations.

:/no : ‖ 25. COLONS

Use a colon to do only the following:

(1) set up a list after an introduction.

EXAMPLE:
Two major source languages form most of the modern English
vocabulary: Anglo-Saxon and Latin. (Also see "Dashes.")

(2) set off formal letter greetings, Bible verses, minutes, and subtitles.

EXAMPLES:
Dear Sir: Romans 12:18–21   2:31 PM
Introducing Hispanic Literature: An Annotated Bibliography

(3) set off longer and more formal quotations, summary words or
phrases, and independent clauses that amplify and explain preced-
ing independent clauses.

EXAMPLES:
Jeremy Bentham's characterization of an unprincipled politician of
his day will serve to set the type: "Sketched out by himself and
finished by his editor and panegyrist, the political character of
Gerard Hamilton may be outlined in a few words: he was determined
to join a party; he was as ready to side with one party as another;
and whichever party he joined, he was as ready to say one thing as
another in support of it."
Only one thing drives my sister crazy: excessive neatness.
"But . . . a complex crisscross may have occurred: while television
may indeed have coaxed Americans to shift leftward in social
matters, the nation seems at the same time to have moved a bit to
the right politically." (Lance Morrow)

(4) separate the names of cities and publishers in footnotes and bibliographic entries for books (see section 12).

EXERCISE. COLONS IN A LETTER

Place colons in the following letter written by a disappointed viewer to the station manager of a local television station. If you think a colon belongs in a given slot, mark a colon in the underlined space. If you decide a colon is not right for a marked space, use a comma, a semicolon, or no punctuation.

Dear Sir_____
    At 7____00 p.m. last Friday, I tuned to your channel expecting to watch one of my favorite episodes of _____ *Hogan's Heroes*. Instead, for no reason that I heard announced on the air, your station broadcast animated versions of two parables_____ one from Luke 12____13–21 and the other from Matthew 13____1–23. I was upset for two reasons_____ I missed an entertainment that has become almost a ritual with me, and I thought your animations were in bad taste. The Gospels deserve portrayal by quality actors and narration by someone who sounds less like Bugs Bunny.

Your disgruntled viewer____

Chuck Hennepin

Chuck Hennepin

SPECIAL HINTS

Colons have very limited use in English, and are used only as shown in this section. (For other punctuation marks often confused with colons, see "Dashes," "Semicolons," and "Commas.")

,/no , ‖ # 26. COMMAS

> **Use commas to join or to separate elements within sentences. Use commas for the following purposes only:**

(1) to join simple sentences with *and, but, for, nor, or, so,* or *yet.*

EXAMPLES:
He looked, but he trembled at what he saw.
She could make a banjo from a broomstick, and she could make a cider that would change your eyes from brown to blue.

(2) to join words, phrases, and short clauses in series, including adjective pairs.

EXAMPLES:

Instead of being tall, dark, and handsome, he was a little short, slightly gray, and somewhat paunchy.

He threw open the tent flap, he snatched up his ax, and he burst from the tent screaming at the bear.

Her reckless, impish manner didn't fit her staid, matronly name— Agatha.

(3) to separate introductory words, phrases, and clauses from the rest of the sentence

EXAMPLES:

Smiling coldly,
With an uncommonly cold and malicious smile,   } he accepted the invitation.
After he smiled with a look of unmitigated contempt,

(4) to separate extra, interrupting elements from the rest of the sentence. (Use a pair of commas for this purpose.)

EXAMPLES:

The scientist {
, overjoyed by her discovery,
, who had been digging for a year at the site,
, indeed,
, reeling with joy,
, to proclaim her discovery,
, an ordinarily calm woman,
} let out a "Whoopie!" that shook the cavern.

(5) to separate extra, contrasting, or qualifying elements from the end of a sentence

EXAMPLES:

He headed north again {
, figuring that he had hesitated long enough.
, although he wished he could avoid the dismal journey.
, disheartened and lonely.
}

BUT

He headed north again $\begin{cases} \text{after deciding that he had} \\ \text{hesitated long enough.} \\ \text{as he usually did this time} \\ \text{of year.} \\ \text{despite his dread.} \end{cases}$

(6) to separate years, parts of addresses, informal letter greetings (salutations), letter closings, and names of states after cities from the main flow of your writing

EXAMPLES:

Dear Judy,

Yours truly,

Lincoln was inaugurated on March 4, 1861, after seven states had seceded from the Union.

(*But:* Lincoln was inaugurated on March 4 of the year the Civil War began. *No comma*)

The President lives at 1600 Pennsylvania Avenue, Washington, D.C., in the White House.

She lived in Seneca Falls, New York, until she went to college.

(Note: In addresses no comma is used between state designations and zip codes.)

EXERCISE 1. PROOFREAD FOR COMMAS IN A LETTER

Put in or remove commas to correct the following letter. Leave correctly used commas in place.

Dear Judy and Brian

Well I finally got here. I'm staying at the U.S. Grant Hotel; my room overlooks a plaza, and San Diego Harbor. You can write to me c/o The Felix Cafe 1236 Fourth Avenue San Diego California, 92101. Until I move on to L.A., and fame as a screenwriter I'm waiting tables at The Felix.

At the moment I'm ok; the room is ugly but cozy. Judy I wish I had your painting, of the canyon to brighten the place up. Now I'm gathering colors on my brush waiting, for the inspiration to know where to put my next brush stroke. When my life is over will I have a finished masterpiece, or an unfinished sketch touched here and there at a few, isolated inspired moments?

I miss you guys the times we had and the times we could be having; but I've got to give this thing, a try. If I can, get one script read by a major company as i have then I can get one accepted. As soon as I can get bus

fare and a week's rent together which shouldn't take me more than three weeks
I'm heading for L.A. Culver City Universal City and a new start on life!
    Be good to yourselves and, each other.
                                        Love
                                        Beth

EXERCISE 2. WRITE AN ANSWERING LETTER

Write an answering letter to Beth to try to cheer her up and reassure her about
her talent and determination. Go over your letter to make sure you have used
commas, semicolons, and periods where they should be.

SPECIAL HINTS

Use commas whenever the normal subject–verb–object word
order of sentences is delayed by introductory elements, interrupted
by extra elements, or added to by contrasting elements at the end.
(To find out how to use commas with quotation marks, see
"Quotation Marks.")

Do not use single commas to separate artificially a subject
from its verb, two kernel sentences (independent clauses), or
elements of a phrase, like a prepositional phrase.

cs ‖ 27. COMMA SPLICE

**Use either a comma with a conjunction, or a
semi-colon, to join independent clauses.**

Joining two sentences with a comma alone is like using string
to splice two pieces of rope together. The splice is only makeshift
and not strong enough for a permanent bond. Single commas are
used to signal the end or the beginning of secondary information
within sentences. (See "Commas," (3) and (5).)

EXAMPLES:
    comma splice: Latin has become a dead language, it lives on
                     only in parts of other languages which it
                     spawned or influenced.

REVISED: Latin has become a dead language, but it lives
             on only in parts of other languages that it
             spawned or influenced. (*comma plus conjunction*)

REVISED: Latin has become a dead language; it lives on
             only in parts of other languages which it
             spawned or influenced. (*semicolon*)

There are only seven conjunctions that can be used with a
comma to join two independent clauses: *and, but, for, nor, or, so,*
and *yet.* (See "Conjunctions.")

SPECIFICS

To fix a comma splice you also have these options:

(1) subordination: Make one clause introductory to the other.

EXAMPLE:
Although Latin has become a dead language,
it lives on in parts of other languages that it spawned or influenced.
(*introductory clause signalled by* although)

(2) separation: Make two sentences.

EXAMPLE:
Latin has become a dead language. It lives on only in parts of other
languages that it spawned or influenced.

(3) conjunctive adverbs: In addition to using a semi-colon, you may
want to specify the logical relationship between clauses by using
words like *however, nevertheless,* and others. (See "Relationships.")

EXAMPLE:
Latin has become a dead language; hence, it lives on only in parts
of other languages that it spawned or influenced. (*conjunctive adverb
at the semi-colon*)

EXAMPLE:
Latin has become a dead language; it lives on, therefore, only in
parts of other languages that it spawned or influenced. (*conjunctive
adverb within the second clause*)

EXERCISE. PROOFREAD TO CHANGE COMMA SPLICES

Use any of the five methods shown above to fix each of the comma splices in the following paragraph. Make no change in correct sentences.

I plan to graduate from this college with my degree in "General Studies," I also plan to make a career out of "life." People expect graduates to specialize in one occupation, I don't want to. Many corporations in Japan and some in the United States make themselves the center of their workers' lives, I don't plan to center my life on work. What matters is who I am, what I am. My job as office worker or mechanic or even my talents as disco dancer or softball player don't define my identity. When people ask me what I "do," I'll say, "I live."

SPECIAL HINTS

Make deliberate connections between your ideas; your readers will appreciate your guidance and pay more attention to your message.

(For more on structuring sentences, see section 4.)

conj ‖ 28. CONJUNCTIONS

Use conjunctions to signal the relationships between pairs of ideas and the relative importance of ideas in pairs.

SPECIFICS

(1) coordinating conjunctions: To link words, phrases, and clauses in pairs and series, use *and, but, for, nor, or, so,* and *yet*. These words link ideas that are equal in importance and often parallel in structure.

EXAMPLE:
"We sometimes lose sight of the fact
that our primary objective is really to be as happy as possible
and
that all our other objectives, great *and* small, are only a means to that end." (Robert J. Ringer)

The two *that* clauses are paired by *and* to signal that we forget both ideas and their importance to us. These two clauses have similar structures: "objective-is-really" and "objectives-are-only." Note, too, that the adjectives *great* and *small* are also coordinated by *and*. (See also "Commas," point (2), for series.)

(2) correlative conjunctions: To emphasize parallel ideas stated in parallel wording, use these pairings based on the coordinate conjunctions: *not only . . . but also . . . , either . . . or . . . , neither . . . nor . . . , both . . . and . . . , whether . . . or . . . ,* and *not . . . but. . . .*

EXAMPLE:

What makes a novel endure in popularity is *not only* its entertainment value *but also* its insight into human nature.

The words, phrases, or clauses that are paired in this direct way do not need to be parallel all the way through, but the beginnings must be parallel: "not only its entertainment . . . but also its insight. . . ."

(See "Subject–Verb Agreement," point (2), for a note about keeping signals of number consistent in such constructions.)

(3) subordinating conjunctions: To link clauses of unequal importance (an independent, or base, clause with one or more dependent clauses), use words like *because, although, until,* and others. Such words are usually quite specific about the logical relationships between ideas within sentences. (See "Relationships" for a complete list.)

EXAMPLE:

Motorcycling can be fun in the hills around Tucson—*unless* it rains, *because* the rains bring the danger of flash floods in the desert gulleys.

The main idea above, emphasized by its placement in the independent clause, is the fun of cycling near Tucson, Arizona. The conjunctions *unless* and *because* signal to the reader that there are reasons why the main statement is not always true—flash floods are not fun, especially for a cyclist.

(4) conjunctive adverbs: To specify logical relationships between independent clauses that you have already joined with a semi-colon, and even to specify logical relationships between sentences, you may want to add words like *however, nevertheless, indeed,* and *certainly.*

EXAMPLE:

The Governor did not like the tax bill; *nevertheless,* he signed it into law. *Certainly,* he thought it was the best tax law he could get from the legislature this year.

EXERCISE 1. SUPPLY CONJUNCTIVES AND SUBORDINATORS

The quotations below contain blanks. By looking at the clauses on each side of a blank you should be able to select a word from the list below to fit the meaning. Try to fill in the blank with the word you think the writer actually used. (Each word listed was used only once. You may use the charts in the "Relationships" section to help you reason out your answer. Making sense is more important for this exercise than being "right.")

thereafter	if	certainly	because
indeed	however	thus	overall

1. "Fitzgerald was comparatively simple to edit _____ he was a perfectionist about his work. . . . _____, Perkins added, 'Scott [Fitzgerald] was especially sensitive to criticism.'" (A. Scott Berg)
2. "_____ ministers were owners of such impressive funeral chapels, what may the tombs of the kings, sons of the gods, have been! _____, the most ephemeral of the pharoahs, starting with Rameses I, were buried in elaborately decorated tombs." (Christiane Desroches-Noblecourt)
3. "To those who loved John Kennedy the transition of power seemed needlessly cruel. _____ it was harsh." (William Manchester)
4. "Most [impatient critics and readers] preferred to ignore the fact that the author of *White-Jacket* was still functioning. _____, Melville had only two slim volumes of poems printed. . . ." (Jay Leyda)
5. "_____, the impression conveyed is that females are invisible. . . . _____, adult women also appear in these [1960's] juvenile books as passive, servile, and almost always a wife or mother." (Pauline Bart)

EXERCISE 2. PARAPHRASING QUOTATIONS TO VARY SENTENCE STRUCTURE

In order to practice varying sentence structures, paraphrase each of the quotations above. Use subordinating conjunctions and, where possible, occasional coordinating conjunctions. The charts in "Relationships" will provide lists of such words. *Paraphrasing* means rewriting so as to put the original sentence's meaning into your own words. Strictly applied, this definition requires you to change all of the sentence structures and most of the words from the original sentences. (See section 7 for a review of paraphrasing.)

EXERCISE 3. MAKE UP SENTENCES OF YOUR OWN

Select at least one conjunctive adverb from each of the nine charts in "Relationships." Use each in sentences or sentence pairs that you make up.

EXERCISE 4. MAKE UP MORE; USE SUBORDINATORS

Repeat Exercise 3 using subordinating conjunctions from the "Relationships" charts.

SPECIAL HINTS

The more complicated your subject, the more you need to specify for your readers the logical connections between your clauses and sentences. Conjunctions help your readers put your ideas together.

(For more hints on structuring sentences, see section 4.)

con ‖ 29. CONNOTATION

Change loaded words in order to change the tone of your writing.

Use words with emotional impact to appeal to your readers' feelings or sense of humor. Try to be especially aware of the emotional impact your words can have on your readers.

EXAMPLES:

    unaware: Obviously, the worst day of the year is Christmas.

    AWARE: *Although most people have fond memories of Christmas,* for me it is a *terrifying* time of year.

The "unaware" writer didn't realize that few readers would consider Christmas the "worst" time of year. The "aware" writer knows that her feelings about Christmas are different from most people's. So her lead sentence, shown above, sets up an explanation of why Christmas terrifies her.

EXERCISE 1. MATCHING TONE WITH SITUATION

Choose the sentence you think is better for each situation described below.

1. Situation: You are writing to a local television interviewer asking her to speak at your college about the value of wording questions carefully.
   a. Because I love the tricky way you set up your victims for the question that kills them, I would sort of like to have you entertain at the college with a speech on how you do it.
   b. Because I admire the cleverness with which you elicit candid responses from your interviews, I would appreciate your speaking at the college about questioning techniques.
2. Situation: You are writing a recommendation for a friend in order to help him get a job.
   a. Ted has limited experience with the exact work required for this job, but his work on similar tasks has been above average.
   b. Ted hasn't done much work like he would on this job, but his work on a similar job has been ok.

EXERCISE 2. LISTING AND ANALYZING CONNOTATIONS

Make a list of the emotionally charged words in the sentences in Exercise 1. Note what impression each one gives or what the impact is.

EXERCISE 3. MAKE YOUR OWN RESPONSE TO THE SITUATIONS

Use your own words to make sentences that give the best impression for each of the two situations in Exercise 1.

SPECIAL HINTS

In each writing you do, make sure that the emotional impact of the words you use matches the attitude you wish to convey to your readers. If your own experience does not tell you that a word has a negative, positive, or neutral connotation, check all of the meanings of the word in a dictionary for clues, especially paragraphs on synonyms. (See "Dictionary," (8).)

d mod ‖ 30. DANGLING MODIFIERS

Use -*ing* phrases and -*ed* phrases to introduce or follow a naming word (noun or pronoun). Make sure the connection between these phrases and the words they "modify" is logical.

EXAMPLES:

dangling modifier: Running within a block of a highway or just a busy street, the carbon monoxide makes the air unbreathable.

REVISED: Running within a block of a highway or just a busy street, *I can hardly breathe* because the carbon monoxide is so thick.

REVISED: *When I run* within a block of a highway or just a busy street, the air seems unbreathable because of the carbon monoxide.

Even though -*ing* and -*ed* words (called *participles*; see "Verbals") are clear statements of activities, the person or thing doing the activity should be pointed out to the reader. In the examples above, it may seem obvious that carbon monoxide does not jog, but eliminating any guesswork and the silly image of a smelly cloud in a running suit helps the reader see the real message— the writer's disgust for air pollution.

EXERCISE 1. PROOFREADING TO REVISE A PARAGRAPH

Revise the following paragraph to eliminate dangling modifiers. Do not change correct -*ing* or -*ed* phrases.

My favorite sportscaster is Bill Russell. Knowing basketball from the inside, the games he calls have that added dimension of the veteran player who knows how it felt playing aggressive but alert basketball, running flat out for an hour. Shredding his microphone with his high-pitched laugh, he seems to enjoy thoroughly the games he helps telecast. Intrigued constantly by the strategy of basketball, his sportscasting reflects his years as a player and especially as a player-coach. His tone always indicates his respect for basketball and especially for the men who play it.

EXERCISE 2. WRITE YOUR OWN PARAGRAPH

Write a paragraph about your own favorite sportscaster or newscaster. Use at least two -*ing* phrases to modify nouns or pronouns (probably subjects of sentences).

SPECIAL HINTS

Especially when you begin a sentence with an -*ing* word, make sure that the person or thing doing the activity is specified right after the comma that separates the -*ing* phrase from the subject of the sentence.

—/no — ‖ 31. DASHES

‖ **Use a dash to emphasize shifts in a train of thought, summary words or phrases, or to interrupt elements of your sentences.**

EXAMPLES:

The future holds promise—but who anymore knows the past well enough to see the promise of the future?

"Government of the people, by the people, and for the people"— this was Lincoln's ideal.

Profits—her main reason for patenting the invention—had shown no sign of leveling off after five years.

All three streets—Park Street, Rio Grande Boulevard, and Wymot Drive—are under construction.

EXERCISE. JUDGING EMPHASIS

For each of the sentences below, decide whether to increase emphasis or to leave the emphasis as it is. To increase the emphasis, replace each comma with a dash.

1. "What we were going through seemed like a kind of Berlitz course in 'Legal,' a language I didn't speak and in which I was being forced to read and think sixteen hours a day." (Scott Turow)
2. We all stood in the rain, a beleaguered but resolute crowd.
3. The baby, who hadn't been fed in five hours, cried ceaselessly.
4. His problem, an ethical dilemma, was whether to replace the missing money with his own to cover his friend's guilt, or to call the police to avoid being named as an accomplice.

SPECIAL HINTS

Use dashes sparingly, perhaps once in a composition, to emphasize shifts in thought or mood. Use dashes only to give impact to carefully chosen words, not to salvage impact from dull or vague wording.

dial ‖ ## 32. DIALECT or LANGUAGE LEVEL

‖ **Use the dialect that is appropriate to your situation, considering your purpose and your readers.**

EXAMPLES OF DIALECTS:

The following comments were spoken by people waiting to ride a roller coaster with two consecutive loops. The rest of each statement comes from students' written comments as they reported what they heard. An explanation follows each sample statement; the italicized words represent the dialect usage.

VULGAR: "_____ no, I won't ride it twice." (Fill in the blank with any of several words not heard during children's TV programs.)

Vulgar words show emotion, but they are usually inadequate for college writing, which requires explanations and details.

NONSTANDARD: "It *weren't* as bad as I thought," said one pale little boy as he wobbled down the ramp.

Nonstandard word usage works best to depict the dialogue of people who have little or no formal schooling.

SLANG: "Be *cool, man.* Hey, I can *dig it,* but can you *dig it?*"

Slang is best used to depict the language of a subculture in written dialogues. But since such words are temporary, either dying out quickly, or becoming standard, avoid using them in the expository sections of your essays.

COLLOQUIAL: "I *ain't gonna* get on that thing. *No way!* Uh-uh!" protested one girl.

Colloquial usage might be accepted in very familiar writing to close friends. In college writing, colloquial wording serves to depict the dialogue of close friends, but it isn't suitable for expository passages because these are usually read by strangers or acquaintances, not just close friends.

REGIONAL: "Say, that thing moves *right* fast," said my Southern friend, Ted.

"Yeah," I answered in my Midwestern tongue. "It does go *lickety-split.*"

Regionalisms are best used to quote dialogue that fixes the speakers to one geographical area.

FAMILIAR: "Fool! I *wanna* 'float like a butterfly *an'* sting like a bee,' not land like a bat *an'* get squashed like a flea."

The language of informal, everyday conversation among friends and acquaintances can appear in an essay as vibrant dialogue, but not in expository passages of essays.

STANDARD: *"I bet a wine drinker invented this two-loop roller coaster,"* suggested one man to his wife. *"The double-loop in the track makes it look like a corkscrew."*

Most writing assignments in college and on the job, writings in most newsmagazines and newspapers, and most business reports, letters, and memoranda are written in standard dialect. Most writing to strangers and to general or unknown readers should be in standard dialect.

JARGON: "The ad said you *pull 3.5 G's* on this thing," said one girl to her date.

Jargon refers to words used in a field of study, occupation, or area of interest. Jargon is used in scholarly journals, technical journals, legal documents, textbooks, manuals, etc. When jargon occurs in writing that is directed to someone not in the field, each jargon word must be defined or its meaning made clear from the context.

FORMAL: One guy who thought he would be funny by making a speech only made me feel more nervous when he turned to the people waiting behind him and said, *"My fellow daredevils, let us take this opportunity to bow our heads in prayer for our safety during this great undertaking."*

When English is used formally (and in seriousness), it is the language of ceremonies, rituals, prayers, as heard in traditional weddings, funerals, dedications of buildings, etc.

Unfortunately, speakers and writers who rely mainly on standard and formal dialects and plenty of jargon words sometimes look on the use of other dialects as though the user were wearing tennis shoes to a funeral. Also unfortunately, speakers and writers who rely mainly on slang, colloquial, and familiar dialects with some regionalisms and vulgarisms scoff at users of other dialects as though they were wearing tuxedos and ball gowns to a baseball game. The answer to the dilemma of usage is versatility and knowing your readers. Being able to use whatever dialect people expect for writing in a given social or educational situation opens the way to any reader.

Most college writing assignments require the use of standard dialect and the technical jargon from some special field, such as sociology, only after careful study.

EXERCISE 1. CLARIFYING JARGON

Rewrite the following letter. Clarify the jargon by putting everything into standard dialect. Imagine that your reader is a nonspecialist whose good will you
want. So be polite and also make the meaning clear. (The name and address
of the addressee have been omitted.)

I infer from your letter that you are looking for guidance concerning the
implementation of the Grand River dam site.

As a geologic engineer with the State of Missouri, I can furnish you guidance
for interpreting where the dam might be sited. But I can not give you guidance
about whether or not it will be environmentally advantageous to construct the
dam.

The main section of the dam is in line with two topographic knobs, which
is interpreted to be the same line where the Quintana Minerals Company has
now deposited tailings from its coal mine. These tailings occur 16 miles south
of Beckwith on State Road 91. Preconstruction aerial photos indicate the dam,
once constructed, will cover State Road 91 all the way back north to the town
of Beckwith and will spread east and west a distance of five miles.

Please call if you need further help.

Sincerely yours,

Emmett W. Watson

Emmett W. "Whizzer" Watson

EXERCISE 2. EVALUATING JARGON

List the qualities that are changed in rewriting the letter in Exercise 1 in
standard dialect. Is it always possible to substitute a single word for jargon?
Or do you have to rewrite an entire section? Which version do you prefer?

EXERCISE 3. PARAPHRASING A TEXTBOOK

Besides being an effective study technique, paraphrasing parts of your textbooks will help make you more sensitive to the spelling, word usage, and
sentence structures of standard dialect. It will also help you see the uses and
the abuses of the technical language some texts are written in. Paraphrase
a paragraph from one of your texts.

(Paraphrasing and summarizing in standard dialect are skills needed
for research papers and exams. See section 7.)

SPECIAL HINTS

Every dialect has its purpose. To depict colorful personalities, write your characters' dialogue in colloquial, regional, and even nonstandard dialect. Your own voice in your essays—in the expository passages—should be written in standard dialect.

dict ‖ ## 33. DICTION AND THE DICTIONARY

‖ **Use a dictionary to check your word usage (diction) and to learn new words (vocabulary).**

Consult your dictionary for information about:

(1) syllable divisions
(2) pronunciation and spelling
(3) part of speech
(4) word parts
(5) definitions

(6) idioms
(7) derived words
(8) synonyms
(9) antonyms
(10) related phrases

To demonstrate each of these ten special cases, let's look at two entries adapted from *Webster's New World Dictionary* for the words *supercilious* and *proud*.

EXAMPLES:

```
su-per-cil-i-ous (soo' per sil' e es) adj. [L.
superciliosus < supercilium, eyebrow, hence (with
reference to facial expression with raised brows)
haughtiness < super-, above + cilium, eyelid]
disdainful or contemptuous; full of or
characterized by pride or scorn; haughty-SYN. see
PROUD-su' per-cil' i-ous-ly adv.-su' per-cil' i-
ous-ness n.
```

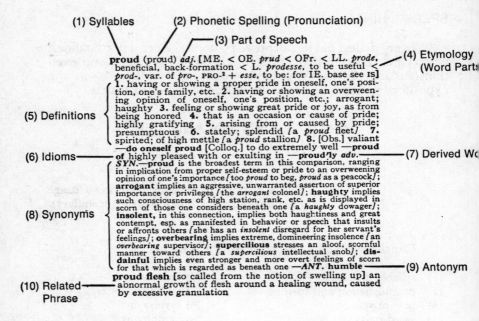

(1) Syllables   (2) Phonetic Spelling (Pronunciation)

(3) Part of Speech

proud (proud) *adj.* [ME. < OE. *prud* < OFr. < LL. *prode*, beneficial, back-formation < L. *prodesse*, to be useful < *prod-*, var. of *pro-*, PRO-² + *esse*, to be: for IE. base see IS] **1.** having or showing a proper pride in oneself, one's position, one's family, etc. **2.** having or showing an overweening opinion of oneself, one's position, etc.; arrogant; haughty **3.** feeling or showing great pride or joy, as from being honored **4.** that is an occasion or cause of pride; highly gratifying **5.** arising from or caused by pride; presumptuous **6.** stately; splendid [a *proud* fleet] **7.** spirited; of high mettle [a *proud* stallion] **8.** [Obs.] valiant —**do oneself proud** [Colloq.] to do extremely well —**proud of** highly pleased with or exulting in —**proud'ly** *adv.*—

SYN.—**proud** is the broadest term in this comparison, ranging in implication from proper self-esteem or pride to an overweening opinion of one's importance [too *proud* to beg, *proud* as a peacock]; **arrogant** implies an aggressive, unwarranted assertion of superior importance or privileges [the *arrogant* colonel]; **haughty** implies such consciousness of high station, rank, etc. as is displayed in scorn of those one considers beneath one [a *haughty* dowager]; **insolent**, in this connection, implies both haughtiness and great contempt, esp. as manifested in behavior or speech that insults or affronts others [she has an *insolent* disregard for her servant's feelings]; **overbearing** implies extreme, domineering insolence [an *overbearing* supervisor]; **supercilious** stresses an aloof, scornful manner toward others [a *supercilious* intellectual snob]; **disdainful** implies even stronger and more overt feelings of scorn for that which is regarded as beneath one —*ANT.* humble

proud flesh [so called from the notion of swelling up] an abnormal growth of flesh around a healing wound, caused by excessive granulation

(5) Definitions

(6) Idioms

(8) Synonyms

(10) Related Phrase

(4) Etymology (Word Parts)

(7) Derived Wo

(9) Antonym

SPECIFICS

(1) **syllable divisions:** If you must divide a word at the end of a line of writing, make sure that you use a hyphen between syllables not in the middle of a syllable. One-syllable words cannot be divided.

EXAMPLES:

super-

cilious   proud

To proofread for word divisions, skim your right margin for hyphens and broken words. If you often have trouble spelling, check key words in a dictionary; look especially for syllables you might have left out.

(2) **pronunciation:** The *phonetic spelling* is a code to help you learn to say new words, like the jargon of a college course. If you can tell how to say a word from looking it up in a dictionary, you will know the word when you hear someone else say it. You will also be able to link the way the word is said with the way it is spelled.

EXAMPLE:

spelling   *phonetic spelling*
supercilious   soo′pər sil′ ē əs

- The syllables are separated in the phonetic spelling so you can learn to say the word step by step.
- Symbols are used to show how to say the vowels and a few consonants. A key printed at the bottom of every other page shows you how to say the sounds of the new word based on similar sounds in familiar words.

fat, āpe, cär; ten, ēven; is, bīte; gō,/hôrn, tōol, look; oil, out; up, fur; get; joy; yet; chin; she; thin, then; zh, leisure; ŋ, ring; ə for *a* in *ago*, *e* in *agent*, *i* in *sanity*, *o* in *comply*, *u* in *focus*; ′ as in *able* (ā′b′l); Fr. bâl; ë, Fr. coeur; ö, Fr. feu; Fr. mon; ô, Fr. coq; ü, Fr. duc; r, Fr. cri; H, G. ich; kh, G. doch. See inside front cover. ☆Americanism; ‡foreign; *hypothetical; <derived from

oo sounds like the middle sound in *tool* (tool).
ə sounds like the *a* sound in *ago*, the *e* sound in *agent*, and the rather dull sound of other vowels that are barely pronounced.
i sounds like the first sound in the word *is*.
ē sounds like the *first* sound in the word *even*.
Also, the *c* in *supercilious* sounds like an *s*.

- The ′ and ′ markers tell which syllables are said with more force than the others. The first syllable in *supercilious* gets some emphasis, but the major force is on the middle syllable.

Another way to show the *sound* of *supercilious*, then, might be: soo – purr – SILL – ee – us. Such a *sound spelling* makes a recognizable rhyme for each syllable of a word. For a writer, though, knowing how to say a word is one step toward being able to spell the word accurately.

(3) part of speech: Most dictionaries use a code of abbreviations like the following to indicate the function that a word may have in a sentence. Words that function as more than one part of speech have definitions clustered after each part-of-speech label. (Each part of speech has a separate section in this handbook.)

adj.	adjective	n.	noun
adv.	adverb	prep.	preposition
conj.	conjunction	pron.	pronoun
interj.	interjection	v.	verb
		vbl.	verbal

Supercilious and *proud* are both adjectives.

Make sure your endings are correct for the functions the words are supposed to have in your sentences. The job of a word in a sentence often determines how the end of the word is spelled—at least for nouns, verbs, adjectives, and adverbs.

EXAMPLES:

proud (adj.)	proudly (adv.)
pride (n.)	prideful (adj.)
supercilious (adj.)	superciliously (adv.)
superciliousness (n.)	

The following sampler of general and scientific endings will help you begin to link particular endings with particular functions of words—a necessity for learning new words for your writing.

NOTE: These endings indicate part of speech when they make separate syllables. Words like *dance* and *size* and *dent* do not contain "suffixes" as separate syllables that indicate the functions of the words. In fact, all three can be nouns or verbs.

ENDINGS THAT INDICATE PART OF SPEECH (FUNCTION)

NOUNS

ENDING	MEANING	SAMPLE USE
-ance -ence	the act, quality, or state of (something)	Although the independ-*ence* of the press is essential, politicians often find the press a hind*rance*.
-er, -or	one who (does something)	The bartend*er* poured the weary doct*or* a drink.
-geny	origin, production, development	Haeckel's theory that "onto*geny* recapitulates phylo*geny*" was orderly, daring, and original, but an oversimplification.
-ism	belief	Commun*ism*, social*ism*, and fasc*ism* have been three influential political philosophies in Europe during this century.
-ology	the science or study of (something)	After studying bi*ology* Tina wanted to major in marine mamm*ology*.

VERBS

ENDING	MEANING	SAMPLE USE
-ate	to form, produce, provide, combine with (in chemistry), cause to be modified	Many a child has tried to mitig*ate* a parent's anger with a cute smile and a "Who, me?" look of innocent surprise.
-fy, -ify	to make	The problems of space navigation are magni*fi*ed for ships that will approach the speed of light.
-ize	to make, to combine (in chemistry)	Developments like the microprocessor continuously revolution*ize* the computer industry.

ADVERBS

ENDING	MEANING	SAMPLE USE
-ly	in a (particular) manner	Melissa stroked the guitar wistful*ly*, singing soft*ly*, near*ly* in a whisper.

ADJECTIVES

ENDING	MEANING	SAMPLE USE
-able -ible	capable of or worthy of (something)	The flow of the river was hardly notice*able*, almost impercept*ible*.
-ant, -ent	doing, having, or being (something)	Many indig*ent* families have become indign*ant* over cutbacks in aid programs.
-escent	becoming; reflecting or emitting light	The old fluor*escent* lamp flickered annoyingly overhead.

ADJECTIVES

ENDING	MEANING	SAMPLE USE
-itious	characterized by (some trait)	Although the time seemed prop*itious* for buying more stock, he decided to sell.
-ous	full of; having a lower valence than -ic elements (in chemistry)	His supercili*ous* treatment of my request showed his loathing of me.
-tight	closed to (something)	He kept his pipe tobacco in an air*tight* container.

(4) word parts: Check the parts of your key words and the parts of terms from your field of study; make sure that your spelling is correct and that you have used the correct ending for the meaning you intend.

Many of the words you learn in college are formed from nearly standardized word parts called prefixes, roots, and suffixes. The more of these common word parts you know, the easier it will be for you to check the spelling, the function (part of speech), and the meaning of the words you are learning to use in your writing. In a dictionary entry, what follows the part-of-speech label is the "family tree" or history of a word, called its "etymology." Often the etymology traces a word's forms back through its history to a prefix and a root word—to word parts.

The origin for the word "supercilious" is shown below.

[L. *superciliosus* < *supercilium*, eyebrow, hence (with reference to facial expression with raised brows) haughtiness < *super-*, above + *cilium*, eyelid]

The word came from *super-*, the Latin prefix meaning "above," and from *cilium*, the Latin root for "eyelid." What's above the eyelid is the eyebrow. Apparently, even the ancient Romans associated raising one's eyebrows with "superciliousness."

You can see how words containing *super-* are related to each other. Such words have something to do with being above or over something or someone. So words like *supervisor, superstar,* and *superiority* are related. Even less common words like *superfluous* and *supercilious* are related by their use of the prefix *super-*. As you become more familiar with prefixes in the languages that have borrowed from Latin, you may even see how words like *supranational* and *soprano* are related to the *super-* words.

A writer who knows word parts would never confuse *inferiority* with *superiority*. Knowing word parts can even aid in spelling collegiate and technical words correctly. (See "Spelling.") Finally, as you probably recall from the previous section on part of speech, knowing standard endings (suffixes) can help with correct usage of newly learned words in your writing.

(5) definitions: Make sure your words are right for the context. Some meanings of a word may fit in only with certain dialects; other meanings may only be appropriate to particular fields of study.

Some dictionaries list definitions by age, listing the oldest of the current definitions first. Other dictionaries list the most common definitions first. *Proud*, for instance, means "having or showing a proper pride in oneself, one's position, one's family, etc." in the oldest of the current uses of the word, as you can see from the definitions listed below.

> **1.** having or showing a proper pride in oneself, one's position, one's family, etc. **2.** having or showing an overweening opinion of oneself, one's position, etc.; arrogant; haughty **3.** feeling or showing great pride or joy, as from being honored **4.** that is an occasion or cause of pride; highly gratifying **5.** arising from or caused by pride; presumptuous **6.** stately; splendid *[a proud fleet]* **7.** spirited; of high mettle *[a proud stallion]* **8.** [Obs.] valiant —**do oneself proud** [Colloq.] to do extremely well —**proud of** highly pleased with or exulting in —**proud′ly** *adv.*

Dialect abbreviations indicate whether the definition of a word is British, colloquial, slang, or even obsolete or archaic usage. For instance, the eighth definition of *proud* indicates that *proud* is no longer used to mean "valiant." An archaic usage, labeled "Arch." in some entries, is a definition that is used rarely. Words like *thee, thou,* and *goeth,* heard in an occasional church service, are archaic.

Abbreviations for fields of study indicate that a word may have different uses in different courses. For example, in botany, the word *cilia* means a hairlike fringe on some kinds of leaves; in zoology, however, *cilia* are hairlike projections that provide motion, such as for lower animals.

Especially for the key words of your thesis and topic sentences, make sure that the meaning you intend is right for the context.

EXAMPLES:

wrong context: She had the typically *supercilious* manner of a wallflower.

RIGHT CONTEXT: Since she has become famous, she has had a *supercilious* attitude.

To make the context clear, you should provide examples of words that label or characterize to support your judgment.

EXAMPLE:
His *supercilious* attitude toward my tennis ability was clear from the way he swivelled his hips when he served, choked up a foot on his racket handle, ran around shots to make backhand returns, and returned my serves sitting down.

(6) idioms: Often words are set by tradition to be used together. Although it enlivens writing to avoid clichés, some terms are set phrases. A lawyer, for instance, may write about being *privy to* his client's secrets; a linguist may write on *privilege of occurrence* for sequences of letters or words.
 The task of using words idiomatically often centers on using the preposition that is set by tradition with the appropriate noun or verb or adjective.

EXAMPLES:
She was majoring *in the field of health education.*
Because he disliked satire, he could not *put up with* a sleazy *take-off on* his favorite novel.

Notice that *in* and *of* cannot be switched in the first example, and "put up for" would sound ridiculous in the second example. Most idioms are learned by reading and hearing them in general conversation, in the media, and in texts and classes in specific fields. Sometimes, however, the use of idioms takes special practice, special care, and the help of a hardbound dictionary, which will include idiomatic expressions. For instance, to "do oneself proud" is a colloquial idiom that one might expect to hear on *The Waltons*. The adjective *proud* is often used with the preposition *of* in standard contexts, as when a father writes to his son that he is proud of the son for working his way through college.

(7) derived words: If you are not sure that a spelling you have written is a word in conventional usage, look it up in a dictionary. If an ending looks questionable, check the end of the entry of the base word.

If, for example, you wondered if you could use *proudful* in a sentence, you should consult a dictionary. Since no such form is listed under *proud*, don't confuse your readers by inventing words that aren't needed. In this case, *proud* or *prideful* already serve as adjectives. Similarly, if you wonder, like comedian George Carlin, whether there is a word *chalant* to describe nervous people as there is a word *nonchalant* to describe calm, self-assured people, consult a dictionary.

Is *nonsupercilious* a word? Since dictionaries often list common, unspecialized words that begin with *non-* or *un-*, a separate listing might be found. Since no such form is listed, the antonym for *proud*, *humble*, might serve better. Unless you are writing about something from your imagination or a commercial product you invented, you need not make up words to name things. If you're not sure whether a form of a word can stand as a word, look for it in the dictionary. If it's there, make sure it can be used in your context. If it's not there, don't use it; look for an actual word that will work in your context.

(8) synonyms: Use dictionary paragraphs about synonyms to enlarge your writing vocabulary and to make sure you are using the most exact word for your context.

Synonyms have similar but not identical meanings. For example, by studying the paragraph below, you can see that the six synonyms listed for *proud* have slight differences in meaning from one another.

> *SYN.*—**proud** is the broadest term in this comparison, ranging in implication from proper self-esteem or pride to an overweening opinion of one's importance [too *proud* to beg, *proud* as a peacock]; **arrogant** implies an aggressive, unwarranted assertion of superior importance or privileges [the *arrogant* colonel]; **haughty** implies such consciousness of high station, rank, etc. as is displayed in scorn of those one considers beneath one [a *haughty* dowager]; **insolent**, in this connection, implies both haughtiness and great contempt, esp. as manifested in behavior or speech that insults or affronts others [she has an *insolent* disregard for her servant's feelings]; **overbearing** implies extreme, domineering insolence [an *overbearing* supervisor]; **supercilious** stresses an aloof, scornful manner toward others [a *supercilious* intellectual snob]; **disdainful** implies even stronger and more overt feelings of scorn for that which is regarded as beneath one

These slight differences in meaning make a considerable difference in a sentence.

EXAMPLE:

inexact usage: The *supercilious*, hot-tempered thug snarled menacingly as Rockford reached for the crowbar.

MORE EXACT   The *insolent,* hot-tempered thug snarled men-
    USAGE: acingly as Rockford reached for the crowbar.

Since thugs are rarely "aloof," but are often insulting and contemp-
tuous (especially the hot-tempered ones), of the six synonyms for
proud, insolent fits the context best.

When you are polishing your word selection, use your dictionary. The note *SYN.,* as in the entry for *supercilious,* will tell you
where to find a paragraph that explains in which contexts to use a
word or a synonym. These paragraphs will help you pick the exact
word you need.

(9) antonyms: Decide if a contrast based on an antonym would help
you state your idea more clearly or forcefully.

Some people learn concepts best by recognizing contrasts or
opposites. It has been said, for example, that a person cannot fully
appreciate wealth without first having experienced poverty. *Wealth*
and *poverty* express opposite or contrasting experiences, so the words
are *antonyms.* "Make love, not war," a famous slogan from the
Vietnam War protests, forces itself on people's memories. This
slogan sets word meanings opposite to each other in an unusual
way.

—ANT. **humble**

The antonym suggested for *proud* is *humble.* Although a proud
person might be overly assertive, a humble person may be mildly
or politely assertive or even unassertive. If a word's meaning is not
clear to you from the definitions and synonyms, look up the
suggested antonym, if one is listed. (Dictionaries rarely give antonyms for technical terms.)

Similarly, if you are looking for the exact word to make a
contrast, look for the antonym entry under your first term.

EXAMPLE:
"Pride," not humility, "goes before the fall."

(10) related phrases: Special idioms are sometimes listed as separate
entries in a dictionary. Check near the words you look up in a
dictionary for such phrases, often colorful or imaginative uses of a
word that can be used to set the tone or focus of your sentence or
even of your whole writing. In *Webster's New World Dictionary* the

entry *proud flesh* follows *proud*. This use of *proud* to mean "swelled up" could be useful in a later writing.

> **proud flesh** [so called from the notion of swelling up] an abnormal growth of flesh around a healing wound, caused by excessive granulation

If you were writing a lament about the fine print in contracts that always seems to hide a catch of some kind, you might look up *catch* to find other words for your main idea. Near *catch* in a recent dictionary you might notice *Catch-22*, which has been taken into the language from the title and main punchline of Joseph Heller's novel from the early 1960's that depicted absurd and useless struggles against nonsensical regulations. Looking for related phrases, then, might lead you to a more exact expression for one of your important ideas or to something like *Catch-22*, the title of a novel that might serve as an example to help you make your point.

SUMMARY

To check your use of words and to learn new words, look in a dictionary to:

(1) make sure you use a hyphen between syllables when you divide a word at the end of a line (the clearest divisions are made between word parts); check words that may be spelled with a hyphen.

(2) make sure the spelling of a word is correct, using accurate pronunciation as one guide to spelling.

(3) make sure your word ending signals to your readers the function of the word in your sentence (for many nouns, verbs, adjectives, and adverbs).

(4) build a familiarity with word parts to check spelling, function, and meaning of a word.

(5) make sure you are using the right word for the context.

(6) make sure you are using the word with the idiomatic preposition or other word partner.

(7) make sure there is such a word in conventional use as the one you have written or have in mind.

(8) select the exact word for your context from paragraphs about synonyms.

(9) construct a contrast based on antonyms.

(10) check for an imaginative related phrase for tone, focus, or a lead for an example.

The following is a series of practice exercises for each of the ten skills listed in the summary above. You will practice one skill at a time. Few of the answers will be obvious because the questions are designed so that you will look up information in a hardbound dictionary. You will find that the words become increasingly harder as you progress through the exercises. You should not expect to learn all about the dictionary in one day, but do your best on these exercises. You can begin to build up the skills you need in order to use more advanced words and technical terms in your courses.

EXERCISE FOR (1). END-OF-LINE DIVISIONS

Rewrite the following words, dividing them as you would if they came at the end of a line in your writing. Check a dictionary for syllables and word parts. Use only one hyphen per word.

1. intolerable	2. through	3. certainly
4. approach	5. resignation	6. quiver
7. misspelling	8. lightning	9. superannuated

EXERCISE FOR (2). LEARNING PRONUNCIATIONS

Use a dictionary to determine the pronunciation of these words.

1. heaume	2. data	3. tomato
4. quay	5. rhinal	6. oneiromancy
7. lymphopoiesis	8. encaenia	9. semioviparous

EXERCISE FOR (3). DETERMINING PART OF SPEECH

Determine the part of speech of the following words. Some words can function as more than one part of speech.

1. store	2. find	3. watch
4. dismal	5. nation	6. servile
7. kingdom	8. bottle	9. label
10. inquire	11. boundary	12. obscure

EXERCISE FOR (4). ETYMOLOGY AND WORD PARTS

Use the word history (etymology) of the words below to find their roots and the meanings of those roots. Besides listing the roots, you should list the other word parts attached to the roots. The dictionary may tell you to look at another word's etymology to find the root and other parts (called "affixes"), so be ready to check in two or three places in your dictionary for each word.

1. biography   2. autobiography   3. bibliography
4. ontogeny   5. recapitulate   6. phylogeny
7. carbohydrate   8. proteose   9. deoxycorticosterone

EXERCISE FOR (5). CORRECT USAGE BY DEFINITION

Pick the better word to use in each of the sentences below. Use a dictionary to help you choose between the alternatives given.

1. $\frac{\text{Thorough}}{\text{Throughout}}$ investigation revealed the cause of the fire.

2. The $\frac{\text{cavalry}}{\text{calvary}}$ charge was repulsed by an artillery $\frac{\text{barricade}}{\text{barrage}}$

3. The clairvoyant had a $\frac{\text{promontory}}{\text{premonition}}$ about an accident.

4. Her hair was $\frac{\text{redolent}}{\text{somnolent}}$ of wild flowers.

5. The $\frac{\text{ambivalence}}{\text{ambiguity}}$ of Errol Flynn's love/hate relationship with his first wife $\frac{\text{intrigued}}{\text{enthralled}}$ the gossip columnists.

EXERCISE FOR (6). IDIOMATIC PREPOSITION USAGE

Use a dictionary to help you choose which of the alternative expressions is idiomatic (conventional) usage for each of the sentences below.

1. Her sharp, even teeth were vaguely reminiscent $\frac{\text{of}}{\text{for}}$ a barracuda's.

2. $\frac{\text{In}}{\text{On}}$ the whole, her performance of the sonata was sensitive.

3. Civil defense authorities warn $\frac{\text{of}}{\text{to}}$ the high casualty rate that would result $\frac{\text{from}}{\text{with}}$ an $\frac{\text{all-for-it}}{\text{all-out}}$ nuclear war.

EXERCISE FOR (7). DERIVED OR MADE-UP WORDS

Determine, by looking up each in a dictionary, which of the words below is accepted by most readers as an actual word.

1. finely   2. rarelike   3. aerie
4. supermach   5. hypersonic   6. irregardless
7. cornucopioid   8. suturistic   9. morphologically
10. ascomycete   11. dirimentous   12. passitivity

EXERCISE FOR (8). SYNONYMS AND CONTEXT

Check in a dictionary for paragraphs on synonyms for any of the alternative words below, or look up the definitions of the alternatives. Then select the best word for the context. List the clues in the sentence that helped you make your selection.

1. The inexperienced, quick-tempered tax accountant _____ about the complicated federal tax regulations. Feeling angry and tired, he decided to take a break from the dead-end work—maybe for a week, maybe to look for a new career.

    snarled   grumbled   griped   raged

2. The _____ liverwort and snail darter became villainous species in the eyes of energy-hungry Americans, because environmentalists used these two endangered species to block construction of two hydroelectric projects.

    innocuous   guileless   innocent   inoffensive

3. The ancient city of Pompeii was destroyed in 79 A.D. by a _____ —the eruption of Mt. Vesuvius, which spread lethal gases through the city and buried it under several feet of volcanic ash.

    disaster   cataclysm   catastrophe   calamity

4. Finding a truly happy person is a _____ event, especially if the person is a character in a soap opera.

    scarce   rare   singular   precious

5. _____ often intimidates opponents but infrequently persuades anyone.

    enmity   belligerence   animosity   bellicosity

EXERCISE FOR (9). ANTONYMS AND CONTEXT

Consult a dictionary for the definitions of the four alternative antonyms (opposites) given. Choose one to fill in the blank for the sentence. Explain why the word you select makes the most sense.

1. Instead of being hot with passion as he had expected, she was _____. She had heard the rumors about him and believed them, though they were false.

frigid   arctic   cold   dead

2. Cornered by the security guard, the spy made a _____ and deadly response to the guard's warning. The guard had mistaken him for a slow, hungry, weak, ordinary junkie trying to steal calculators to finance a fix.

sudden   quick   prompt   spry

3. Cowardice, not _____, leads to the unethical life.

boldness   intrepidity   fearlessness   resolution

4. A harmonious relationship was impossible for the family; indeed, within the family and without, their relationships were _____.

discordant   quarrelsome   riotous   unpeaceful

5. In spite of the propaganda circulated by the dictator's supporters that made him seem laudable, his regime had been one of the most _____ in a century of cruel despots.

heinous   odious   execrable   atrocious

EXERCISE FOR (10). MAKING SENTENCES BASED ON IDIOMS

Many of the most common words in the language occur in phrases. If your dictionary does not contain the phrases listed below, check in a library for a dictionary of phrases. Make up a sentence for each phrase below to help you remember its meaning.

1. first water	2. Main Street	3. open shop
4. work basket	5. work ethic	6. work song
7. open city	8. open stock	9. fish ladder

The following exercise is a review of the previous ten exercises. You may not need a dictionary to find synonyms and antonyms (8's and 9's), but you will need a hardbound dictionary to help you solve most of the problems.

EXERCISE A. A SUMMARY EXERCISE: REVISE A PASSAGE FOR DICTION

To give you more realistic practice with using a dictionary to sharpen your word usage, rewrite the paragraph below. The numbers above the underlined words correspond to the numbered bits of advice in the summary on page 187 (the numbers match the parts of this section and the exercises above). Use a dictionary to "follow the numbers" and revise this paragraph.

(8)
Several *groups* hang out in our busy library. The engineering students
(8)   (8)
lean over their formulas and slide rules. The pre-med students *drill* each other
(8)   (6)
about the *nuances* of anatomy and once *on* a while glance around to see any
(8)
fine *bodies* that might pass by their study tables. The secretaries are wired
(8)   (5)
to the audio-visual study *places*, practicing *transgression* with their pads and
(1) (2)
pencils. A couple of *pre-pharmasy* students camp over in the corner as if
(2)   (9)
grimly convinced that *perseverence*, not _____, will carry them through
(8)
Chem 1. One student sits with his head perched on the *edge* of his econ text
(7)   (3)   (6)
as if the content of the book were *subjugatable* by *osmotic*. Nearest *from* the
door the browsing students stand and sit, their homework done or
(4)   (10)
succesful ignored, looking as satisfied and casual as *cats*.

SPECIAL HINTS: THE 10-ITEM VOCABULARY RECORD

To use the flood of new words you learn each week in your
classes, you need to be able to use a dictionary and your textbook
glossaries in the ten ways demonstrated in this section. For words
that merit special study (because you deduce that they'll show up
on an essay exam or written project for a course), use a system
like the one below to master the words.

SAMPLE VOCABULARY RECORD

		Part of		
(1) *Syllables*	(2) *Pronunciation*	(3) *Speech*	(4) *Parts & Meanings*	
on-tog-e-ny	ahn-TAHJ-uh-nee	n.	onto-	organism
	(än täj′ ə nē)		-geny	development

(5)   *definition*: development of an individual organism
(6)   *partner*: of?
(7)   *derived forms*: ontogenesis (n.); ontogenetic, ontogenic (adj.)

(8)   *synonyms*: life cycle
(9)   *antonyms*: phylogeny
(10) *special usage*: "Ontogeny recapitulates phylogeny" was Ernst Haeckel's faulty
      claim that the stages an individual embryo goes through reproduce (sum-
      marize) the stages of evolutionary development for the species, like frogs or
      man.
      Sample use: My brother is studying the ontogeny of a hybrid tulip he made
      for his high-school science project.

... ‖ 34. ELLIPSIS

Use an ellipsis, or three spaced periods in a row, to signal that unimportant or irrelevant information has been removed from a quotation. An ellipsis can also indicate an unfinished or implied idea, especially in dialogue. Use ellipses sparingly.

EXAMPLE:

original passage: Ants are more like the parts of an animal than
                    entities on their own. They are mobile cells,
                    circulating through a dense connective tissue
                    of other ants in a matrix of twigs. The circuits
                    are so intimately woven that the anthill meets
                    all the essential criteria of an organism. (Lewis
                    Thomas)

quotation with ellipsis   *quotation without ellipsis*
   "Ants are . . . like   Ants can be com-
. . . mobile cells."   pared to "mobile cells."

The quotation on the right above demonstrates one way to avoid the rather formal and sometimes awkward use of an ellipsis by paraphrasing. Nevertheless, the ellipsis can be used to condense a quotation by removing pronouns and bridging sentences, by leaving out unnecessary modifiers, and by omitting sentence parts like endings that would only prolong the quotation and lessen its impact.

SPECIFICS

(1) long quotations: When you must quote a passage longer than one
     paragraph, use a line of periods across the page to indicate where
     you have omitted a sentence or more. Omission of a line of poetry
     is also signaled by a line of periods.

     EXAMPLE:
     After the first powerful, plain manifesto
     The black statement of pistons, without more fuss
     But gliding like a queen, she leaves the station.
     . . . .
     Ah, like a comet through flame, she moves entranced,
     Wrapt in her music no bird song, no, nor bough
     Breaking with honey buds, shall ever equal.
                                   (Stephen Spender, "The Express")

     The example above shows the opening and closing of a poem. This
     quotation might appear in a paper that compared openings and
     closings of Spender's poems to analyze the forcefulness of his key
     images; hence, the middle of the poem would not be relevant and
     could be left out.

(2) dialogue: Ellipsis may be used to show pauses or to indicate
     unfinished sentences of dialogue.

     EXAMPLE:
                      pauses: "The house . . . the house," he wheezed as he
                                 gasped for breath, "it's . . . fire!"
     unfinished sentence: "He said he would mail the check," whimpered
                                 Louise, only now beginning to realize she had
                                 been deceived, "but maybe he. . . . Oh! why did
                                 I trust him?"

     The fourth period in Louise's lament above indicates that the
     sentence ended after the unspoken words.

EXERCISE 1. ELLIPSIS TO DELETE INTERRUPTERS

Copy the following quotations. Use an ellipsis to omit the unnecessary material between the commas in each quotation.

1. "Dara was not really for either side any longer, she said, although she pro-
   fessed a great liking for Dad." (Roger Zelazny)
2. "Downstairs, when the lift door had opened, he constructed an ingratiating
   smile for the wine-swilling *Gauleiter* and his lumpish woman, discovering that
   his appetite had fled." (William Walling)
3. "Humankind, archaeology has long since made clear, began trying to pen-
   etrate tomorrow as soon as it dawned on men that there was one." (Frank
   Trippett)

EXERCISE 2. PARAPHRASING TO AVOID ELLIPSIS

Use paraphrasing and parts of the quotations from EXERCISE 1 to quote from
each sentence without using ellipsis. (For a review of paraphrasing, see section 7.)

SPECIAL HINTS

Omit only unessential words from quotations, but be certain
to signal the omission with an ellipsis. If an ellipsis ends a quotation,
don't forget the fourth dot for the period of the sentence. Do not
use an ellipsis to begin a quotation; it isn't necessary.

end ‖ 35. ENDINGS

‖ **Bring your writings to a close.**

Merely stopping after your last point is like rolling a bowling
ball off a table and not letting your readers hear it hit. The
momentum of your essays, even on an exam, should lead to a
forceful ending. Lengthy reports, essays, and research papers
certainly require a conclusion that ties everything together.

Compare the approaches used in the following two endings
of essays on pollution.

EXAMPLES:
1.   "The clouds, the thick, heat-trapping clouds have blocked most of the
   light and made the air unbreathable. Beneath the clouds, the metallic-smell-

ing surface smolders dully, a grey-brown, devoid of animal and plant life, and hopeless of ever supporting life. The unprotected traveller on such a surface would be vaporized by the heat, if not choked by the air."

This fictionalized account of the appearance of the planet Venus from its surface presages the doom that could await the earth if pollution continues unchecked. If we begin now to counter the careless destruction of our environment, this description will never be used for the earth. If we do not. . . .

2. If we start now to regulate our industrial production more carefully, to re-cycle more of the waste products of our consumer technology, to renew our polluted lakes and incendiary rivers, to develop clean and effective mass transit systems, to cut timber selectively and reforest our hillsides, and to style buildings in harmony with the natural countryside, then soon we may once again be able to call America "America the Beautiful."

The first ending used a shocking comparison to conclude a persuasive essay. The sentence that trails off at the end of the essay forces the reader to finish the thought by supplying the implication. The second ending summarizes a rather lengthy research paper on pollution, that was titled "America the Polluted." The planned contrast between the title and the allusion to a famous song makes the paper feel finished. Using parallel phrases to conclude the paper compresses the ending considerably. In this case, what is lost in smoothness is gained in forcefulness.

Some common techniques for creating endings include

(1) summarizing with an echo of the thesis or title
(2) presenting a solution to the problem you have described in detail
(3) urging readers to do something—read further, write someone
(4) quoting or making a succinct and quotable statement
(5) (for short writings) merely echoing key words of the thesis

EXERCISE 1. GLIB ENDINGS

Summarize the faults of the following ending sentences and suggest another for each topic.

1. If you don't vote for my candidate, you're crazy!
2. In conclusion, I would like to ask that you vote *for* the proposed bond issue.
3. So, if you ask me, I think Medicare is no good.

EXERCISE 2. PROFESSIONAL ENDINGS

Pick an issue of a magazine you enjoy reading, or that attracts you as you browse through your library's current issues. Leaf through several articles, but look especially at the last two or three paragraphs of each article. How do they end? Briefly summarize your findings, quoting important sentences to support your judgment about what the writers are doing to end an article.

EXERCISE 3. JOURNAL ENDINGS

Pick a professional journal in your field or area of interest. Use the procedure given in Exercise 2, including a summary of your findings. What do professional journal writers do to end their articles, other than list "References" or "Notes"?

SPECIAL HINTS

The end of your writing is not the place for second thoughts, apologies, beginnings of new topics, overstated claims of what your essay has accomplished, or a word-by-word repetition of your thesis. Neither is your ending the place to distract your reader with digressions and quibbles, nor is it the place to insult the reader. A good ending is as forceful and specific as the best paragraph in the rest of the essay, but most of all a good ending "finishes off" your essay in the way that artisans put the final touches on their creations.

es ‖ 36. ESSAY EXAMS

Use a compact structure to write essay exam answers.

In Section 4 of this text, which examines styles of writing, it is suggested that a highly compressed writing style serves best on essay exams. Section 4 ends with exercises designed to help you study compression or density. The section on outlining shows the value of using outlines as study devices and suggests making a "scratch" outline before starting an answer. The section on repetition shows four effective ways to keep your essay answers coherent. The "interlocking paragraphs" method is a special application of the structure of a standard school theme, discussed in Section 2 of this text. In short, to write a good exam essay, you must use a highly compressed style that favors *-ing* and *-ed* ("Verbal") phrases to flesh out your sentences. You must use a theme structure that includes "interlocking" or obvious transition sentences. You must also constantly use major terms of the topic to keep your topic in the forefront of your essay. But how?

36a. Studying for an Essay Exam

In preparing any exam, but especially an essay exam, teachers have to focus on the relationships between ideas in the material. In short, they need to see the organization behind the information. So how should you study for an essay exam? You should constantly paraphrase and summarize the commentary of your teachers and your text according to the organizing principles that each uses.

To study for an essay exam, then, use the chart of "Common Organizing Principles" in Section 3 of this text. Any of these twenty-two principles might be used to organize a lecture, textbook chapter or section—or exam question. Summarize the information that seems to "go together," especially the information and ways of looking at information stressed by your teacher. Summarize the major concepts, condensing your class notes, text notes, and laboratory or outside reading notes to about ten percent of their original length—the key terms and brief definitions, main people and their identities, major trends and their characteristics, items stressed by the teacher and their significance.

36b. Preparing for an Essay Exam

Read your text chapters, underline and summarize major ideas, and study the summary and any problems or questions given by the author (look closely at these before and after reading because they signal main ideas). Take notes during class by paraphrasing your teacher's comments and including answers to nonroutine questions. Each week, write down what you consider to be the ten most important concepts you have studied for the subject. Make notes on how these major concepts are related; decide which concepts you would ask about, and try to write your own exam questions. Pick the toughest question and try to write an answer, using your text and notes only when you must to get organized. During the days before the exam, read your text's chapter summaries, then your own summaries of text and notes, then your notes on how major concepts relate, then your sample questions, and finally your sample answers.

This procedure does not guarantee that you will write the same exam your teacher does, but it does parallel the thought process your teacher goes through. Furthermore, paraphrasing and summarizing cause you to practice the condensed writing style you need for the exam.

36c. Taking an Essay Exam

Consider the general suggestions made at the beginning of this section, but also be confident and resolute. Confidence usually builds with studying, especially if you feel organized and saturated with information when you enter the testing room. Experience with exams can also build confidence, but everybody, regardless of experience, is nervous before an exam. During the exam period, don't get flustered by delays, noise, or other distractions. You don't have the time, and you can't control conditions, anyway. What you can control is what you know and what you can do.

If you have been writing as part of your studying, your hands and forearms should be in good shape so you can write constantly and rapidly for an hour or more. But try to have an energy food before the exam (carbohydrates) because you'll put out a lot of energy.

During the test, examine the questions carefully. Read the directions, and look to see whether you have a choice on what to answer. Look to see which questions are most important (count the most toward your grade); then plan your largest block of time to work on the most valuable questions. Leave time at the end for picking up quick points if there is a set of short-answer, low-value questions.

Treat identification and short-answer questions as if they were long essay questions. That is, give the same information but give only the most important details. On longer essay questions, look to see if you must evaluate information or just summarize it. If you must evaluate, do so briefly, using most of your time to show what you know, not what you think.

EXAMPLES:
The following two "short answer" identifications received full credit. The first lists characteristics; the second reasons through cause and effect. Don't expect to recognize the terms unless you have had more than basic psychology courses, but notice the density of terms.

Sample A: *Neo-Behaviorism*

Neo-Behaviorism flourished 1925–1960. Its data base included animal behavior (Norwegian white rats and occasional pigeons during the war). The data base was generated using classical conditioning, such as determining a reflex and attaching a signal to it (as Pavlov did); instrumental learning, as in a Skinner box, which reinforced desired behavior; and learning to distinguish between two simultaneously presented stimuli. The Neo-Behaviorist methodology included statistical designs (control group or factorial designs, usually), presumed a quantitative view of evolution (supposing that animal behavior could be generalized to humans who were different from animals only in degree or proportion but not kind); defined operationally (operationism), i.e., a dependent variable was defined in terms of the method of measurement. Methodology was influenced by logical positivism in that only measurable phenomena were regarded as valid for study. Associationism presumed stimuli were linked to responses, other stimuli, or reinforced responses. Neo-Behaviorist theory ranged from the deductive hypotheses of Hall to the pure description of results of Skinner, who eschewed theorizing.

Sample B: *Self-Regulated Processing and Feedback*

Humans may be regarded as self-regulated information processing systems because they respond to environmental stimuli and continue operation on a task until they reach a "stop" signal—their goal or a realization that they must abandon an approach that isn't working.
Information is the reduction of uncertainty, i.e. information helps a decision maker to reduce available alternatives. Redundancy exists when information is available from more than one source, so it is a function of prior

knowledge. Feedback is used to regulate behavior and includes positive feedback ("continue") and negative feedback ("desist").

EXERCISE 1. MAKING YOUR OWN TEST

Find out which of your teachers plans to use essay exams or essays on exams this term. Follow the suggestions under "Preparing for an Exam" in this section. If you can, show the teacher one of your "tests" or your list of key terms; find out if your selection shows that you are thinking along the lines your teacher wants in the course.

EXERCISE 2. PRACTICE-TEST WITH A PARTNER

In a course for which you will have an essay exam, find someone you can study with whose intelligence you respect (seems at least as informed and studious as you are). Suggest writing a test for each other about two weeks before the real test. Give each other a choice of three questions, write one essay, and evaluate each other's answers for information density, accuracy, and style. (Your opinions may be different from your instructor's, but your thinking and practice—and getting another perspective besides your own—are what matters.)

EXERCISE 3. A STUDY BUDDY

In each course for which you will have an exam, especially lecture courses, get acquainted with someone who seems to take notes regularly. Take notes regularly yourself, but agree to share or photocopy each other's notes if one of you misses a class. Plan to attend all classes; there's no substitute for hearing information and an instructor's interpretation first hand.

SPECIAL HINTS

Constantly process your reading, listening, and notes for major ideas and supporting details. Outline or summarize major concepts; relate major concepts according to the common organizing principles. Make up your own practice tests; write occasional practice answers. Be unflusterable during the test.

!/no ! 37. EXCLAMATION MARKS

**Use an exclamation mark to indicate state-
ments that are shouted in dialogue or statements of extreme surprise, outrage, or other
strong emotion.**

EXAMPLES:

Look out!   Quiet!   You're kidding!

Use the exclamation mark sparingly; overuse weakens its
impact. Ordinarily, your choice of words, not your punctuation,
should show your emotions.

EXERCISE 1. PUNCTUATING A PASSAGE: ! OR .

Put an exclamation mark or a period in the underlined spaces below.

"Run, Giselle____ Nan____ Pass the ball, push the pass with both hands.
Defense, Linda____ Hands up, up____ Good steal—go____ Go____" Even in practice, making a steal and driving for the lay-up felt like being onstage in a
spotlight belting out a red-hot jazz solo____ For a moment, I was the focus of
the coach's constant encouragement____

"Good shot, Bess____" Every time the coach praised me, long distance
across the court, I could tell she wanted me to make first team as much as
I did myself. But when I finally did make it, she wasn't there to see it____

EXERCISE 2. WRITING ABOUT SHOUTING

Write a paragraph or two about a time when someone was yelling for you or
at you. Use exclamation marks after the most emphatic statements. (Don't
forget to use quotation marks to the *right* of the exclamation mark when you
quote what someone shouted.)

SPECIAL HINTS

In most college writing, exclamation marks should be used
only when you are quoting what someone shouted.

frag ‖ 38. SENTENCE FRAGMENT

You will avoid writing sentence fragments if you make sure that all the units you have punctuated as sentences do these three things:
* **express a complete idea**
* **contain at least one subject–verb combination**
* **do not contain only one subject–verb combination with a subordinator (such as _although, if, unless, when,_ and others).**

SPECIFICS

(1)   verbals: Do not use a word that ends with *-ing* as a verb by itself. (See the verb form chart in "Passive Verbs.")

   EXAMPLES:

   fragment: Daydreaming constantly as if in a stupor.
   SENTENCE: He *was daydreaming* constantly, as if in a stupor.
   SENTENCE: He daydream*ed* constantly, as if in a stupor.
   SENTENCE: Daydreaming constantly, as if in a stupor, he usually missed his bus.

   Verbal phrases (based on a participle) modify nouns or pronouns. They help add information to sentences but are not sentences by themselves. Either reword a verbal phrase to make it a sentence or join the phrase to a sentence as a modifier.

(2)   subordinate clauses: Do not use a clause that starts with a subordinator as a sentence, but join it to a sentence. (For a list of subordinators, see the charts in "Relationships.")

   EXAMPLES:

   fragment: Until he saw that there was no hope of staying afloat.
   SENTENCE: *He kept bailing* until he saw that there was no hope of staying afloat.
   SENTENCE: *He saw* that there was no hope of staying afloat.

   Subordinate clauses modify verbs or nouns in sentences; they cannot stand alone. A clause is subordinate if it starts with a subordinator like *until* or *that*. *Removing* the subordinator from a fragment would leave a complete sentence, as shown in the latter sample sentence above.

(3) lists: Ordinarily, a list, such as a list of examples to support a point, lacks a subject–verb combination, and so should not be punctuated as a sentence.

EXAMPLES:

> fragment: Many scientists convinced Roosevelt to start the Manhattan Project. Such as Albert Einstein, Vannevar Bush, and Leo Szilard.
>
> SENTENCE: Many scientists convinced Roosevelt to start the Manhattan Project, such as Albert Einstein, Vannevar Bush, and Leo Szilard.

One way to avoid such fragments would be to give the list within the base clause, in this case, right after the word *scientists*, with a comma before and after the list.

EXAMPLE:

> SENTENCE: Many scientists, such as Albert Einstein, Vannevar Bush, and Leo Szilard, convinced Roosevelt to start the Manhattan Project.

(4) missing subject or missing verb: Sometimes, to fix a fragment, you need to supply a subject or a verb in order to make a complete subject–verb combination. Pronoun subjects and verbs related to *be* are often left out, an omission that accidentally forms a fragment.

EXAMPLES:

> fragment: I going to major in chemistry, so can be a pharmacist.
>
> SENTENCE: I *am* going to major in chemistry, so *I* can be a pharmacist.

Especially when you are recopying or revising a writing, make sure that your subject–verb combinations have all their parts.

(5) fragmentary clauses: Each of the types of fragments above can, of course, occur in clauses that form sentences. A verbal phrase, a subordinate clause, a list, or part of a subject–verb combination can never do the work of a base clause (independent clause).

EXAMPLES:

> fragment: Encased in concrete and lead, but some old ones are reportedly breaking open in the sea.

SENTENCE: *The nerve gas drums were* encased in concrete and
lead, but some old ones are reportedly breaking
open in the sea.

The first part of the sentence needed a subject and part of
the verb in the fragmentary version, but the second part of the
sentence has a complete subject—verb combination.

EXERCISE 1. REVISING A PARAGRAPH

Revise the following paragraph so that sentence and clause fragments become complete sentences or clauses.

A "resort" beach can be a strange place. Because of zoning laws in
coastal towns, I guess. A mile of beach on the Atlantic can have several
"atmospheres." Like the arcades, the residential ocean front, the hotels with
their boardwalks and private beaches, and the open beach that is "unde-
veloped" property. Walking any distance on a beach. Can see different clus-
ters of people gathered for different kinds of "fun in the sun"—or at least near
the sun.

EXERCISE 2. SENTENCE COMBINING

Join the following sentence groups to make longer sentences. Use at least
one subordinator, such as *while, because,* or *unless.* Use at least one sentence that begins with an *-ing* word. You may add and omit words as you
wish to make new sentences. Before beginning, you may wish to review the
lists of subordinators in the charts in the "Relationships" section.

1. Some people go crazy at sales.
2. Some people buy anything.
3. The thing is marked down.
4. The thing is useless.

5. My uncle bought a plaque on sale.
6. The plaque had a fish on it.
7. The fish was three feet long.

8. My mother bought a lamp.
9. The lamp was at a sale.
10. The lamp was gaudy.
11. The lamp body was a dragon.
12. The dragon glowed in the dark.

EXERCISE 3. DESCRIBE A PLACE

Write a paragraph about what you notice about people when you go, for example, to a beach, a lake, a ski lodge, a train station, a cafeteria, or a movie. Be sure to use subordinators and participial modifiers, but double-check to make sure that there are no fragments in your paragraph.

SPECIAL HINTS

Make sure that everything you punctuate as a sentence contains at least one independent sentence. If you use a subordinator, then the whole unit should have two subject–verb combinations: one in the independent clause, one in the subordinated clause. Since readers take in information one bit at a time, you should put a complete "bit" or thought between your beginning capital letter and your ending period, exclamation mark, or question mark.

hy/no hy ‖ 39. HYPHENS

‖ **Use a hyphen to do only the following things:**

(1) Divide a word at the end of one line to continue it on the next line. Use at least two letters on the first line and divide the word between syllables. [See "Dictionary" (1).]

EXAMPLES:

ex-
ponential   pro-
liferate

(2) Link words in front of nouns when the words act as a modifying unit.

EXAMPLES:
    modifying unit: Sending the fullback off-tackle was their bread-
                      and-butter play.

        not a modifier: Sending the fullback off the tackle on either side was a winning play for them.

                     The waitress brought the bread and butter.

      In the example, *off-tackle* modifies the gerund *sending*, a verbal noun; *bread-and-butter* modifies *play* in the first example in the same way as *winning* does in the second example. If the hyphens were left out, the sentence in the first example could be misread.

(3) Separate words in the process of being compounded. Consult a recent dictionary for use of the hyphen with such words as these:

NOT YET COMPOUND WORDS	COMPOUND WORDS AND DERIVED WORDS
self-delusion	selfless, selfish
all-powerful, all-clear	coauther, cooperate
ex-officio, ex-president	exponent, express
home-brew, home-grown	homesick, homestead
anti-UN	antiaircraft, antiwar

(Words with *anti* and *pro* are hyphenated only if a capital letter follows the hyphen: *proactive, pro-British.*)

(4) Separate compound numbers from twenty-one to ninety-nine and fractions.

EXAMPLES:

seven-eighths	forty-four
twenty-two	the twenty-second crab
one-fifth gone	eight ten-thousandths
two-thirds majority	fifty-one percent

(5) Simulate halting speech, spell out words and numbers in dialogue, suspend numbers in a series.

EXAMPLES:

"B-b-b-broke!" sobbed the infant.

"Receive is spelled r-e-c-e-i-v-e," said the secretary confidently.

"The correct stock number is 8-4-2-9-1-X," replied the sales representative.

Three-, four-, and five-syllable words probably contain affixes.

(6) Distinguish a word with a separate prefix from a word with similar spelling.

EXAMPLES:
re-cover (*cover again*)   vs. recover (*get back, retrieve*)
un-ionized (*not having ions*) vs. unionized (*belonging to a labor union*)
(See "Dash" to contrast the use of dashes and hyphens.)

EXERCISE. SUPPLYING HYPHENS IN A PARAGRAPH

Supply hyphens where they are needed in the following paragraph.

She skated with the self assurance of an all pro line
backer lunging at air after the quarterback has just side
stepped his all out blitz. Although I had known her for
twenty-two years, I had never noticed her make it or break
it attitude stronger than when she put on her ice skates.
She attacked the ice in a half angry, half frustrated stag
ger that invariably sent her crashing headfirst into the
side of the rink or sprawling feet first onto the ice.

SPECIAL HINTS

When a prefix is attached to a capitalized noun or a number,
a hyphen separates them. Use a standard dictionary to look up
syllable divisions and possible compound words.

infl ‖ 40. INFLECTIONS (-*S, -ED, -ING,* ‖ -*ER, -EST*)

‖ **Give special study to these five word endings.**

Although some words, like the personal pronouns, change
in spelling to indicate the functions they serve in a sentence, these
five endings are the most troublesome for many student writers.
They indicate quantity, time, or comparison.

SPECIFICS

(1) *-s*: Use an *s* at the end of most nouns to show your reader when you are writing about more than one.

EXAMPLES:

one:	bee	ark	file	treat	glove
more than one:	bees	arks	files	treats	gloves

(See "Plurals" for more information on when to use an *s* with nouns. Contrast the use of *'s* to show possession by studying "Apostrophes.")

An *s* ending on a verb signifies that you are writing about someone else who is doing something now, or who does something regularly or continuously.

EXAMPLES:

Fred services computers for IBM.
Gracie looks happy now, but she was miserable when Curt left.

(See "Subject–Verb Agreement" for more information about when to use the *s* signal on your verbs.)

(2) *-ed*: Use an *ed* at the end of most verbs and verbals that refer to the past in some way. Verbs that end in *ed* are called *regular*, like *called, hugged, divided*, and hundreds of others. (See "Irregular Verbs" for a list of verbs that use *ed* rarely or not at all.)

EXAMPLES:

The team manager lugged water and towels out to the thirsty, tired, sweaty football players.
Durrell had sued for a divorce, but she has now changed her mind.

(See the charts in "Passive Verbs" for more complete directions and examples on when to use the *ed* ending on your verbs, like *lugged* and *has changed*. Take a look at "Verbals" (1) for uses of *-ed* like that in the participle *tired*.)

(3) *-ing*: The *ing* ending is used in verbs and verbals to refer to present action or action in progress at some time.

EXAMPLES:

His cheek was still stinging from the glancing blow she struck him with the frisbee.

(For use of *-ing* words as participles, study the section on participial modifiers in "Verbals." For use of *-ing* words in verbs, like *was stinging,* see the "Progressive" column on the charts under "Passive Verbs.")

(4) *-er* vs. *more* or *less*: Use *-er* as an adjective or adverb ending in a comparison, or use *more* or *less* before longer adjectives, adverbs, or participles to make a comparison. Never use the *er* ending with *more* or *less*. *More* and *less* can also be paired with *than* to state comparisons, as can adjectives and adverbs ending with *er*.

EXAMPLES:

faulty comparison: Councilman Bennett's plan would be more cost-lier than the mayor's.

COMPARISON: Councilman Bennett's plan would be *more expensive* than the mayor's.

COMPARISON: Councilman Bennett's plan would be *costlier* than the mayor's.

Some words, like *unique,* cannot be used in comparisons. Other words, like *dead, empty, titanic,* and *huge,* might be used in idioms ("deader than a doornail"—a cliché) or in colloquial or nonstandard uses: "This place is deader than the county morgue."

Use the *er* ending, *more,* or *less* to compare two and only two items.

(5) *-est* vs. *most* or *least*: Use *-est* to end an adjective or an adverb in a statement about the superiority of one item over at least two others. Use *most* or *least* before longer adjectives and adverbs to indicate superiority. Never use the *est* ending with *most* or *least*.

EXAMPLES:

faulty statement of superiority: Carlotta is the most bestest backgammon player I know.

REVISION: Carlotta is the *best* backgammon player I know.

REVISION: Carlotta is the *luckiest* backgammon player I know.

REVISION: Carlotta is the *most adept* backgammon player I know.

Some clichés are based on a faulty use of these "superlative" forms, like "the hostess with the mostest," but such uses are hardly welcome in college writing assignments, which usually ask you to show your individuality in constructing ideas, not in using odd forms of adjectives or adverbs.

EXERCISE 1. EDITING FOR -S

Put an *s* in only one of the two blanks in each of the following sentences.

1. The boy___ run___ fast during practice.
2. After the train___ explode___, the sabotage team will make its getaway.
3. The clock___ tell___ time accurately enough for most amateur athletic events.

EXERCISE 2. EDITING FOR -ED OR -ING

Put either an *ed* or an *ing* into the blank in each sentence below. Your choice will be determined by when the action is happening and the meaning of the sentence.

1. Smil_____ as nonchalantly as he could, he tried to remove his foot from the waste basket gracefully.
2. A menac_____ shark circled the dinghy for hours.
3. As he turn_____ and duck_____, he could see the vase smash_____ against the wall and shatter_____ into a hundred pieces.

EXERCISE 3. CHARTING COMPARISON AND SUPERIORITY

Fill in the open slots in the chart below with the correct use of *-er, -est, more, most, less,* or *least* for each adjective, adverb, or participle. Use a dictionary if you need help.

PART OF SPEECH	QUALITY OF ONE PERSON	COMPARISON BETWEEN TWO	SUPERIORITY AMONG THREE OR MORE
adjective	tall		tallest
adjective		livelier	
adverb	lively		most lively
adjective		less abrasive	
adverb			fastest
adverb	coldly		

PART OF SPEECH	QUALITY OF ONE PERSON	COMPARISON BETWEEN TWO	SUPERIORITY AMONG THREE OR MORE
participle			least shaken
adjective	good		
adverb			best
adverb	badly		worst
adjective	many		
adjective	indecorous		

SPECIAL HINTS: USING INFLECTIONS

These are the signals readers are trained to expect:

-*s*: When you write about current action involving someone other than yourself or your reader, chances are that either your subject *or* your verb will use the *s* ending to indicate the number of things or people you are writing about, as Exercise 1 above demonstrates. Never use the *s* signal for number on both your subject and your verb. Although subjects or verbs may end in *s* because of normal spelling, the *addition* of the *s* indicates number:

EXAMPLE:
    The bus stops here.

(*normal spelling*) (*s added to stop to signal current action of someone or something other than the writer or the reader*)

-*ed*: When you write about action that happened in the past, you will use the *ed* ending on most verbs.

-*ing*: The present participle ends with *ing*. It is used in progressive verbs (verbs used to indicate action in progress at some point in time) and as an adjective.

    They were swimming when the threatening storm struck.

    (*progressive verb*) (*present participle used as an adjective*)

-*er*: When you compare two people or things, use *er* on the end of short adjectives and adverbs. Use *more* or *less* before longer adjectives and adverbs—without the *er* ending. Comparisons often include the word *than* (not *then*).

-*est*: Use the *est* ending on short adjectives and adverbs; use *most* or *least* before longer adjectives and adverbs—without the *est* ending. Use *est* endings or *most/least* only to indicate superiority of one item over at least two others—never for a comparison of only two items.

int ‖ 41. INTERJECTIONS

Words used to indicate names, pauses, brief answers, and sometimes exclamations should be used in dialogue that represents informal conversation—not in ordinary college writing nor in dialogue that represents formal or standard usage.

EXAMPLES:

"*Hey, you!* Get off that ledge!"

"Who, me? *Why, officer,* I was just sunning myself."

"*Oh, sure,* I suppose you get a heck of a tan at night like this."

"*Well,* actually, I'm not sunning myself. I'm just trying to see Nova Scotia."

"From Ohio? *Hey,* are you drunk or something?"

"*Nope,* I'm just a human homing pigeon getting my bearings."

As you can see from this brief conversation between a bewildered police officer and a smug but lonely drifter, interjections can be forceful or mild. The forceful interjections end with an exclamation mark; the milder ones end with a comma that joins them to the following sentence. Interjections, which occur often at the beginnings of sentences, are extra comments used in informal sentences.

EXERCISE. A CONVERSATION

Write a conversation between two people walking barefoot on a beach, lake shore, or street. Use interjections at the beginnings of sentences that they use to react to things they see, hear, smell, or find. ("Hey, look at that." "Oo, that's pretty.") Remember to start a new paragraph each time the speaker changes, as in the example above. [See also "Quotation Marks" (5).]

SPECIAL HINTS

Generally, interjections do not have a place in standard, occupational, or formal writing. Interjections that you use in your writing, therefore, should occur in the context of dialogue, quoted comments, or quoted thoughts.

irvb ‖ 42. IRREGULAR VERBS

Make sure that you are using the conventional form of the verb for the point of view and time you intend.

SPECIFICS

(1) *is, has, does*: The chart below shows how three verbs change form to indicate the point of view for current action.

the writer (self):	I	am	have	do
the reader (other):	you	are	have	do
a third person or a thing:	he, she, it	is	has	does
the writers (selves):	we	are	have	do
the readers (others):	you	are	have	do
third persons or things:	they	are	have	do

(2) *was, have, did*: The chart below shows the same three verbs making fewer changes to indicate point of view for *past* action.

the writer (self):	I	was	had	did
the reader (other):	you	were	had	did

a third person or a thing:	he, she, it	was	had	did
the writers (selves):	we	were	had	did
the readers (others):	you	were	had	did
third persons or things:	they	were	had	did

(3) forms of *be*: Whereas regular verbs use only three spellings to show all possible times and persons, the unusual verb *be* includes all of these spellings: *am, are, be, been, is, was, were.* The chart below contrasts the several changes of *be* to show person and time with the few changes of a regular verb—*act.* (For a review of the various verb forms that show different times, see "Tense Shift and the "Verb Form Chart" at the end of "Passive Verbs.")

DISTANT PAST USE THESE INDICATORS OF PERSON	WITH THIS FORM OF *BE*	WITH THIS FORM OF *ACT*
I, you, he, she, it we, you, they	had been	had acted

CONTINUING PAST USE THESE INDICATORS OF PERSON	WITH THESE FORMS OF *BE*	WITH THESE FORMS OF *ACT*
I, you; we, you, they he, she, it	have been has been	have acted has acted

SIMPLE PAST USE THESE INDICATORS OF PERSON	WITH THESE FORMS OF *BE*	WITH THIS FORM OF *ACT*
I; he, she, it you; we, you, they	was were	acted

PRESENT USE THESE INDICATORS OF PERSON	WITH THESE FORMS OF *BE*	WITH THESE FORMS OF *ACT*
I you; we, you, they he, she, it	am are is	act acts

FUTURE

USE THESE INDICATORS OF PERSON	WITH THIS FORM OF *BE*	WITH THIS FORM OF *ACT*
I, you, he, she, it we, you, they	will be	will act

DISTANT FUTURE

USE THESE INDICATORS OF PERSON	WITH THIS FORM OF *BE*	WITH THIS FORM OF *ACT*
I, you, he, she, it we, you, they	will have been	will have acted

Note that only three spellings of *act* are used for all functions: *act, acts, acted*. Regular verbs end with *ed* for all time indications except the present. Irregular verbs, though they do not vary as much as *be*, use three different spellings, on the average, to indicate their times.

(4) similar verb forms: In the list of irregular verbs under "Special Hints" in this section, meanings are given for verbs whose forms are sometimes confused with other verbs of similar spelling. Since most of these words are used frequently in English, most have developed one set of meanings when they take objects and another set when they do not. Sometimes you can use the ability of a verb to take an object to tell its forms apart from similar verb forms.

EXAMPLES:
Einstein has *laid* the basis for perceiving the universe in a new way. (*meaning = put in place; object = basis*)
The city of Troy had *lain* undiscovered for centuries. (*rested; no object*)
Editha resigned herself to her existence; the symbol of her resignation was donning an apron to *set* the table. (*meaning = place things on something; object = table*)
The sociologist was asked to *sit* on a panel about "futuristics." (*meaning = occupy a chair; no object*)

Along with confusion between similar irregular verb forms, some irregular verbs resemble other regular verb forms. In such cases, meaning alone makes the difference, since both forms might take objects.

EXAMPLES:

found: Watson and Crick *found* the structure of DNA.
          (*meaning* = *"discovered,"* so *founded* could not be
          used)

founded: According to legend, Romulus and Remus
          founded Rome. (*meaning* = *established*)

EXERCISE 1. REVISING FROM PRESENT TO PAST

Revise the following paragraph by changing it from present to past tense.
Use the list of irregular verbs under "Special Hints" to help you.

Whenever I become depressed, I run. Sometimes I awake in the middle
of the night and just lie in bed restlessly mulling over the problems of the
previous or upcoming day. When I think instead of sleep, I lose my rest anyway; so I get up and run. Sometimes I run to some place, like the airport—
a five-mile trip one way for when I'm really depressed. By the time I catch
my second wind, I forget my problems, or at least they shrink enough so that
they no longer sting my conscience. As I plod along, the regrets and inse-
curities that sit heavily on my shoulders gradually fall away as I draw myself
down deep within my spirit in the hypnotic rhythm of the run. I am meditation
in motion; I fly along the concrete. Time freezes, and distance steals beneath
my feet.

EXERCISE 2. REVISING FROM PAST TO PRESENT

Write a paragraph about something you used to do for enjoyment; then rewrite
it as if it were happening now. For practice, use as many irregular verbs as
you can.

SPECIAL HINTS: IRREGULAR VERBS REFERENCE LIST

Be sure you know which meanings go with which spellings
for the verbs you use. Consult a good dictionary to check the many
meanings that these irregular verbs have. Make sure you do not
try to force an object after a verb that does not take one. (See
"Transitive and Intransitive Verbs.") Also, when a verb needs an
object in order to be clear, supply it.

Use the checklist below to help you indicate time with
irregular verbs. The present or base form is used for present and
future times. The past form shows the simple past, such as the

forms you used in Exercise 1 above. The past participle is used with *has, have, had,* and *will have* to indicate the distant past, the continuing past, and the distant future. (See (3) above and "Tense Shift" to study the way in which the times of verbs relate to each other.) The present participle, used in "progressive tenses" (see "Passive Verbs"), is not normally shown in verb charts, since the addition of the *-ing* ending is all that is needed to form the present participle from the present form. Most of the verbs listed have meanings with objects and other meanings without objects. Consult a standard dictionary for the principal spellings of verbs not listed below. (If no spellings for past and past participle are listed, these are formed by adding *-ed* to the verb you looked up.)

PRESENT	(Meaning)	PAST	PAST PARTICIPLE	TR = takes object INTR = no object
arise		arose	arisen	intr
awake		awoke	awaked	tr
be		was, were	been	intr
bear	(*carry*)	bore	borne	tr and intr
beat		beat	beaten	tr and intr
become		became	become	intr
begin		began	begun	tr and intr
bend		bent	bent	tr and intr
bid		bade *or* bid	bidden *or* bid	usually tr
bind		bound	bound	tr and intr
bite		bit	bitten *or* bit	tr and intr
bleed		bled	bled	tr and intr
blow		blew	blown	tr and intr
break	(*smash*)	broke	broken	tr and intr
bring	(*carry*)	brought	brought	tr
build		built	built	tr and intr
burst	(*explode*)	burst	burst	tr and intr
buy	(*purchase*)	bought	bought	usually tr
catch		caught	caught	tr and intr
choose		chose	chosen	tr and intr
cling		clung	clung	intr
come		came	come	intr
creep		crept	crept	intr
cut		cut	cut	tr and intr
deal		dealt	dealt	tr and intr
dig		dug	dug	tr and intr

PRESENT	(Meaning)	PAST	PAST PARTICIPLE	TR = takes object INTR = no object
dive		dived or dove	dived	usually intr
do		did	done	tr and intr
draw		drew	drawn	tr and intr
dream		dreamed or dreamt	dreamed or dreamt	tr and intr
drink		drank	drunk	tr and intr
drive		dɪove	driven	tr and intr
eat		ate	eaten	tr and intr
fall	(*descend*)	fell	fallen	usually intr
feed		fed	fed	tr and intr
feel	(*touch*)	felt	felt	intr
fight		fought	fought	tr and intr
find	(*discover*)	found	found	usually tr
flee		fled	fled	tr and intr
fling		flung	flung	tr and intr
fly		flew	flown	tr and intr
forbear		forbore	forborne	tr and intr
forbid		forbad or forbade	forbidden	tr
forget		forgot	forgotten or forgot	usually tr
forgive		forgave	forgiven	usually tr
freeze		froze	frozen	tr and intr
get		got	got or gotten	tr and intr
give		gave	given	tr and intr
go		went	gone	usually intr
grow		grew	grown	tr and intr
hang	(*suspend*)	hung	hung	tr and intr
hang	(*execute*)	hanged	hung	tr and intr
have		had	had	tr
hear	(*listen*)	heard	heard	tr and intr
hide	(*conceal*)	hid	hidden or hid	tr and intr
hit		hit	hit	tr and intr
hold		held	held	tr and intr
hurt		hurt	hurt	tr and intr
keep		kept	kept	tr and intr
know	(*understand*)	knew	known	usually tr
lay	(*put*)	laid	laid	usually tr
lead	(*guide*)	led	led	tr and intr

PRESENT	(Meaning)	PAST	PAST PARTICIPLE	TR = takes object INTR = no object
leave	(*depart*)	left	left	tr and intr
lend		lent	lent	usually tr
let	(*allow*)	let	let	usually tr
lie	(*recline*)	lay	lain	intr
light		lighted *or* lit	lighted *or* lit	tr and intr
lose	(*not win*)	lost	lost	tr and intr
make		made	made	tr and intr
mean	(*intend*)	meant	meant	tr and intr
meet	(*encounter*)	met	met	tr and intr
pay		paid	paid	tr and intr
prove		proved	proved *or* proven	usually tr
put		put	put	usually tr
quit		quit	quit *or* quitted	tr and intr
read		read	read	tr and intr
ride		rode	ridden	tr and intr
ring	(*chime*)	rang	rung	tr and intr
rise		rose	risen	intr
run		ran	run	tr and intr
say		said	said	usually tr
see		saw	seen	intr
seek		sought	sought	usually tr
sell		sold	sold	tr and intr
send		sent	sent	usually tr
set	(*put*)	set	set	tr and intr
sew		sewed	sewn *or* sewed	tr and intr
shake		shook	shaken	tr and intr
shave		shaved	shaved *or* shaven	usually tr
shed		shed	shed	tr and intr
shine	(*give light*)	shone	shone	tr and intr
shoot		shot	shot	tr and intr
show	(*exhibit*)	showed	shown *or* showed	tr and intr
shrink		shrank *or* shrunk	shrunk *or* shrunken	usually intr
shut		shut	shut	tr
sing		sang	sung	tr and intr
sink		sank *or* sunk	sunk	tr and intr

PRESENT	(Meaning)	PAST	PAST PARTICIPLE	TR = takes object INTR = no object
sit	(*occupy a seat*)	sat	sat	usually intr
sleep		slept	slept	tr and intr
slide		slid	slid	usually intr
sling		slung	slung	tr
slink		slunk	slunk	intr
speak		spoke	spoken	tr and intr
speed		sped *or* speeded	sped *or* speeded	intr
spend		spent	spent	usually tr
spin		spun	spun	tr and intr
spit		spit	spit	tr and intr
split		split	split	tr and intr
spread		spread	spread	tr and intr
spring		sprang *or* sprung	sprung	tr and intr
stand		stood	stood	tr and intr
steal		stole	stolen	tr and intr
sting		stung	stung	tr and intr
stink	(*give off odor*)	stank *or* stunk	stunk	intr
strike		struck	struck *or* stricken	tr and intr
string		strung	strung *or* stringed	tr and intr
swear		swore	sworn	tr and intr
swim		swam	swum	tr and intr
swing		swung	swung	tr and intr
take		took	taken	usually tr
teach		taught	taught	usually tr
tear	(*rip*)	tore	torn	tr and intr
tell		told	told	tr and intr
think	(*consider*)	thought	thought	tr and intr
thrive		thrived *or* throve	thrived *or* thriven	intr
throw		threw	thrown	usually tr
thrust		thrust	thrust	tr and intr
understand		understood	understood	tr and intr
wake		woke *or* waked	waked	tr and intr
wear		wore	worn	tr and intr

PRESENT	(Meaning)	PAST	PAST PARTICIPLE	TR = takes object INTR = no object
weave		wove *or* weaved	woven *or* wove	tr and intr
weep		wept	wept	tr and intr
wet		wet *or* wet-ted	wet *or* wetted	tr and intr
win		won	won	tr and intr
wring		wrung	wrung	usually tr
write	(*inscribe*)	wrote	written	tr and intr

ms ‖ 43. MANUSCRIPT FORM

Set up your writings, especially the first page, for the convenience of your reader.

(1)   first pages: The first page of each writing you hand in should state in the upper right corner, your name, the course and section number, the instructor's name, the assignment, and the date.

EXAMPLE:
Ronda Jones
English 111-07A
Mr. Hibbison
Comparison of Sources Essay [MLA style omits this line.]
November 17, 1982

(2)   cover pages: A research paper, especially after the freshman year, should bear a cover page. Some instructors prefer not to have cover pages on longer papers, including research papers; if your instructor does not want a cover page, use the format above on your first page, then center your title after skipping two lines.

　　　If you use a cover page, center your title a third of the way down, center your name beneath the title after skipping two lines. At the bottom third of the page, center the course and section number, the instructor's name, the name of the college, and the date. (Of course, follow any variations of this pattern your instructor gives you.)

EXAMPLE:

Why Foods Are the Best
Vitamin and Mineral Source

Kathryn Cook

English 102-81A

Mr. Hibbison

J. Sargeant Reynolds
Community College

March 14, 1981

(3) logistics: As a matter of courtesy to your instructor, submit your
writings typed or neatly handwritten on $8\frac{1}{2}''$ × $11''$ paper, on one
side only (no squeezing). Leave margins of $1\frac{1}{2}$ inches on each side
and at the top and bottom. Skip lines only if your instructor wishes
you to do so on handwritten work. Double-space throughout
typed work. Number each page at the top right corner, starting
with page 2.

Avoid torn-out paper. Use neither typing stock from pads
nor lined paper from spiral notebooks: these snag on other papers.
If your writing is more than one page long, bind your pages with
one staple or paper clip in the upper left-hand corner.

Use blue or black ink to handwrite; use only black ribbon to
type (half-and-half ribbons make two-tone letters).

If you make last-minute changes, do so as neatly as possible,
such as by a single cross-out with the correction written above.
Avoid last-minute changes on homework by thoroughly proofreading your final draft; if there are too many changes, recopy.

The tools of writing are not expensive (except for typewriters)
Following the guidelines above shows respect for your instructor;
neatness does not make good writing, but it does make convenient
reading.

EXERCISE. PRICING SUPPLIES

Price loose-leaf binders, pens, loose-leaf paper, staplers, staple refills, and
paper clips at your nearest book or stationery supply store. Estimate the cost
of these supplies for one term, multiply by the number of terms you expect
to be in college, divide by the number of courses you plan to take, divide by
the number of assignments you can count on writing for each course (include
one exam per course, five lab reports per lab course). What's the cost per
assignment?

SPECIAL HINTS

The format of a manuscript may seem like a picky issue. But
the issue is who will be inconvenienced. Matters of form should
be your last consideration, but they should be on your list of tasks
for each assignment. Don't be paranoid about form, but do show
that your instructor's convenience means something to you.

| **mis mod** | # 44. MISPLACED MODIFIER |

Make sure that your modifiers are as close as possible to the words they modify. Modifiers can be words, phrases, or entire clauses.

EXAMPLES:

misplaced modifiers: The chemist handed the beaker to her assistant with the potassium cyanide in it carefully.

REVISED: The chemist *carefully* handed the beaker *with the potassium cyanide in it* to her assistant.

Although adverbs like *carefully* and prepositional phrases like *with the potassium cyanide* and *in it* can sometimes be moved away from the words they explain and still make sense, the clearest practice is to keep such modifiers just before or just after the words they explain.

EXAMPLE:

misplaced clause: The lawsuit involves a plate-glass window in a local department store which he walked through with minor cuts and scratches.

REVISED: The minor cuts and scratches he got *when he walked through a plate-glass window at a local department store* form the basis of his lawsuit.

The *which* clause in the first sentence above should be positioned after *window* so that readers do not have to double back after reading the sentence to figure out where the cuts and scratches came from. The revision shows one way to link these injuries to walking through the window (rather than walking through the store).

SPECIFICS

(1)   modifiers that look two ways: Make sure that your modifiers explain either what is before them or what is after them.

EXAMPLES:

unclear modifier: She decided only after she had seen him to break off their relationship.

REVISED: She decided to break off their relationship *only
            after she had seen him kissing another woman.*

REVISED: She decided she would not break off their
            relationship *until she had seen him one last time.*

The "unclear" example gives too little information for a reader to tell what happened first—her decision, her seeing him, or her breaking off their relationship. The revisions give two possible interpretations of what happened first. The repositioning of modifying phrases and the addition of more detail both work together to clarify the unclear version.

(2) split constructions: Proofread your sentences, possibly out loud, to make sure you have not awkwardly split a unit of meaning.

EXAMPLES:

awkward splits: The Russians have, judging from their fondness
                   for making headlines and their experiments
                   with long-duration space flight, decided to soon
                   attempt to build and maintain a permanent
                   space station.

REVISED: The Russians *apparently have decided* to attempt
                   to build and maintain a permanent space station
                   soon, judging from their fondness for making
                   headlines and their experiments with long-
                   duration space flights.

Splitting the verb phrase *have decided* and *to attempt*, an infinitive, asks the reader to postpone understanding until a clause and an adverb have passed by. Few readers are so patient.

EXERCISE. REVISING A PARAGRAPH

Revise the paragraph below to eliminate misplaced modifiers.

When I was, before I came back to college, working for a few years, one thing that used to annoy me really was the high-school clique. Being single in a new town is difficult without having to prove to a hopefully new female acquaintance anyway that I shared my adolescence with her but we didn't know it. That mentality maybe exists in the discos and the cowboy bars mostly, or so I thought, but I even found it in the laundromats. I, when I, with some reluctance, admitted that I was not a graduate of an in-town high school, got a look as if I stupidly had washed colors and whites in hot water together—with bleach. I decided to eventually stop trying to become acquainted with "clique mentality" women, but that narrowed my field certainly.

SPECIAL HINTS

Reading your work aloud can help you spot places where you have split constructions, needlessly postponed parts of phrases or clauses, or awkwardly positioned a modifier.

msh ‖ 45. MOOD SHIFT

Use your verb form to indicate whether you are making a statement, giving a command, or making a wish. Don't switch moods, especially from factual verb forms to command verb forms.

EXAMPLES:
Factual statements (indicative mood)
Yuichiro Miura *skied* down the South Col of Mount Everest, *fell*, and *survived*.
Commands (imperative mood)
Hit the dirt!
Remove the old putty with a putty knife.
Grasp the handle of the club firmly.
Wishes and if's (subjunctive mood)
If I *were* taller and quicker, I would consider trying out for a professional basketball team.
I wish that I *were* smarter, but I realize how hard some smart people work to be "like everyone else."

SPECIFICS

(1) formal suggestions: Especially in formal situations, subjunctive forms are used to make requests, recommendations, and resolutions. Use

the subjunctive form *be* or the present form of a verb, often after the joining word *that*.

EXAMPLES:
"I move," he shouted, "that the amendment *be* accepted by acclamation."
Be it therefore resolved that the president of this organization *act* as liaison to the national in matters of organization and funding and that the president *report* to this local annually.

Notice that subjunctive forms, like *act* and *report* in the example above, do not take the usual *s* ending.

(2) idioms: Some established wordings in English use the subjunctive form *be* or a present verb form without an *s* on the end.

EXAMPLES:
Be that as it may, we will not support the bill.
We will fight if need *be*.
Come what may, he refused to go.
"Lest she *succumb* to the wiles of that lounge lizard," declared the actor in his best melodramatic voice, "I shall offer my own wiles that she *be* able to choose the better lizard."

(3) informality: In informal situations or when writing to people you know well, you may use the regular (indicative) forms if the subjunctive forms seem too distant or "out of tone."

EXAMPLES:

formal:	I wish that I *were* richer than Phil.
informal:	I wish (that) I *was* richer than Phil.
formal:	If that lie *be* not treason, I *know* not what is.
informal:	If that lie *is* not treason, I do not *know* what is.

(4) modals: Use modal verbs to spell out opinions, speculations, possibilities, wishes, and other statements that are not facts. The meaning of each modal, and how to use it, are shown in the following list.

Can   expresses a judgment, opinion, or fact about physical or mental ability.

EXAMPLES:
He *can* pole-vault eighteen feet.
She *can't* understand your attitude about drinking.

Could   also indicates a judgment or opinion about physical or
mental ability, but is more polite or more tentative than
can. *Could* is often used with *have* to make judgments about
past actions.

EXAMPLES:
He knew what he *could* do.
She *could* have broken the stereo, but she did not.
"*Could* you wait outside, please," the nurse asked.

May   indicates possibility, permission, wishes, and conditions.

EXAMPLES:
possibility:	He *may* refuse the Nobel Prize.
permission:	"You *may* begin the bombardment," the general announced calmly.
a wish:	"*May* you get all that you deserve," she said coyly.
condition:	"The few have died violently," the chaplain's eulogy began, "so that the many *may* live in peace."

Might   does the job of *may* but is more tentative, even doubtful,
about possibilities.

EXAMPLES:
doubtful possibility:	The new serum *might* work.
very doubtful possibility:	*Might* the Bengal tiger be saved, or will it join the two-thirds of all the species that have ever lived by becoming extinct?
seeking permission:	"*Might* I have the car tonight, Dad?" I asked, expecting a flat refusal.
wish:	"I wish I may, I wish I *might*, Have the wish I wish tonight."
a condition:	We kept fighting, relentlessly but hopelessly, telling ourselves that we fought "so that those who have gone before *might* not have died in vain."

Must   expresses necessity, obligation, probability, or certainty. The equivalent phrases *has to* and *have to* specify a current necessity or obligation; *had to* indicates a past necessity or obligation.

EXAMPLES:

necessity or inevitability:	"He raised his bony fists above his head and shook them. 'They put on loudspeakers and shouted that we *must* surrender. We refused.'" (Pearl Buck)
current obligation:	We *have to* pay by the first of the month or give up the furniture.
probability:	"You *must* be kidding," she scoffed.
certainty:	Then there *must* be justice after all.

Ought   is always used with an infinitive starting with *to*. *Ought to* indicates a compelling duty or desire or an expectation.

EXAMPLES:

a desire:	You *ought* to check those calculations.
a duty:	"You *ought* to go to your daughter's graduation," he stated flatly.
expectation:	The coffee *ought* to be ready by now.

Shall   is used in formal and legal documents to express the future and to show determination or necessity.

EXAMPLES:

"*Shall* I wait, madam?" the butler asked stiffly.
The parties *shall* abide by the terms of this contract in perpetuity.
"I *shall* return." (General Douglas MacArthur)
"Blessed are the meek, for they *shall* inherit the earth." (Matthew 5:5)

Should indicates duty, propriety, or expectation. *Should* is perhaps the most familiar word for stating opinions.

EXAMPLES:

"We *should* be on watch," said the guard, "but I don't think we *should* have much trouble on a night as cold as this."
Americans *should* be more energy-conscious.

Will   expresses the future, especially determination to do something. *Will* also indicates willingness, ability, habit, or expectation.

EXAMPLES:

future:	"We *will* be married tomorrow!" they gasped together.
willingness:	I *will* serve on your committee.
ability:	She *will* easily clear $20,000 profit on her house.
expectation:	The price *will* be higher next year.

Would   expresses a condition, usually in the past or future, that is the opposite of what is fact or of what happened.

EXAMPLES:

I *would* not accept such a position if I were the negotiator.
"I *would* have been there, but I couldn't get a ride," he apologized.

EXERCISE 1. A DRAFT RESOLUTION: ALCIBIADES

For practice using subjunctive verbs, draft a resolution to the United Federation of Planets' ruling council. Make your resolution in favor of sending a rescue expedition to the two inhabited planets of the Alcibiades star system. The sun in that system has begun its red giant phase and is becoming too cool to sustain life, and its expansion is threatening the two planets.

EXERCISE 2. AN EDITORIAL: SAVING ALCIBIADES

For practice using the modals, which express opinions and judgments, write an editorial to the United Federation news service in favor of (or in opposition to) the life-saving mission resolved in Exercise 1. State the moral obligation to save lives, the necessity for careful planning of the mission, and the possibilities for failure of the mission in your editorial.

SPECIAL HINTS

Use subjunctive and modal verbs to express your opinions, wishes, guesses, and make other nonfactual statements. These words not only specify the nature of your opinions, as shown in the list of modals above, but they help to qualify your opinions and make them appear more reasoned and thoughtful.

Use command verbs (imperative forms) to give commands, directions, and instructions. When giving instructions, be especially careful not to switch between command verbs (*do, cut, carry, polish, choose,* and many others) and regular (indicative) verb forms that are used to describe a process (*he does, she cuts,* and so on).

The forms of regular verbs (indicative forms) are listed on the charts in the section on "Passive Verbs."

n ‖ 46. NOUNS

> **Use nouns to do only the jobs listed below. Nouns take familiar endings, such as *-dom, -tion, -ity,* and others, or they take no particular ending (suffix). Do not use adjective endings on words that do the following tasks.**

SPECIFICS

(1)   subjects: Use nouns to indicate what a sentence is about, especially who or what is acting.

EXAMPLES:
Freedom yields to no tyranny. (*subject of verb yields*)
They want the *city* to buy the condemned building. (*subject of infinitive to buy*)

(2)   subject complements: Use nouns that follow linking verbs and verbals to complete the meaning of a previous noun or a pronoun.

EXAMPLES:
I am *Mr. Stevenson.* (*completes I*)
He took on the responsibility of being *treasurer.* (*completes responsibility*)

(3)   objects: Use nouns to indicate who or what is the focus of the action specified by the verb. Nouns also end prepositional phrases.

EXAMPLES:
Freedom enlarges mankind's *spirit*. (*object of verb*)
They wanted to buy the *house*. (*object of infinitive*)
We gave *Jim* a standing ovation. (*indirect object*)
Against one *wall* leaned a rusted shotgun. (*object of preposition*)
"They call me *Mr. Tibbs!*" (*object complement*)

(4) possessives: Use nouns to specify the owner of something. (See "Apostrophes" for a review of when to use apostrophes on nouns.)

EXAMPLE:
Harry's bugle, filled with shaving cream, never sounded better.

(5) direct address: Use nouns to specify who is being talked to. This use of nouns usually occurs in dialogue. Use a comma or a pair of commas to separate direct address from the rest of the sentence. (See "Commas" (3), (4), and (5).)

EXAMPLE:
"*Friends, Romans, countrymen,* lend me your ears."

(6) appositives: Use nouns rather than entire relative clauses to identify someone or something further. (See "Commas" (5) for punctuation of appositives.)

EXAMPLE:
Geri, my *cousin*, my *friend*, and my *confidante*, was killed while she was trying to photograph the Lebanese civil war, another violent *conflict* fought in the name of religion.

EXERCISE 1. A DOZEN PRACTICE SENTENCES: NOUN FUNCTIONS

Using the examples above as guides, write two sentences for each of the six noun functions, for a total of twelve sentences.

EXERCISE 2. A DOZEN PRACTICE SENTENCES: NOUN TYPES

Study the list of noun types in "Special Hints" below. To increase your understanding of these types, write three sentences for each, for a total of twelve sentences. Is it possible to write a sentence that has only one type of noun in it?

SPECIAL HINTS: NOUN TYPES

Every object, living thing, place, activity, person, and concept has a name. Those names are nouns. Use this checklist of nouns to help you understand how versatile nouns are. (See "Plurals" for an explanation of how to form noun and pronoun spellings for plural.)

common nouns:	category names that are not capitalized, like *bird, house, treaty, person, backgammon, idea.*
proper nouns:	capitalized individual and brand names, like *Tweety, Versailles, Treaty of Paris, Pablo Neruda, Existentialism* (See also "Capital Letters.")
compound nouns:	two nouns or an adjective and a noun that have been joined in spelling or are thought of as a unit, like *pigeonhole, United Nations, capital punishment, headache.*
collective nouns:	nouns that use singular forms but depend on their context to determine their number, like *orchestra, family, congregation.*

EXAMPLES:

singular:	The *orchestra* is playing a waltz.
plural:	The *orchestra* are tuning their instruments.

ns ‖ **47. NUMBER SHIFT**

Make sure that your subject and verb agree about the number of people or things you are writing about. In addition, to avoid confusing your readers, make sure that all the words in your passage share that agreement. (To study the signals that show agreement between subjects and verbs, see "Subject–Verb Agreement.")

EXAMPLES:

confusing:	I'm not polluting; we clean up litter that other people have strewn along the roadside.

CONSISTENT: *I'm* not *a* polluter; in fact, *I* even help *my* friends pick up other people's litter strewn along the roadside.

The italicized items in the consistent example emphasize that the writer is a single identity, distinct from his friends and from other people. For readers who may have only one or two seconds to figure out the message, there is no time to sort out conflicting signals about how many people are at the focus of the sentence. Instead of a confusing shift from *I* to *we*, the consistent sentence uses *I, am, a, -er* (no *s*), *I*, and *my* as signals to refer to the writer throughout the first half of the sentence. For your readers' sakes, choose a focus and give consistent signals about it.

SPECIAL CASE

Not everybody is male. Use plural forms when you do not know the gender of your subject. Switching from singular pronouns like *everybody, each, anyone, someone,* and others to plural pronouns like *they, their, them* gives conflicting signals about the number of people concerned. The result is that both number and gender are confused.

EXAMPLE:

confusing: Let each person vote according to their conscience about what he deems just.

CONSISTENT: Let *all people* vote according to *their* consciences about what *they* deem just.

CONSISTENT (AND SINGULAR): Let each person vote by conscience about what seems just.

The singular sentence "writes around" number signals.

EXERCISE 1. REVISING A PARAGRAPH

Revise the following paragraph to make number references clear. If something is referred to first as singular and then as plural, make all references to the same things either all singular or all plural. (See "Plurals" for a list of singular and plural pronouns.)

I love a parade. They're exciting to watch, but it's even more exciting to march in one. Everybody carries his banners and flags; the bands struts by while the people on the sidewalks smile, wave, clap, and cheer. Parades give everyone his own special memories, and for a time everybody senses their togetherness.

EXERCISE 2. PICKING PRONOUNS

Pick the pronoun in each group below that signals a number different from the others in the group.

A. I   my   ourselves   me   mine
B. themselves   them   their   he   they
C. all   many   several   some   someone
D. its   neither   her   few   one
E. this   yourselves   him   another   each

SPECIAL HINTS

Singular means that only one item is being counted (or none). Singular signals include all singular pronouns, all nouns without the plural *-s, -es,* or internal spelling change signals (see "Plurals"), and the articles *a* and *an*. *Plural* means that more than one item counts. Plural signals include all plural pronouns, all nouns with the plural *-s* or *-es* endings or a plural spelling and plural adjectives (see demonstrative and numerical adjectives in "Adjectives").

Make sure that the count given by all the words in your sentences is accurate.

num ‖ 48. NUMERALS

Generally, write out numbers (including fractions) that can be written in one or two words. Otherwise, use numbers in the following ways:

(1) dates: Write dates as numbers except in formal invitations. Use 1st, 2nd, 3rd, and other such "ordinals" only when the year is not included.

EXAMPLES:
May 1st   *but*   May 1, 1942
11/1/78 *(for filling out forms)*
Nov. 1, 1978 *(informal)*
November 1, 1978 *(more formal)*
1 November 1978 *(military and technical style)*

(2) times: Write hours as numbers if a.m. or p.m. is used and if the minutes are shown.

EXAMPLES:
8:15 a.m.   *but*   eight o'clock
at 8:15   *but*   around eight
12:00 a.m.   *but*   twelve midnight
1300 hours *(military style)*

(3) addresses: Write numbers in numerals, not words.

EXAMPLES:
602 4th Street, Tucson, AZ 85721
1712 N. Huron Ave., Apt. 12B

(4) pages, chapters, scenes, and the like: Write numbers in numerals, not words.

EXAMPLES:
page 15   pp. ix–xvi   pp. 285–287
Chapter 15   ch. 15   ch. XV
Act IV, scene 1, lines 5–7   IV, 1, 5–7
Romans 12: 1–10
vol. 14, no. 2

(5) technical uses of numbers: Write numerals, not words.

EXAMPLES:
186,000 mi/sec   95th percentile
40° N.   16°C.
78%   18 ft.
623 km $5.99

Note: Since dates and addresses are read in grouped numbers, no commas are used within year dates or street numbers. Amounts of money that can be written in a word or two are written out as words.

EXAMPLES:
1100 B.C.
1492
thirty thousand dollars
    (For a review of abbreviations that are sometimes used with numbers, see "Periods.")

EXERCISE 1. PICK A NUMBER

Pick the correct forms in each sentence below.

1. Her train arrives at 8:10. / eight ten.

2. He ran the 100 / hundred in only 10.2 / ten point two seconds.

3. The company should clear 10,000,000 / ten million during this fiscal year.

4. The house she designed is at 10035 Canyon Drive. / ten zero thirty-five Canyon Drive.

5. Look it up in Leviticus 4:6. / chapter four, verse six.

EXERCISE 2. EDITING A PARAGRAPH

In the following passage, all numbers have been written as words. Where appropriate, convert words to numerals.

    On July twelve, nineteen hundred and eighty-two, more than twenty-five hundred runners participated in the annual ten thousand meter run. The fastest time was posted by Ross Whitmore, thirty-five minutes and seventeen seconds. Whitmore is a member of Electricians' Local six zero two.
    The fastest time by a woman was posted by Eileen Jamison of Dewburg, forty-two minutes and fifty-six seconds. Eileen is a member of the nineteen eighty-two graduating class.
    A crowd of about seven hundred people stayed at the Seventeenth Street start/finish line for most of the afternoon to cheer in the entrants through the seventy-five degree heat.
    Trophies and complimentary t-shirts were awarded by The Shirt Factory, one thousand and fifteen First Street, for the top three times for men and women.

SPECIAL HINTS

Whenever possible, do not flood your readers with numbers. If your subject calls for many numbers, round them off if you can, so that they are not all given as numerals. Be consistent, however, in dealing with comparable numbers—if the first dollar figure you report is in words ("about eighty dollars"), later figures should be written as words ("actually about ninety dollars").

OM or ∧ | **49. OMITTED WORDS OR PHRASES**

Carefully proofread your writing to catch omitted words and phrases. Neatly write in the omitted words above the space where they should go. Mark the space with a caret, a symbol that looks like an upside-down V: ∧

SPECIFICS

(1) negatives: Leaving out words like *not, never, nothing, hardly,* and other negative words reverses your intended meaning.

> EXAMPLES:
>
> reversed: George III did take the colonists' threats seriously before the Boston Tea Party.
>
> INTENDED MEANING: George III did *not* take the colonists' threats seriously before the Boston Tea Party.

(2) subjects, verbs, and objects: Leaving out subjects, parts of verb phrases, or objects puts huge holes in your sentences.

> EXAMPLES:
>
> missing subject and verb part: Trapped in the cave, but he was rescued after a day.

COMPLETE: *He* was trapped in the cave, but he was rescued after a day.

missing object: She said.

COMPLETE: She said *that she had discovered the 650th isotope.*
She said, *"I think I've found another isotope of lead."*

(3)   articles: Even in directions and instructions, you need to use the words *a, an,* and *the,* and pronouns like *your* to reinforce other context clues about your point of view, the number of things you are writing about, and how general the discussion of your topic is.

EXAMPLES:

misleading: Place wrench on plugs carefully so as not to crack.

CLEAR: Place *your* wrench on *the* plugs carefully so as not to crack *them.*

(4)   comparisons: State both halves of a comparison in similar wording.

EXAMPLES:

misleading: Communication with dolphins is as important as aliens.

COMPLETE: Communication with dolphins is as important *as communication with* aliens.

(5)   prepositions: Include prepositions so that your sentences do not become distorted.

EXAMPLES:

distorted: Let's stop the restaurant.

ACCURATE: Let's stop *at* the restaurant for a shark-burger.

ACCURATE: Let's stop the restaurant *from ignoring the fire codes.*

(6)   lost phrases and clauses: Sometimes phrases and longer wordings get left out of sentences as an oversight.

EXAMPLES:

lost: We dumped mercury into the rivers of North America along with zinc, kepone, insufficiently treated sewage, and what else.

COMPLETE: We dumped mercury into the rivers of North
             America along with zinc, kepone, insufficiently
             treated sewage, and *who knows* what else.

EXERCISE. EDITING A PARAGRAPH

Insert omitted words into the following paragraph. Also, cross out words and
phrases that were copied twice.

It was 5:05 a.m. and I was trudging out to to to try to start my car in the
middle of an ice storm. When I tried to put the key into the car door, after
chopping my way through a layer of ice, the was frozen. Luckily, the other
door wasn't even locked. I must have have forgotten to lock it the before. As
I reached across the front seat the front seat to unlock the passenger, I noticed
a bundle of old clothes in the back seat. It moved! I had a runaway in the
back of my car, nearly frozen, lost, feverish, and hungry.

SPECIAL HINTS

After writing a rough draft (or even a final draft), read each
sentence to yourself (out loud, if conditions permit). Start with
the last sentence and go through all the sentences in your writing
from last to first. Although your mind may try to read the words
you intended rather than the words you actually wrote, try to read
only the words written on the paper.

open ‖ 50. OPENINGS

**The opening section of a paper should do all
of these things:**
(1)   announce your subject
(2)   reveal your attitude about your subject
(3)   attract your readers' interest
**(4)   announce the organization of your sup-
        port section.**

Compare the approaches taken in the following two openings.

EXAMPLES:

1.   *TITLE:*   The Terror of *The Exorcist*
        LEAD-IN: Fritz Leiber once wrote, "So long as man progresses, the area of the unknown will continue to grow, both inside and outside the mind, and wherever the unknown is, there will be monsters." Certainly the possession of a twelve-year-old girl by the devil, as it is presented in the movie, *The Exorcist,* is monstrous. The terror that viewers, including myself, feel during the movie arises from a confrontation with the unknown, in demonic possession. The violence
        THESIS: caused by the possession has no known limits, and that violence is out of all proportion to the power of the human characters in the story.

2.   *TITLE:*   The Terror of *The Exorcist*
        LEAD-IN: To hear a child use vulgarity is sometimes comical. Watching a child commit social errors may be unpleasant at the time and yet be something to laugh about years later. In *The*
        THESIS: *Exorcist,* however, these actions were more than unpleasant and were definitely not funny when they were performed by a possessed child.

Both of these writers used a title to announce their topic. Yet their attitudes, or "slants" are somewhat different. The first writer wrote about feeling terrified because of the violence in the story; the second writer felt terror at the distorted childishness of the possessed main character. The first writer uses a quotation to engage the reader's interest—an old technique that should be used infrequently. The second writer relies on a striking generalization that runs counter to the usual attitude about public vulgarity, even in a child. Finally, both writers predict how their supporting paragraphs will be organized. The first writer starts by discussing the unlimited violence depicted in the movie and then contrasts that with the limitations of the human characters. The second writer plans to review the items in the movie that make the viewer feel unpleasant and then explain how elements of humor are used in the movie to provoke terror in the viewers.

Here are some common techniques for making openings interesting:

1. asking a question (one that your essay will answer)
2. contradicting a typical attitude or stereotype
3. startling readers with a fact, generalization, or statistic
4. using a "once-upon-a-time" anecdote (see Figure 2-9)
5. using a quotation or reference to a famous event to set the tone or reveal your attitude

These techniques are most useful when you need to make a special effort to attract your readers' attention.

EXERCISE 1. REWRITING WEAK OPENINGS

For each incomplete statement below, use your imagination to discover ways to include the four features of a good opening. Then rewrite the statements.

1. My topic for this paper is air pollution.
2. When you think about it, you'll realize that smoking isn't good for you.
3. Everybody ought to have a hobby.
4. Getting through the first year of college is hard.
5. People shouldn't use charge accounts so much.

EXERCISE 2. PROFESSIONAL OPENINGS

Pick up an issue of a magazine you enjoy reading, or one that attracts your attention as you browse in your library's current issues (perhaps *Rolling Stone, Ebony, Time, New Republic*). Leaf through several articles, but look especially at the first two or three paragraphs. How do articles in such magazines begin? Briefly summarize your findings, quoting important sentences to support your analysis of how writers begin articles.

EXERCISE 3. JOURNAL OPENINGS

Pick a professional journal in your field or area of interest. Follow the procedure given in Exercise 2, including a summary of your findings. What do professional journal writers do to begin their articles?

SPECIAL HINTS

Your subject and your stated attitude toward your subject form your *central idea*. Since you will often discover your real attitude toward your subject as you write your first draft, you should revise your opening after you finish your first draft. The organization of your essay and the structure of your thesis statement should match. (See Sections 1 and 2 and the sections "Outlining" and "Structure" in this handbook.)

out ‖ 51. OUTLINING

> **Use an outline to plan a writing, to reorganize a rough draft, or to check the organization of a final draft. Outlining requires you to list your supporting ideas under your main ideas and list your main ideas under the thesis or controlling focus of your writing.**

SPECIFICS

(1) the scratch outline: Scratch outlines are most useful when you have little time to plan and when you know your topic thoroughly, such as during the first few minutes of an essay exam.

Since the purpose of a scratch outline is to get your ideas in order, use phrases and merely indent to indicate a supporting example or detail.

EXAMPLE:

topic—women returning to college
marriage & family before college
so college = social
so college = interrupted
freedom to return to col.
need for col. for higher pay on job
colleges adapting to returning women
demands on woman & family
guilt vs. rewards

When you are familiar with a topic, each phrase in a scratch outline such as this should be the heart of a topic sentence, hence the heart of an entire paragraph.

(2)   the phrase outline: Use a phrase outline to plan rough drafts or in-class essays on topics that are somewhat unfamiliar. A phrase outline follows a strict form in order to lay out the organization of an entire writing. Notice the Roman numerals, the capital letters, the regular numerals, and the indenting in the example below.

EXAMPLE:
I.   Introduction
      A.   thesis: reasons, problems, and rewards that go with woman's return to college
      B.   background
           1.   marriage, not career, as earlier main concern
           2.   college for social motives earlier
           3.   interruption of college for marriage
II.   Support Section
      A.   freedom to return to college
           1.   mobility
           2.   longer life span
           3.   labor-saving devices
           4.   nursery schools and day-care centers
           5.   children in school
      B.   need for more education
           1.   low-paying jobs for women with little education
           2.   career interests
      C.   colleges adapting to returning women
           1.   special counseling
           2.   women's studies
           3.   scholarships
           4.   flexible-time study programs
      D.   demands on woman and family
           1.   help with housework
           2.   rewarding support
      E.   guilt vs. rewards
           1.   initial confusion
           2.   loss of time for
                a.   family
                b.   home
                c.   community
                d.   amusement

3.   respect from instructors
4.   commiseration with other returnees
5.   acceptance by younger students
III.   Conclusion: challenge but fulfillment

In the example above, each section marked with a capital letter contains the outline of a paragraph. Making a phrase outline helps you decide which paragraphs need more support and which topics have so much support that they could be split. Since a formal outline helps you divide your topic, having only one letter under a Roman numeral or one regular number under a capital letter would defeat the purpose of dividing the topic. Each list on an outline should be stated in parallel wording as much as possible, so that you can see clearly the relationships between phrases. For instance, items 3, 4, and 5 under 2.E. in the above example (the rewards) are listed in parallel form—noun + prepositional phrase. Finally, a phrase outline lets you see how specific your support section is. In the example above, the paragraph that develops from section 2.E. will be the most specific paragraph in the essay because of the number of items listed under point 2, "loss of time." Many instructors advise planning your writings down to this fourth level of specifics (represented by small letters) to make sure you use enough detail to be clear to your readers.

(3)   the sentence outline: Use the sentence outline to plan your message about each of your topics. Since every entry in this outline is a sentence, you include verbs and objects that specify your attitude and your key details, as well as a phrase that states your topic.

EXAMPLE:
Thesis: A mature woman returns to college for a variety of reasons, and she encounters many of the same problems and satisfactions as her fellow returnees.
I.   When she was "college age," the primary concern of the returning student was getting married and starting a family.
    A.   Going to college was a social choice.
    B.   Getting married usually interrupted college.
II.   The returning woman student is freer to pursue her education and a career.
    A.   With greater mobility than ever before, she is not tied only to her home and family responsibilities.

   B.   Since she is likely to outlive her husband, she must
        prepare for years alone.
   C.   Labor-saving devices make homemaking less time-con-
        suming than when she was first married.
   D.   Nurseries and day-care centers will tend younger chil-
        dren.
   E.   School-age children give her more free time.
III.   The returning woman student needs more schooling to enter
       the work force and have a chance at higher pay.
IV.   Colleges are adapting to the returning woman student.
   A.   They provide special counseling.
   B.   They offer women's studies courses.
   C.   Companies and colleges make scholarships available for
        returning women.
   D.   Flexibly scheduled courses help the returning woman
        balance her varied responsibilities.
V.   Returning to college places demands on the woman and on
       her family.
   A.   She leaves the security of her home life.
   B.   The family needs to share the work of maintaining the
        home.
VI.   The returning woman student may feel guilty about her
       absence from home.
   A.   She has less time for her family, her community, and
        herself.
   B.   The welcome of the instructors, other older students,
        and younger students helps her overcome her initial
        confusion.
VII.   Returning to college is a challenge, but the fulfillment the
       returning woman receives makes the problems matter less.

        Although the wordings of topic sentences (the sentences
marked with Roman numerals) may change considerably, this kind
of composition plan is very thorough and enables you to put
problems of organization aside and concentrate on your writing
style as you write a draft that follows the outline.

(4)   the paragraph outline: This type of outline is essentially a listing of
your topic sentences that helps you plan or check the order of your
paragraphs. A look at a list of your topic sentences can tell you if
your support is organized in the most effective way. Save your
strongest points for last—this makes the greatest impression on

your reader and lends force to your writing. Yet you should open with an important point to capture your readers' interest.

EXAMPLE:
Thesis: The mature woman returns to college for a variety of reasons, but she encounters many of the same problems and satisfactions as her fellow returnees.

1. While men pursued higher education chiefly to prepare for their life's work, until the last decade a woman's decision to go to college has been more of a social choice.
2. As a young student, her college days were very likely to have been interrupted by marriage.
3. The physical mobility of today's family accounts for the related lack of close family ties.
4. The business and professional worlds now include women of all ages in increasing numbers.
5. The early and middle 1960s saw the beginning of the return of such women to higher education; the colleges have responded.
6. Leaving the security and familiarity of the home puts a strain on the older wife and mother.
7. Because of her absence from the home, a woman may experience strong guilt feelings.
8. Leaving home and family for college is a challenge to both the woman and her family, but the fulfillment and gratification she gains make it all worthwhile.

EXERCISE 1. OUTLINE A TEXTBOOK PASSAGE

Pick a section from one of your textbooks—at least five or six paragraphs under one heading—and make a topic sentence outline for the passage. (Underline the topic sentence in each paragraph, and write a summary sentence for each paragraph that does not have a topic sentence. Then list your results.)

EXERCISE 2. OUTLINE A MAGAZINE PASSAGE

Write a sentence outline for an article in a magazine (or a section of several paragraphs).

EXERCISE 3. OUTLINE A JOURNAL PASSAGE

Try to write a phrase outline for a journal article in your field or area of interest.

EXERCISE 4. OUTLINE AN ESSAY ANSWER

Design an essay exam question for any of your subjects this term; make a scratch outline of your answer.

SPECIAL HINTS

As well as being an effective planning aid, outlining is also useful for checking the structure of a rough draft.

Use the scratch outline for quick planning of essay exam answers. Use the phrase outline for in-class essays on somewhat unfamiliar material that requires more planning. Use the sentence outline for thorough planning of your writings, especially for organizing writings on unfamiliar topics so that you can concentrate on style. Use the paragraph outline (also called the topic sentence outline) to check the general order of your paragraphs for effect.

¶/no ¶ ‖ 52. PARAGRAPHING

¶ **Start a new paragraph here.**
no ¶ **Do not start a new paragraph.**

Most paragraphs present a blend of general and specific information, with the specifics given to make the general statements clear. When the general point—usually stated in a topic sentence—has been supported, it's time to move on to the next point.

EXAMPLE:
Of all the Indians who live in what anthropologists call the Southwest Culture Area, Tarahumaras have changed the least over

the last 300 years. They are truly a mirror on the past. To see them is to pay a visit to most Arizona tribes about 100 years ago. They are corn farmers, about 50,000 of them, who live in widely scattered settlements and whose houses are separated from one another by the limits of shouting distance. They are also pastoralists who raise sheep and goats for their manure, wool, and hair. Oxen are yoked to wooden plows. They are foragers who supplement their diet of corn, beans, squash, chilis, and a little meat by gathering potherbs and by fishing the numerous streams and rivers of their mountain fastness. (Bernard L. Fontana)

The first sentence in the sample above, the topic sentence, is amplified by the two sentences that follow. The rest of the paragraph specifies how the Tarahumaras' life style compares to those of the historical Indians of the area. To indent after the words "100 years ago" would make a paragraph of generalities and a following paragraph of specifics, violating what most readers expect a paragraph to do—state a point and explain it in clear, specific terms. When the point is made, it's time for the next point. In the example above, Fontana lists the ways that the Tarahumaras subsist; after he mentions fishing, his list of examples is sufficient. His task for the paragraph is done.

EXERCISE 1. EDIT A PASSAGE

The following essay is printed as one paragraph. Decide where you would start a new paragraph and underline the topic sentence for that paragraph. (Review the section "Topic Sentence Placement.")

SOUPING UP A CAR IS STUPID

I think that "souping up" a car is stupid for several reasons. First of all, boys who put all their money into a car to make it look nice and maybe run faster are foolish. All those fancy things like chrome valve covers, clear distributor caps, mag or Fenton rims, extra-wide tires, air shocks (when they are not usually needed), and hydraulic air lifters are superfluous. Unsouped cars, however, without all that mess on them, probably run better and are more economical. The more flashy parts on a car, the less miles to the gallon they get. Also, imagine all of the maintenance work that would have to be done to these hot rods. Everytime a part falls off, is damaged, or is too used, it goes to the garage, and the owner is charged double because it was a special part. A normal car, though, would not have to be tuned up or taken to the garage as often. And then after a souped-up car gets all the nice "under-the-hood" extras, more money and time go into installing hood locks, which are designed to "lock the hoods" (the friendly neighborhood J.D.'s) out of the car. Again, one can see the advantage of a normal car, which has no hood locks. Furthermore, the average car owner can spend that extra money in different ways, such as buying clothes or investing it. Another reason hot rods are stupid is that the driver is usually very self-centered. Guys who own these kinds of cars are the ones who need attention. They must think that people will look at them in awe and stare. The souped-up car driver thinks that a cool car makes a cool guy, and to me that's not cool. It's fake. Some of those people are selfish, conceited, and snobby. They have to prove themselves better than the normal car owners by driving flashy wheels. On the other hand, the normal car owner is not apt to be on an ego trip. Since he doesn't have a fancy car to cruise town in, the normal car owner develops a better personality and does not let the car be his personality, like the souped-up car owner does.

(Cheryl Frasher, student)

EXERCISE 2. WRITE YOUR OWN PASSAGE

Write a couple of paragraphs on something you think is phoney.

EXERCISE 3. OUTLINE YOUR PASSAGE

Do a phrase outline for Exercise 2. (See "Outlining.")

SPECIAL HINTS

Outlining can help you decide when it's time to start a new paragraph. Usually, when you plan a particular kind of support for each of your general statements, it's easier to decide when your support section in a paragraph is finished.

For practice recognizing different levels of sentences, see "Abstract and General Words."

( ) 53. PARENTHESES

Use parentheses in pairs to enclose extra information or numbering of lists within sentences.

Put an exclamation point or question mark inside parentheses only if an entire command, statement of surprise, or question is enclosed in parentheses within another sentence. If a regular statement is enclosed within another sentence—an awkward practice that should be avoided—do not capitalize the first letter and put no period at the end of the enclosed sentence.

EXAMPLES:

extra information: He was glad (although he pretended to be humble) that he had won the award.

list: There are a few things that I must do to hit a good forehand in racquetball: (1) "sense" the target area, the bottom right corner, (2) plant and point my left foot, (3) snap my wrist, (4) shift my weight forward, and (5) turn my hand forward on the follow-through.

enclosed question: She knew the troubles he had been having (With his constant complaining, who didn't know his litany of "bad luck"?), but she could see no way to help him.

enclosed statement: Genetic research could lead to cures for cancer (most scientists think that will take decades), stronger and more productive grains, and even rapid learning in animals and humans.

statement not enclosed: Genetic research could lead to cures for cancer. *Most scientists, though, think that will take decades.* It could also lead to stronger and more productive grains and even rapid learning in animals and humans.

SPECIFICS

(1) overusing parentheses: If you find yourself using parentheses to
     add several explanations, revise your writing to make the explana-
     tions into modifiers.

     EXAMPLES:

           awkward: There (hovering above the house) was a huge
                       glowing (actually it was pulsing from dim to
                       bright) metallic-looking sphere.
           REVISED: The sphere hovering above the house was huge.
                       It had a metallic look, although it pulsed from
                       dim to bright.

(2) dashes, parentheses, or commas: To set off a word, phrase, or clause
     that interrupts a sentence, you may use dashes, parentheses, or
     commas for specific purposes. Dashes call attention to the interrup-
     tion. Commas identify the interruption but do not emphasize it.
     Parentheses play down the interruption as if it were a digression
     from the real sentence. Notice how the impact of the sample
     statement below changes with changes in the punctuation.

     EXAMPLES:

     The sound of the Big Bang—a kind of background static—seems
     to radiate with equal strength from all over the sky.
     The sound of the Big Bang, a kind of background static, seems to
     radiate with equal strength from all over the sky.
     The sound of the Big Bang (a kind of background static) seems to
     radiate with equal strength from all over the sky.

The emphatic dashes cause readers to pause, the commas
barely slow the reader down, and the parentheses almost invite
the reader to skip the enclosed phrase altogether.

EXERCISE 1. SETTING OFF INTERRUPTERS

Set off the underlined parts of sentences below using commas, dashes, or
parentheses.

1.   As a prank he had switched coats with me his sleeves were several
     inches too short for me but no one at the formal dinner seemed to notice.

2. My cousin a volunteer fireman for several years assisted in one of the field tests for residential smoke alarms.

3. "One of the pleasures of reading is seeing [an] alteration on the pages, and the way by reading it you have made the book yours." (Paul Theroux)

4. "If it weren't for the ever-present film of impurities coating the surface the oxides, nitrides, and absorbed gasses all metal atoms would bond to each other when brought together." (Western Electric ad)

5. "We traveled around the islands in Nixe the black, hand-built fishing boat of Fritz Angermeyer a German settler on the islands." (Kenneth Brower)

EXERCISE 2. WEIGHING PARENTHESES

Explain what signal the author of the following passage seems to give by placing the second sentence in parentheses.

"It has so far proven impossible to assign numerical values to stress levels as against other factors, but most researchers now agree that stress does play a role in the onset of coronary disease. (It is also involved in the onset of disease and disability as a whole—including accidents—for reasons not yet understood.)" (John Man)

SPECIAL HINTS

The usual punctuation for extra words, phrases, and clauses used in sentences to explain a term further is a comma or comma pair, depending on the insert's position in the sentence. (See "Commas" (3), (4), and (5).)

pass ‖ 54. PASSIVE VERBS

Use verbs that communicate action. Use the chart under "Special Hints" at the end of this section to help you construct active verbs.

Passive verbs weaken a passage and make it limp. Passive verbs can also conceal blame or responsibility; such constructions should show politeness, not cover up for someone. Passive verbs are best used to stress the helplessness of a victim, but can rarely sustain an entire paragraph. Compare the two passages below.

EXAMPLES:

(1)	(2)
Freedom *beckoned* to me through the slats in the side of the red panel truck that *hauled* the prisoners toward Bakirkoy. In the *dimming* light of dusk I *could see* that there *were* still such wonderful things in life as women, trees, and open horizons. (Billy Hayes with William Hoffer)	I *was beckoned* to *by* freedom through the slats in the side of the red panel truck in whith the prisoners *were hauled* toward Bakirkoy. In the light, which *was being dimmed* *by* dusk, *it could be seen by* me that there *were* still such wonderful things in life as women, trees, and open horizons.

The forms of *be* (*am, are, be, been, being, is, was,* and *were*) indicate no action. Passage 1 moves along with active verbs, and is nearly free of forms of *be*. Passage 2, however, stumbles awkwardly along and sounds much more formal than passage 1. Passages like 2 ought to stress action, but they often turn passive. Deadening verbs like *was, were, being,* and *be* join with the other trappings of passive constructions, such as *by, it, there,* and *in which,* and remove the life from a writing.

SPECIFICS

(1) progressive verbs: Composed of forms of *be* used with *-ing* words, progressive verbs stress action in progress—that is, action happening at a particular moment.

EXAMPLES:
He *was shaving* when I called.
The surgical team *has been operating* for five hours.

(2) tenses: Active and passive forms indicate six basic time frames from the distant past through the present to the distant future.

Each of these time frames may indicate a rather general time period or use progressive forms to specify a particular instant in time.

Study the examples on the charts under "Special Hints" to see what your options are for stating the times of actions. In your own writing, you should use the forms in the "Active" and "Active Progressive" columns most of the time. Most of the "Passive Progressive" verbs sound very awkward, so they should be used only rarely.

EXERCISE 1. REWRITING SENTENCES

Rewrite each sentence below to stress action or responsibility.

1. It slipped out of my hands. (*Show a person doing an action.*)
2. Dinosaurs were able to live only as long as the climate in which they lived was stable. (*Stress the action.*)
3. The executive is a person who makes decisions on important matters, usually after consultation with workers and managers who are familiar with their sides of the issue. (*Substitute an action for is and adjust the rest of the sentence to go along with your substitution.*)
4. The football game's play-by-play was called with the galloping cadence of a thoroughbred that was running all-out for the finish.

EXERCISE 2. REWRITING A PARAGRAPH

Rewrite the paragraph below to change verbs into past passive and past progressive passive forms. Use the "Verb Form Chart" under "Special Hints" to help you and to check your work.

I responded strongly to absurd trivialities. Our bar used plastic swizzle sticks embossed with the phrase, BUNDLES FOR BERLIN; some pilot's old man manufactured such things and had given us a trillion gross of them, though as yet we had by no means the capability of carrying anything as far as Berlin. I studied the shiny red globe on one end of such a stick, as if it were a marvel of nature, a salmon's egg or an immense dewdrop on a rose petal, and I experienced a kind of ecstasy; then I felt with my finger tips the sharp edges of the thing, and I took extraordinary pleasure in my sense of touch. I bent the stick. It broke. I felt intensely sad, as if I had snapped something of great value. (John Hersey)

EXERCISE 3. EVALUATING ACTIVE VS. PASSIVE CONSTRUCTIONS

Look over your work on Exercise 2 and describe the effect of changing the verbs to passive forms. What is gained or lost with the verb changes?

SPECIAL HINTS: CONVERTING PASSIVE TO ACTIVE

In all writings, whether personal narratives or lab reports, active verbs keep straight who is responsible, who acts, and what action occurs. Use the forms of *be* only to stress current action or action in progress: *She is running for state legislator.* It is acceptable to use *is* to link terms with definitions (Hemoglobin is. . . .), but such uses occur only once in a while. Search for the action in your sentences and stress it with active verbs.

- Convert nouns to verbs:
  She *is* a good judge of character.

  She usually *judges* character accurately.
- Avoid *there is/are*:
  There is no justification for a raise.

  You need more up-to-date facts and figures to justify a raise.
- Tell who does what:
  The attempt to increase activity fees was squelched.

  Most of the *students voted* against increasing activity fees.

If you really get stuck trying to convert passive verbs into active ones, follow this diagram and model conversion.

passive: subject + be + past participle + by + doer

active: doer   + verb + object

EXAMPLE:

passive:	A good time	was	had	by	all.
active:	All	had	a good time		

As the following chart demonstrates, passive constructions force readers to focus on the acts that are done, whereas active sentences focus on the "doers."

VERB FORM CHART

TIME (TENSE)	ACTIVE VOICE	ACTIVE PROGRESSIVE	PASSIVE VOICE	PASSIVE PROGRESSIVE
past perfect: (distant past)	*had* + past participle	*had* + *been* + present participle (*-ing*)	*had* + *been* + past participle	*had* + *been* + *being* + past participle
	He *had sung* my song before that show.	He *had been singing* my song just as she had walked in.	The game *had been played* in the rain.	The game *had been being played* just as the lightning had struck the stadium roof.
present perfect: (action started in the past; often action that continues in the present)	*has* *have* + past participle	*has* *have* + *been* + present participle (*-ing*)	*has* *have* + *been* + past participle	*has* + *been* + *being* *have* + past participle
	He *has sung* my song in every performance. They *have sung* my song.	He *has been singing* my song during shows since I gave it to him, and he will keep using it as long as it is well received.	The game *has been played* already. Both games *have been played* already.	The game *has been being played* in its present form since 1902.
past: (action completed in the past)	past tense form	*was* *were* + present participle (*-ing*)	*was* *were* + past participle	*was* *were* + *being* + past participle

Tense				
	He *sang* my song yesterday.	He *was singing* my song just as she walked in.	The game *was played* at night.	The game *was* already *being played* as we arrived.
present: (action happening now; can show future with an infinitive; recurring action)	present tense form He *sings* my song as if he *means* every word.	*am* / *is* / *are* + present participle (-ing) He *is singing* my song better than I have ever heard him sing it.	*am* / *is* / *are* + past participle The games *are played* every Friday evening.	*am* / *is* / *are* + *being* + past participle The games *are being played* this year for the United Fund.
future: (often near future)	*will* + present tense form He *will sing* an encore.	*will* + *be* + present participle (-ing) He *will be singing* professionally for several more years.	*will* + *be* + past participle The game *will be played* tonight.	*will* + *be* + *being* + past participle The game *will be being played* by the time we get there.
future perfect: (often distant or specific future time)	*will* + *have* + past participle He *will have sung* his encore and taken his curtain calls by 11:00.	*will* + *have* + *been* + present participle (-ing) He *will have been singing* for ten years this May.	*will* + *have* + *been* + past participle The game *will have been played* for the championship by a week from Tuesday.	*will* + *have* + *been* + *being* + past participle The championship game *will have been being played* for a half hour by the time we get there.

. or per ‖ 55. PERIODS

Use a period at the end of most sentences, except for exclamations and direct questions. Use a period in many abbreviations.

EXAMPLES:

exclamation:	"It's a bomb!" he shouted hysterically.
direct question:	"It's a bomb?" they gasped in disbelief.
statement:	She said matter-of-factly, "It's a bomb."
abbreviation:	Dogs were domesticated around 9,000 B.C.

Each sentence in the examples above ends with a period—even those that quote other sentences. Of course, when an abbreviation comes at the end of a sentence, no additional period marks the sentence end.

SPECIFICS

(1) abbreviations that are never spelled out: Before someone's name, never spell out *Mr., Mrs., Ms.* or *Dr.* Also, the abbreviations *Sr.* and *Jr.,* which are used after a man's full name, never are spelled out.

EXAMPLES:
Dr. and Mrs. Benton have arrived.
George Willington, Jr., was in charge of arrangements for the stockholders' meeting.

(2) business letters and formal documents: Except for the abbreviations listed in (1), don't abbreviate in business letters and in formal documents, including the inside address of a business letter.

(3) names of organizations and government agencies: The names of organizations and governmental or political agencies are commonly abbreviated without periods.

EXAMPLES:

YMCA	NATO	UN	WCTU	CARE
FDA	FTC	FCC	CAB	AACJC
AFL-CIO	UAW	WHO	NAACP	SGA

Out of courtesy to your readers, however, the first time you refer to an organization or agency you should spell out its entire name and put the abbreviation you will use from that point on in parentheses after the name.

EXAMPLE:

Over the years, the International Association of Poets, Playwrights, Editors, Essayists, and Novelists (PEN) has been instrumental in aiding Soviet dissident writers. PEN expresses particular concern over measures that suppress creative expression in the name of national security.

(4) measurements and scientific terms: Abbreviations that represent units of measure or scientific terms ordinarily do not use periods.

EXAMPLES:

	Hz	mph	mev	NaCl	H_2O	LIFO
	FIFO	UFO	bbl	Zr	ob/gyn	hp
but—oz.	g.	gal.	l.	mi.	lb.

(5) times and places: Abbreviations for times, like *a.m., p.m., A.D., B.C., C.E.,* take periods. Abbreviations of geographical features take periods, such as *Mt., Mass., Rd., Ave.* and others.

EXAMPLE:

His strange note said, "Meet me on the corner of Hector Ave. and 6th St. in Boston, Mass., on June 2, 1995, C.E., at 2:12 p.m."

For other uses of periods with abbreviations, consult a hardbound dictionary. Most hardbound dictionaries have sections on abbreviations in the back.

EXERCISE. EDITING PARAGRAPHS

Place periods where they are needed in the paragraphs below. Remove periods that are used where they should not be. Leave correct uses of periods alone.

1. The United Nations operates several important agencies. U.N.I.C.E.F., for instance, collects money to help the children of the world. It is perhaps more famous to Americans than are the United Nations Institute for Training and Research (UNITAR) and the United Nations Industrial Development Organization (UNIDO)

2. According to one theory, which was based on the calculations of Archbishop James Ussher, the world was created at 9:00 am on Dec 25, 4,004 BC. Physicists like the late Dr George Gamow, however, theorize a far more ancient creation

3. To cover a distance of 10 LY in any reasonable time would require travelling at about 180,000 m.p.s. or close to the speed of light. At that speed, however, according to one scientist, each hydrogen atom that collided with a spacecraft would slam into it with a force of 6 m.e.v.

SPECIAL HINTS

Periods are usually not used with abbreviations of organizations, agency names, compass directions, chemical symbols, units of measurement, and scientific terms. Consult a hardbound dictionary if you are not sure whether to use periods in an abbreviation. (See also "Ellipsis.")

ps ‖ 56. PERSON SHIFT

Choose pronouns that consistently indicate your focus. The focus of your writing will be your subject, your reader, or yourself.

EXAMPLES:

shifting focus: We dumped atomic waste into the ground along a geologic fault line and caused earthquakes. They have built atomic reactors on geologic faults. You can't even tell if you're buying a product from someone who endangers the environment.

CONSISTENT FOCUS:	*We Americans* have allowed the dumping of atomic wastes into the ground along a geologic fault, a procedure that caused earthquakes. *We Americans* have allowed atomic reactors to be built on geologic faults. *We Americans* as *consumers* cannot even tell if *we* are buying a product from a company that endangers the environment.
CONSISTENT FOCUS:	*One agency,* unaware of the effect of *its* procedures, dumped atomic waste in the ground, unwittingly causing slippage along a geologic fault line. A *few utilities* have built atomic reactors on top of geologic faults. Because *average Americans* can know so little about how American agencies and companies operate, *consumers* cannot even tell if *they* are buying from a company that endangers the environment.

The writer of the paragraph that shifts focus has not decided who bears the responsibility for endangering the environment. The writer of the first consistent paragraph has used pronouns and nouns to indicate his belief that we all share the responsibility for endangering the environment. The writer of the last paragraph has used nouns and adjectives to indicate his modified belief that companies are responsible for endangering the environment; he has also used an adjective, a pronoun, and two nouns to present Americans as victims of their own ignorance.

SPECIFICS

(1) *you*: Only letters and instructions are written *to* someone. Ordinarily, then, do not use the word *you* in essays, reports, or exam answers. Using *you* to generalize is informal; college writing usually requires that generalizations start with nouns.

EXAMPLES:

informal:	You never can tell when you might find yourself treading oil.
STANDARD:	Beach freaks can never tell when they might find themselves treading oil.

(2) *one*: Just as *you* is overly informal for most college writing, *one* can be too formal for some topics. Many writers try to avoid using *one* because it sounds so impersonal and because it often leads to the use of *his* later in the sentence, a use that some writers consider biased. To avoid impersonality and assuming a gender (and to avoid the awkwardness of *his/her*), simply use the plural forms of nouns and pronouns.

EXAMPLES:

impersonal:	One can become familiar with the antipollution agencies in the state.
impersonal & biased:	One should familiarize himself with the antipollution agencies operating in his state.
STANDARD:	*People* should familiarize *themselves* with the antipollution agencies operating in *their* state.
STANDARD (AND SINGULAR):	Each citizen should find out about statewide antipollution agencies.

(3) *us* vs. *them*: Writers must constantly distinguish between themselves and their topics, as shown in the "Consistent Focus" examples at the beginning of this section on "Person Shift." Especially in comparison and contrast writing, writers need to double-check their nouns and pronouns for consistent references to one topic and other references to their second topic. In position or belief papers, also, writers must distinguish their views from those of opponents. Again, careful use of nouns and pronouns maintains clarity for the reader.

EXERCISE 1. REVISING FOR CONSISTENCY

Revise the following paragraph so that the point of view is consistent: Explain how you repaint a room (I choose paint. . . .), give directions to your reader (Choose a paint. . . .), *or* explain how any painter might do the job. (A painter has to choose a paint. . . .)

Repainting a room, like a bathroom, is a tiresome chore. You have to choose your paint carefully; enamel paint lasts longest in bathrooms and kitchens. I liked a kind of soft orange for the bathroom, but my wife liked yellow. Choose a color you don't mind waking up to. After a painter chooses his color and type, he has to remove the loose, old paint. Then you can smoothe the surface with no bubbles or chips to loosen your paint a year from now.

EXERCISE 2. WRITE YOUR OWN DIRECTIONS

Continue to follow the directions from Exercise 1 in the point of view you
established. (As an alternative, write a paragraph of directions on a subject
of your choice.)

SPECIAL HINTS

Decide what the focus of your writing will be—your subject,
your reader, or yourself. Use the checklist below to make sure
that the pronouns you use consistently reveal that point of view.

If your focus is your subject use:	*If your focus is your reader use:*	*If your focus is yourself use:*
he, she, it, they; each, everyone, none, some, few, others, etc.	your, you (informal); no pronouns (formal) ("Follow these instructions to assemble. . . .")	I, me, my, mine, myself *If your focus is yourself as part a group use:*
		we, us, ours, our

pl ‖ 57. PLURALS

**Use the conventional signals to indicate sin-
gular and plural. *Singular* means that one item
or less is being counted. *Plural* means that
more than one item is being counted. Nouns
and pronouns have singular and plural forms.**

EXAMPLES:
unconventional: beachs, ourselfs, country's, foots
CONVENTIONAL: beaches, ourselves, countries, feet

SPECIFICS

(1) plural nouns: The following are the main patterns for spelling noun plurals in standard English.

a. Most nouns signal the plural by adding *s* to the singular form.

EXAMPLES: smiles, oceans, seas, hellos, plates

b. Nouns that end with *s, x, z, ch, tch, sh,* and some nouns that end with *o* form plurals by adding *es* to the singular form.

EXAMPLES: lasses, taxes, buzzes, beaches, latches, bushes, echoes (*but not hellos*)

c. A few nouns form plurals by changing letters near or at the end of the singular form and adding *es*, especially nouns that end with *f, fe,* or *y.*

EXAMPLES: selves, lives, countries, shanties

d. A few nouns form plurals by changing middle vowels.

EXAMPLES: feet, men, women, teeth, geese

e. A few nouns, especially names of game animals, use identical spellings for singular and plural.

EXAMPLES: sheep, deer, trout

f. Three nouns use *-en* or *-ren* as a plural signal.

EXAMPLES: oxen, children, brethren

g. Some nouns that are borrowed from other languages retain their native plurals.

EXAMPLES: criterion——criteria   thesis——theses
          fella——fellahin   beau——beaux

For foreign noun plurals and for any plurals you are unsure of, look up the singular spelling in your dictionary to find the plural. Dictionaries usually give the plural spellings of words from categories c through g above.

(2) collective nouns: Some words that end in *s* indicate single things.

EXAMPLES:
Please hand me the scissors. (*one pair*)
Economics is the toughest subject for me. (*one subject*)
The measles is a debilitating disease for older people. (*one disease*)

The numerical value of some collective nouns depends on the context of the sentence. These forms are spelled as singulars.

EXAMPLES:

The *group is* united in *its* determination to raise oil prices this year by ten to fifteen percent.

The *group are all* determined to raise oil prices this year by ten to fifteen percent.

(3) pronouns: The types of pronouns that have singular and plural forms are listed on the chart below. Personal pronouns and indefinite pronouns use completely different words to indicate singular and plural, generally. Some indefinite pronouns can be used before nouns as additional indicators of numerical value.

a. personal pronouns

singular	*plural*
I, me, my, mine	we, us, our, ours
you, your, yours	you, your, yours
he, him, his she, her, hers it, its	they, them, their, theirs

b. -self pronouns

singular	*plural*
myself	ourselves
yourself	yourselves
himself, herself, itself	themselves

c. indefinite pronouns

singular	*plural*
another, anybody, anyone, anything, each, either, every, everybody, everyone, everything, much, neither, nobody, no one, nothing, one, somebody, someone, something	both, few, many, several *reciprocals* (used as objects only) each other, one another

d. indefinite pronouns that can be singular or plural: all, any, more, most, none, some

e. demonstrative pronouns

singular	*plural*
this	these
that	those

EXERCISE 1. CONVERTING NOUNS AND PRONOUNS

Underline the nouns and pronouns in the paragraph below. For the singular nouns and pronouns, write down what their plurals would be. For the plural nouns and pronouns, write down a singular form.

But now he could ring for Mrs. Bolton. And she would always come. That was a great comfort. She would come in her dressing-gown, with her hair in a plait down her back, curiously girlish and dim, though the brown plait was streaked with grey. And she would make him coffee or camomile tea, and she would play chess or piquet with him. She had a woman's queer faculty of playing even chess well enough, when she was three parts asleep, well enough to make her worth beating. So, in the silent intimacy of the night, they sat, or she sat and he lay on the bed, with the reading-lamp shedding its solitary light on them, she almost gone in sleep, he almost gone in a sort of fear, and they played, played together—then they had a cup of coffee and a biscuit together, hardly speaking, in the silence of the night, but being a reassurance to one another.

(D.H. Lawrence)

EXERCISE 2. EDITING A PARAGRAPH FOR NUMBER

After reviewing "Number Shift," proofread the paragraph below and correct misuse of singular and plural forms of nouns, pronouns, and adjectives.

I prefer studying astronomy to studying biology and chemistry. Although all three science are somewhat related, the sciences of life both have its own views of the little world. Astronomy offers me a view of the larger universe, larger than but engulfing our frail, blue worlds. It's actually easier for me to see the paisley shape of parameciums in the heaven than to see it under a lab microscope. All people have his favorite exercise for getting the kinks out of their imagination. I'm like a large number of sci-fi buff who imagine themself cruising between the stars or marooned on distant planet. Although these are the imaginative side of astronomy, these leap outward in my imagination keep me going through the hours of computer analysis and sorting of data that astronomy can entail. Those leap are missing, for me at least, when I study biology and chemistry.

EXERCISE 3. ANALYZING YOUR OWN PARAGRAPH

For further practice using singulars and plurals consistently, write a paragraph comparing one activity, animal, person, event, or idea to two others that are related. Underline each noun and pronoun you use, and then label each as singular or plural.

SPECIAL HINTS

Use both context and form to indicate number. Most writers use context clues like *a, an,* and often *the, one, this, that, another* and other singular forms before singular nouns. Before plural nouns, writers use words like *two, some, many, these,* and *those* to indicate plural forms.

Use the patterns listed under "Specifics" to help you keep numbers clear.

prep ‖ 58. PREPOSITIONS

Use prepositions to signal associations of position, motion, time, and so on. Such signals between your verbs and nouns or between some nouns and other nouns help to make your writing specific and to lead your readers through your sentences.

EXAMPLES:

position: The house *on* top *of* the hill stood *next to* an old, burnt-out barn.

time and motion: *During* the day the dog ran *past* the postman, jumped *over* a fence *into* our neighbor's prize flowers, tracked mud *up* the stairs *to* the children's rooms, chewed *through* his leash twice, barked *at* every car that went *by* the house, and generally became a terrible nuisance.

EXERCISE 1. SEEING RELATIONSHIPS

For the following sentences, tell what relationship—time, motion, position, or simply belonging—the underlined prepositions show. Also list which words are being related by each underlined preposition. Some prepositions can even show comparison, cause/effect, or contrast. (See "Relationships.")

1. After the holocaust of World War II, the Jews scattered throughout Europe and America were determined about reestablishing a homeland.
2. The cost of medical care has gone up like a rocket since 1950.
3. No one but an educated person can resist the tyranny of words.
4. She was against her opponent's ideas, but she stood by his right to free speech.
5. Throughout the last 150 years, our society has been driven toward the idea that "Biggest is best."
6. Because of the emergence of OPEC and China, this century may be remembered as the era of the internationalizing of the earth—or as the era of "every faction for itself."
7. "Well, sir," said the bemused volunteer, "Mr. Caston is one of our oldest contributors, so I filed him under 'O' for 'old.'"
8. Along with the qualities of perseverance and tact, Mr. Denton has demonstrated honesty and ingenuity during his tenure at this company.
9. Submarines can cruise beneath the surface of the sea for weeks without depleting their air supply.
10. A man in reasonably good shape should be able to run a mile within twelve minutes.

EXERCISE 2. WRITING TEN SENTENCES

Using the charts in the "Relationships" section, select at least one preposition from each group (such as *about* from the "specifying" group or *under* from the "classifying" group) and use each in sentences of your own—for a total of ten sentences. You may want to use a dictionary to check your use of the prepositions in the contexts of your sentences.

SPECIAL HINTS

Although prepositions mainly indicate space and time, they can specify a variety of relationships between nouns and other nouns or between verbs and nouns. Overuse of prepositions, however, flattens a writer's style.

pro ‖ 59. PRONOUNS

Use pronouns to represent nouns that you have clearly identified for your readers. The types of pronouns and what they can do are summarized below.

SPECIFICS

(1)   demonstrative pronouns: Use *this, that, these,* or *those* as substitutes for single nouns or just before nouns as adjectives.

EXAMPLES:

pronouns: Whose skis are *those*? *Those* are Phil's, but *these* are Jennifer's.

adjectives: *This* boat came from *that* dock.

Never use the four demonstrative pronouns to "keep things vague."

EXAMPLES:

vague: This person I know has a house, but this person wants to sell this house.

MORE EXACT: My friend wants to sell his house.

MORE EXACT: Brenda and her husband have their house up for sale.

(2)   indefinite and reciprocal pronouns: Use indefinite pronouns either when generalizing or when you are not sure or need not specify the identity and gender of the people you are writing about. (For a list of indefinite and reciprocal pronouns, see "Plurals" (3).)

EXAMPLES:

indefinite: "*Many* are called, but *few* are chosen."

indefinite: The coat could be *anybody's*.

reciprocal: "This is my commandment, that you love *one another* as I have loved you." (John 15:12)

(3)   interrogative pronouns: Use *who, whose, whom, which, what, whoever, whomever, whichever,* and *whatever* for direct and indirect questions.

EXAMPLES:

direct question:	*Whoever* heard of a peanut butter and peach sandwich?
direct question:	To *whom* are you referring?
indirect question:	She asked *what* the noise was all about.

(4)   personal pronouns: Use personal pronouns to establish a point of view in your writing and to refer to previously identified people and things. (See "Person Shift," "Pronoun Agreement," and "Pronoun Reference.")

(5)   relative pronouns: Use *who, whose, whom, which, what, whoever, whomever, whichever, whatever,* and *that* to make clauses that identify nouns or act as nouns.
Use *which, that,* and *what* to refer to things.
Use *who, whose, whom* and sometimes *that* to refer to people.

EXAMPLES:

noun identifier (essential):	The artist *who painted that mural* was a revolutionary.
noun identifier (unessential):	The Brooklyn Bridge, *which was constructed in 1883,* has been sold often but never legitimately.
noun clause:	She was indifferent to *what was going on.*

(6)   -self pronouns: Use the *-self* forms of personal pronouns to intensify nouns or pronouns; also use the *-self* forms to refer reflexively back to nouns or pronouns from later in the sentence.

EXAMPLES:

intensive:	I myself will deliver the package.
reflexive:	I will deliver the package myself.

EXERCISE 1. DESIGN A QUIZ

Make up a five-question, true/false quiz on a subject of your choice in order to practice using words like *some, all, many, most, every,* and other indefinite pronouns.

EXERCISE 2. DEMONSTRATING COMPARISONS AND CONTRASTS

Write a paragraph of comparison and contrast to practice using *this, that, these,* and *those.* Use *this* and *that* in specific statements contrasting members of two groups, such as *this car* and *that car: This car's red interior makes it look sporty, but that car's olive interior nauseates passengers instead of exciting them.* Use *these* and *those* in more general statements that contrast the groups, such as *these cars* and *those cars: Generally, these cars get better mileage than those.*

EXERCISE 3. WRITE A DIALOGUE

To practice using the *-self* pronouns, write a dialogue between two people who are arguing about their relative importance to the company they both work for. You could assume, for instance, that both people are competing for promotion to head of their department.

EXERCISE 4. WRITE A SHORT-ANSWER ESSAY TEST

Use *who, whose, whom, which,* and *what* to make up a quiz of five direct questions about a subject of your choice. The questions should set up one-paragraph answers (which you may wish to provide for the sake of study).

SPECIAL HINTS

For correct use of pronouns, review "Apostrophes," "Case," "Number Shift," "Plurals," "Person Shift," "Pronoun Agreement," and "Pronoun Reference."

p agr ‖ 60. PRONOUN AGREEMENT

Make the pronouns that you substitute for nouns agree with those nouns on three things.
- **whether your focus is yourself, your reader, or your subject (which *person* you are writing about)**
- **whether your topic is considered male, female, or inanimate (which *gender* your topic has)**
- **whether you are writing about one item or more than one (what *number* your topic has)**

SPECIFICS

(1) person: Pronouns and nouns working together help to establish your point of view, to identify who is writing, and who or what is the focus of the writing.

EXAMPLE:

unfocused: The people who buy the products must trust the government's or the company's standards of quality; you can't be sure, though, that the product you take off the shelf has been inspected thoroughly.

FOCUSED: The *people* who buy the products must trust the government's or the company's standards of quality; *they* can't be sure, though, that the product *they* take off the shelf has been inspected thoroughly.

FOCUSED: *We consumers* must trust the government's or the company's standards of quality; *we* can't be sure, though, that the product *we* take off the shelf has been inspected thoroughly.

Save *you* for letters, instructions, and directions. Decide if you are generalizing about others or if you are writing about yourself, either alone or as part of a group. (See "Person Shift" for practice and for a list of pronouns to match your point of view.)

(2)   gender: If you know the identity of your subject, you can specify
      whether your subject is male, female, or inanimate. Although it is
      traditional to refer to ships, planes, and other craft as though they
      were female, the use of neutral pronouns is growing more popular.
      Whichever pattern you choose, be consistent.

EXAMPLES:

inconsistent: When the *Titanic* sank on her maiden voyage,
                     many of its passengers died because the radio
                     operator on the nearest ship had gone to bed.
CONSISTENT: When the *Titanic* sank on *her* maiden voyage,
                     many of *her* passengers died because the radio
                     operator on the nearest ship had gone to bed.
CONSISTENT: When the *Titanic* sank on *its* first voyage, many
                     of *its* passengers died because the radio oper-
                     ator on the nearest ship had gone to bed.

      As the last example demonstrates, using neutral pronouns to
refer to things involves canceling out a personification of the thing.
Referring to the *Titanic* as *he* rather than *she* does not eliminate a
bias toward one gender.

(3)   number: Make the number of persons and things you visualize as
      you write equal to the number of things you report to your readers.
      Singular signals indicate that a reader should visualize one item or
      less; *plural* signals tell a reader to visualize more than one item. (See
      "Plurals" for a list of these signals.)

EXAMPLES:

unequal: We shipped nerve gas across the country on
                     rickety railroad tracks to dump them into the
                     ocean.
EQUAL: We shipped *drums* of nerve gas across the
                     country on rickety railroad tracks to dump *them*
                     into the ocean.
EQUAL: We shipped nerve *gas* across the country on
                     rickety railroad tracks to dump *it* into the ocean
                     in concrete and lead containers.

      In the first example the writer misleads the reader by using
them to refer to the *gas*. The reader may visualize the train and the
aging tracks, but no clue has yet been given to visualize a set of

containers for the nerve gas. The second example, although clearer, may still make the reader think of dumping railroad tracks into the ocean. The third example keeps the numbers of things to visualize consistent by treating the containers separately. Mentioning the containers, by the way, prevents the reader from imagining the dumping of several railroad tank cars into the ocean. (See "Number Shift" for an exercise on number.)

(4)   relative pronouns: For the words *who, which, what, whom, whoever, whomever, whichever, whatever, whose,* and *that,* number and person are relative. In other words, when you write a relative clause, look to what it modifies to determine person and number. The gender of the noun or pronoun modified by a relative clause will tell you whether to use *who, whom, whose, whoever,* or *whomever* (always for referring to people) or *which, what, that, whichever,* and *whatever* (usually for referring to nonhuman species and things) to make your relative clause.

EXAMPLE:

unequal number:	Such "unilateral" treaties, which is an "agreement" that only one side has consented to, are rarely effective.
EQUAL NUMBER:	Such "unilateral" trea*ties,* which *are* "agreements" that only one side has consented to, *are* rarely effective.
EQUAL NUMBER:	Such *a* "unilateral" treaty, which *is an* "agreement" that only one side has consented to, *is* rarely effective.

In the examples above, notice that the form of the verb in the *which* clause is determined by whether *treaty* or *treaties* is the noun that the *which* clause modifies.

EXERCISE. REVISING FOR CONSISTENCY

Revise the following passage so that person, number, and gender are consistent. You may change some pronouns to nouns to help the reader visualize who is doing what.

This morning when I got up, there was an elephant on my lawn. They aren't usually there, of course, so I was surprised. There he stood with its trunk pulling at my newly planted shrubbery. "Those a hedge that won't be,"

I thought to myself. Since these sort of thing had never happened to me before, I didn't really know how to handle them. What could I call—the police, the circus, or the zoo? How could I get her to stop eating my shrubs and leave? Luckily, my kids weren't awake yet; he'd probably want to keep it, but she'd wind up feeding it.

Then I noticed a policeman and some guy in gray work clothes peering around my neighbor's hedge. I thought at first he had come to arrest him for destroying my shrubs, but then I saw the guy in work clothes raising a rifle to shoot it—kind of a severe penalty for eating shrubs. I couldn't let them kill him, so I ran outside waving at him like a maniac. "Don't shoot! I invited it here. It's all we had for his breakfast." I dove for the rifle just as it went off.

When I looked up my wife was staring at me over the edge of the bed. When I told her, I knew it wouldn't believe I had just tried to save an elephant who was eating a bush that wasn't there.

SPECIAL HINTS

Checking for pronoun agreement means making sure that the personal pronouns you use give consistent and clear signals to your readers about the focus of your writing, the number of your topic, and the gender of your topic. Make sure what you visualize gets translated into these consistent signals so that your readers may visualize what you have in mind.

p ref ‖ 61. PRONOUN REFERENCE

When you use a pronoun, make sure that it substitutes for only one noun and that the reader can easily tell which noun is represented by your pronoun.

SPECIFICS

(1) pronouns that could refer to either of two nouns: If a pronoun doesn't refer clearly to only one noun, revise your sentence to clear up the ambiguity.

EXAMPLES:

unclear: Hertzsprung and Russell noted the relationship between stars' color and brightness, but he had discovered it first.

REVISED: Although both Hertzsprung and Russell noted the relationship between the colors of stars and their brightness, *Hertzsprung had published his findings more than a decade before Russell.*

Since *he* could refer to either Hertzsprung or Russell in the unclear example, the name should be used instead of the pronoun, as the revision did. Notice also that revising *discovered it* to *published his findings* avoids confusion about what *it* represents. To be clear, a pronoun should refer to the nearest noun.

(2)   pronouns that are placed too far from their nouns: You should place pronouns close to the nouns they stand for. If too many other nouns get in between, the reader can get lost momentarily.

EXAMPLE:

too far: Margaret, sand cupped in her hands, stared blankly at the ocean as it sifted through her fingers.

REVISED: Margaret stared blankly at the ocean as the *sand* cupped in her hands *sifted through her fingers.*

REVISED: The *sand,* which Margaret held in her cupped hands, *sifted through her fingers* as she stared blankly at the ocean.

Many writers have been led into pitfalls by the use of *it*, so many avoid using *it* by using other sentence structures that are often more specific and clearer.

(3)   pronouns that refer to no stated noun: Make sure there is a noun nearby in your passage that your pronoun can represent.

EXAMPLES:

absent noun: Sheila is fascinated by the biographies of famous scientists, but she does not want to major in it.

REVISED: Sheila is fascinated by the biographies of famous men and women of *science*, but she does
not want to major in *it*.

REVISED: Sheila is fascinated by the biographies of famous scientists, but she does not want to major
in science.

Especially when you use *it*, check to see if your reader can
easily tell what noun is replaced by *it*.

(4)   pronouns that are overworked: Some student writers and would-be
professionals tend to overwork the pronouns *this*, *that*, and *which*.
Pronouns should not be forced to represent entire clauses or
sentences; such use sacrifices clarity (the reader's convenience) for
a shortcut phrasing (the writer's convenience).

EXAMPLES:
overworked: I heard the speaker say, "The welfare system
is being abused!" and I don't think we should
put up with this.

REVISED: I heard the speaker say, "The welfare system
is being abused!" and I don't think we should
put up with such unproven claims.

REVISED: I heard the speaker say, "The welfare system
is being abused!" and I don't think we should
put up with abuses of a system that was designed
to help those who need help.

One way to avoid overusing *this*, *that*, and *which* is to use a
summarizing noun.

EXAMPLE:
Many people complained that the space program served no useful
purpose. *This complaining* has decreased lately because of the wider
publicity given to medical and industrial spin-offs from the space
program.

(5)   pronouns that are vague: The words *it*, *they*, and *you* should represent
people and things that are clearly identified in a passage. Make sure
you are not using these words to avoid identifying people and
things.

EXAMPLES:

vague: It says in the newspaper that it could be a long
           time before inflation can be reduced.
REVISED: An editorial in *The New York Times* projects high
           inflation for the next two years.

Besides substituting nouns for *it* in the vague sentence, the
revision specifies a definite time period and avoids a passive verb.
Often, pronouns, nouns, and verbs are what need fixing in a vague
sentence.

EXERCISE. REVISING SENTENCES WITH CONTEXT

Clarify the pronoun references in each of the following paragraphs by revising
sentences with unclear pronouns.

1. A friendship can happen in such a way that one person must always give
   extra in order to maintain it. This could cause one to lose a friend forever,
   for this person starts to feel hostile, although it may not show on the
   surface.
2. To increase his food supply, early man imitated the desired result of the
   hunt in hopes that it would bring about that result. This is definitely shown
   in his art, depicting the capture of a deer in a hunt, possibly followed by
   incantations or ceremonies; and it is likely that the work of producing
   them was carried on while the actual hunt was in progress.
3. Both Susan B. Anthony and Gloria Steinem have been praised for their
   fostering of women's civil and economic rights, but she has been the
   more effective in influencing employers to exercise them.

SPECIAL HINTS

Although most readers could eventually figure out most
pronouns references, a reader should not be forced to do a
geological survey of each sentence to find the true connection
between the surface of words and the underlying meaning. Make
your pronouns each stand for only one noun, and make sure that
noun is clearly stated as near to the pronoun as possible. Be
especially careful when using *it, they, you, which, this,* and *that.*

?/no ? ‖ 62. QUESTION MARKS

Use a question mark to end every direct question and to express uncertainty about a statement.

SPECIFICS

(1) question words: *Who, whom, whose, what, where, when, why, how, how much, how often, do, does, did, will, is, are, was, were, has, have, can, may,* and other modal verbs (see "Mood Shift") often introduce direct questions and cause ordinary word order to be turned around.

EXAMPLES:
Whose book is this? Why is the sky blue?
When is "the Millenium"? How often are you audited?
Does the plant meet current emission standards?
Is the symphony considering changing conductors?
Has the ceremony been postponed?
Can any government in America balance its budget and provide adequate services?

(2) questioned statements: A question mark can be placed at the end of a statement that is being challenged as inaccurate or hard to believe.

EXAMPLES:
"The ignition is shorted out?" he asked in disbelief.
"The door was locked when you left?" she asked, beginning to feel frightened.

Most uses like this will occur in dialogue, usually in response to a previous speaker.

(3) expected answers: Another form of question that should be used mostly in dialogue sets up an expected answer by tagging a question clause onto a statement.

EXAMPLES:

"She sings well, doesn't she?" asked the old lady, hoping for a compliment for her daughter.

"We don't have to pay for this, do we?" he asked the repairman while thinking of his low bank balance.

EXERCISE 1. PUNCTUATING SENTENCES: ? OR .

Complete the sentences below by putting a question mark or a period in each underlined space. Keep in mind the question forms that are used most often in dialogue.

1. How many whales beached last year __
2. "We won, didn't we __" she asked hopefully __
3. Few people believe how many whales beach every year __
4. It didn't snow __
5. "It didn't snow __" They knew the answer and felt almost cheated by the sky.
6. "Are you studying geology __"
7. He asked to borrow my calculator in a panic __
8. She wanted to know whether we accepted delivery on the defective components __
9. She finally felt safe when the fireman got her down to the bottom of the ladder __
10. Wouldn't similar conditions trigger another earthquake __

EXERCISE 2. DIALOGUE: A UFO SIGHTING

For more practice using question marks, write a dialogue as follows: One person claims to have seen a UFO, but a second person is not easily convinced that the "UFO" was really an alien spacecraft. Try to use all three question situations and even indirect questions. (See the "Special Hints" below.)

SPECIAL HINTS

Make sure you use both word order and a question mark to set off direct questions for your readers. Sometimes, especially in statements challenged by a speaker of dialogue, a question mark alone can indicate a question: *"The car won't start?" she said, as if surprised.* Be certain *not* to use a question mark for *statements* that express doubt or uncertainty. When you write these statements, called indirect questions, use *whether, if,* and question words in the middle of a sentence.

> INDIRECT QUESTIONS:
> She asked *whether* it was raining.
> He wondered *if* the sandworms would attack.
> They asked *how* he could endure running in a marathon.

Note that indirect questions do not use the word order for direct questions—verbs like *was, would,* and *could* appear in the position normal for a statement.

" *or* quo ‖ 63. QUOTATION MARKS

Use quotation marks around all word-for-word statements made by someone other than you, the writer. Quotation marks around a statement signify that the statement is repeated just as it was stated originally, without changes in any of the words.

(See "Ellipsis" for directions on how to leave out irrelevant words. See "Brackets" for directions on how to add words needed to make a statement clear and grammatically correct. See section 7b for more on quotations.)

Quotation marks are also used to set off titles of poems, songs, articles, essays, chapters, subtitles or subheadings, short stories—for composed works published as part of a larger work. You should also use them to set off slang words, sarcastic words, first uses of new words, or key words that you expect will be new to your readers.

SPECIFICS

(1) quotations: If a statement that you quote word-for-word is four
lines or less in length, it should be written into your regular
paragraphs. Longer quotations do not take quotation marks; they
are set off by skipping a line before and after the quotation and
using narrower margins, at least a half-inch narrower on the left
side of the quotation.

EXAMPLES:

short quotation: According to Timothy Bay, "Major oil companies make large corporate contributions to the
CSLP [Center for Short-Lived Phenomena] to
ensure immediate and comprehensive reporting of pollution incidents."

long quotation: Imagine yourself in the 18-million-vol-
ume Library of Congress, but with no card
catalogues, no Dewey decimal system, no alphabetical arrangement of the books according
to author or subject matter. Every single book
that has ever been printed in America is there,
haphazardly arranged on the shelves. In a
world drowning in information, computer illit-
erates may feel the same sense of bewilderment.
(Kathleen McAuliffe)

Most teachers will want long quotations to be double–spaced. Also,
the author should ordinarily be identified in the main text of your
writing, just before you begin the longer quotation.

(2) titles: In general, titles of brief works or works that are part of a
larger publication are set off with quotation marks.

EXAMPLES:

poem:	"We Are Seven"
song:	"Blowin' in the Wind"
article:	"Computer Lib"
story:	"The Necklace"
section of a magazine:	"Publisher's Page"
chapter in book:	"The 800th Lifetime"
subtitle in chapter:	"The Unprepared Visitor"

(3) new words and unfamiliar terms: Unusual uses of words should be
     set off by quotation marks.

     EXAMPLES:

      slang: "He was so angry," whispered Becky, "that I
                       thought he was going to 'hulk out' or some-
                       thing."

    sarcasm: As I got up, brushing the slime and mud from
                       my first suit, the fresh brat who had tripped
                       me chuckled, "Well, you certainly are an 'earthy'
                       person."

  new term: Alvin Toffler characterizes space colonization
                       as a "high-stream" technology.

Titles, words used as slang, and words used as sarcasm are
always set off with quotation marks. New terms, however, need to
be marked by quotation marks only once, when first used.

(4) punctuation with quotations: English teachers will request that you
     always put periods and commas *inside* quotation marks. Many
     business and secretarial science teachers ask students to put periods
     and commas *outside* quotation marks *always*. Different readers are
     trained for different signals. Punctuate with periods and commas
     according to your readers' training.

     Exclamation marks, question marks, and semicolons go inside
     of quotation marks only if they are part of the quotation.

     EXAMPLES:

"You won't?" they asked.

"I won't!" he screamed.

According to our agent, they "asked him politely"; he refused
obstinately.

Why didn't you sing "Auld Lang Syne"?

The entire production company is thrilled about adapting Stephen
Crane's "The Open Boat"!

(5) writing dialogue: There are two sets of "rules" for writing dialogue—
     script style and prose style. In both, a new paragraph starts each
     time the speaker changes, but paragraphs and identities of speakers
     are indicated differently in the two styles.

     One major difference between the two styles is layout. Prose
     dialogue indents every time the speaker changes, and can rely on
     context, rather than names, to keep the identities of the speakers

known. In script dialogue, the speaker's name appears at the beginning of what the speaker says. Another important difference is that prose dialogue can center on one point of view, like Diane's in the example below. Script dialogue can "focus" on one character only by having the character say more, as Linda does in the script example below.

Prose dialogue can include interpretive or explanatory comments by one speaker or the writer. Therefore, prose dialogue uses quotation marks to signal where spoken statements start and stop. Script dialogue only occasionally inserts an explanatory word, such as "running" or "hopefully." Prose style is usually better for including background comments that can help the reader understand the situation. To enable the reader to draw conclusions, you can either use script style or prose style with very few interpretive comments.

For the sake of contrast, the following conversation is written twice—once in script style, then as prose dialogue.

EXAMPLES
Script style:

Linda (running): Diane, wait! I'm glad I caught up with you before we had to go in for the test. You've got to help me. I have to pass this test, but I didn't have time to study at all last night.
Diane: Out with Barry again, huh? Naughty, naughty.
Linda: Oh, Di, this is serious. Yeah, I was out with Barry—out at the hospital. He wrecked his car last night, broke his leg, cuts on his arms and face. I was with him or waiting for him most of the night. I couldn't think, let alone study.
Diane: Oh, Linda, I'm sorry; but what I can I do?
Linda (hopefully): Sit next to me. It's an objective test, just—
Diane: Linda! We could both get a zero if we get caught, or worse.
Linda: Are you still mad at me for what I said about you and Curt? Di, we're friends. Besides, you won't be in trouble; just don't protect your answers.
Diane: No, I'm not mad at you; but it's cheating, Lin.

Prose style:

Linda came running toward me down the hall. I wanted to avoid her; I was still upset about her snide attitude toward Curt. She caught up.

"Diane, wait! I'm glad I caught up with you," she said, catching her breath, "before we had to go in for the test. You've got to help me. I have to pass this test, but I didn't have time to study at all last night."

She looked like she'd been doing something all night. "Out with Barry again, huh?" I chided. "Naughty, naughty." Her whole body sagged; something must have been wrong.

"Oh, Di, this is serious." Her voice trembled. "Yeah, I was out with Barry—out at the hospital. He wrecked his car last night, broke his leg, cuts on his arms and face. I was with him or waiting for him most of the night. I couldn't think, let alone study."

I could remember Barry's handsome face, but I didn't want to think of him hurt. He had been a good friend to me because of Lin; and I knew how much she loved him. "Oh, Linda, I'm sorry; but what can I do?"

"Sit next to me. It's an objective test, just—"

"Linda!" I hate to admit it, but I was scared—and shocked. We were both disgusted by cheaters. I tried to get out of it. "We could both get a zero if we get caught, or worse."

"Are you still mad at me for what I said about you and Curt? Di, we're friends. Besides, you won't be in trouble; just don't protect your answers."

I was still upset with her; but I felt sorry for her, too. I felt helpless and torn. "No, I'm not mad at you; but it's cheating, Lin."

EXERCISE. DIALOGUE: SETTLING A DILEMMA

Finish the dialogue between Diane and Linda in the prose style. Use explanatory comments from Diane's point of view to show her motives and what she thought about her eventual decision to help Linda or not. (For an exercise on titles of longer and shorter works, see "Underlining.")

SPECIAL HINTS

Talking is usually signified by quotation marks to show when a spoken statement starts and especially to show when the spoken statement ends. If you use someone's written or spoken words, you must place quotation marks around everything quoted word for word.

Dialogue can add vividness to a writing. Note that script style does not use quotation marks or explanatory comments. Prose dialogue can help your reader visualize (and hear) your ideas in action—a technique especially suited for narrative writing, anecdotes, and scenarios.

rela ‖ 64. RELATIONSHIPS

Use words that show the relationships between your ideas. The more complicated your topic, the more your reader needs transitional words and phrases to bridge ideas.

Section 3 presents more than twenty different organizing principles that are used at various levels of writing—sentences, paragraphs, essays, and even longer writings. For instance, the time and space signals used in autobiographical writing, or any narrative or description, spell out for readers the where and when of what's happening.

In each of your writings, you will draw conclusions, state generalizations, or make summarizing comments. Readers appreciate guiding words that signal each of these functions.

You can pick up any popular magazine or best-selling book and see how the professionals use these common, little words. In the passage below, taken from Charles E. Silberman's best-selling book *Criminal Violence, Criminal Justice,* the relating words are emphasized with underlining.

EXAMPLE:

In some ways, the [high] crime statistics understate the magnitude of the change that has occurred, for they say nothing about the nature of the crimes themselves. Murder, for example, used to be thought of mainly as a crime of passion. . . . In fact, most murders still involve victims and offenders who know one another. . . . . . .

. . . .

On the other hand, robbery ... has always been a crime committed predominantly by strangers.

Although most readers would have little trouble recognizing Silberman's contrast between murder and robbery, conscientious writers include enough bridges between ideas so that readers can *anticipate* relationships, as Silberman has done with the words *for, for example,* and *in fact* in the passage above.

EXERCISE 1. SEEING RELATIONSHIPS IN A PASSAGE

Use the charts under "Special Hints" in this section to determine the relationships specified by the underlined words and phrases in the passage below. Some words will appear on more than one chart, so use the context of the passage to determine its actual function.

To begin with, a star is born out of a mass of dust and gas, which swirls slowly and which under its own gravitational pull comes slowly together. As this mass of dust and gas . . . comes together, the gravitational pull becomes more and more intense, so the process hastens.

As the cloud condenses, the temperature and pressure at the center get higher and higher until finally they become high enough to break down the atoms at the center and initiate nuclear fusion. At this moment of nuclear ignition, the developing star is born.

A star the mass of our Sun might take thirty million years to reach nuclear ignition, while a star with ten times the mass of the Sun might condense to nuclear ignition in only ten thousand years.

On the other hand, a star with only one-tenth the mass of the Sun might take a hundred million years to ignite.

Naturally, the stars we see in the sky have already reached nuclear ignition. Once they have reached it, they continue to produce and radiate energy at very much the same rate for a long period. (Isaac Asimov, *The Collapsing Universe*)

EXERCISE 2. REVISING RELATIONSHIP SIGNALS

Using the same charts under "Special Hints" that you used in Exercise 1, pick a word or phrase that could replace each of the underlined words and phrases in the passage from Dr. Asimov's book.

EXERCISE 3. REVISING AN ESSAY TO ADD RELATIONSHIP SIGNALS

The passage below is the framework for an essay on how easy it is, but sometimes very costly, to put things off. Rewrite the passage, adding your own ideas, changing sentence structures, and specifying relationships between ideas. The "listing/process chart" will give you ideas on how to get from paragraph to paragraph to present each example of putting something off.

Household chores are easy to resist. Vacuuming the floor can wait. Dirt doesn't accumulate quickly. Dust won't be noticeable. A sink full of dirty dishes can wait; there are many places a person can go out to eat.

A car doesn't require daily cleaning. Waxing the paint will preserve the finish and make dirt easier to remove. Changing oil is a maintenance requirement. Every car needs oil. Without oil a car won't have lubrication.

Painting your house helps preserve the wood; the paint seals out moisture. Two coats of paint are usually preferred. A primer is used as a first coat; it adheres well. The second or finish coat should be an enamel.

Plants need water to grow. In outdoor gardens, a hose is used to water the plants. A good garden hose will cost about ten dollars. Guarantees usually come with quality hoses.

Dogs require good nourishment. As a dog grows, he needs a different diet. Some dog foods can be mixed with water.

A person should not forget to pay bills. Interest on loans and credit is very high today. Penalties are charged on overdue bills. An accumulation of bills will result in going broke. Credit cards must be used carefully to avoid needless buying.

Buying a lot of food on sale will save money. A freezer is great for storing food; it uses very little electricity.

Don't put off until tomorrow what can be done today.

SPECIAL HINTS

Engineers don't ordinarily build bridges where there is already a smooth road. Similarly, you don't need to provide bridging words and phrases (and clauses) where your ideas are likely to be clear to your readers. But since your readers can't get inside your head, they need to be shown the connections between ideas that you may be making almost without knowing it.

The charts that follow list samples of words and phrases that you can use to signal the connections between your ideas. A comma is shown when one must be included after a word or phrase. Capitalized transitions are likely to begin a concluding sentence or paragraph.

RELATING WORDS AND ORGANIZING PRINCIPLES

ILLUSTRATING AND SPECIFYING

prepositions	subordinating conjunctions	coordinating conjunctions	conjunctive adverbs	transitional phrases
about		both . . . and . . .	accordingly,	by the way,
as		either . . . or . . .	besides,	for example, (e.g.)
besides		neither . . . nor . . .	especially,	for instance,
like		not only . . . but also . . .	incidentally,	in particular
of			indeed,	such as
to			namely,	that is, (i.e.)
with				This point can be clarified . . .
				explained . . .
				made clearer . . .
				to be specific,
				to elaborate,
				to enumerate,
				to explain,
				to illustrate,
				to list a few

RELATING WORDS AND ORGANIZING PRINCIPLES

prepositions	subordinating conjunctions	CLASSIFYING AND DEFINING		
		coordinating conjunctions	conjunctive adverbs	transitional phrases
in	if	nor	accordingly,	belonging to this group
like	unless	or	actually,	in like fashion (*or* manner)
of	when		indeed,	in other words,
out	where		in fact,	in plain terms,
under			in truth,	in short,
			likewise,	This means . . .
			namely,	to paraphrase,
			obviously,	under this heading
			of course,	
			really,	
			specifically,	
			surely,	
			truly,	

RELATING WORDS AND ORGANIZING PRINCIPLES

prepositions	subordinating conjunctions	COMPARISON AND AGREEMENT		
		coordinating conjunctions	conjunctive adverbs	transitional phrases
along with	as	and	certainly,	by the same token,
among	as if	or	likewise,	in like fashion (*or* manner)
between	as though		similarly,	in support of
behind			surely,	in the same way
by			undoubtedly,	in a similar way
for				
in				
into				
like				
of				
to				
toward				
with				

RELATING WORDS AND ORGANIZING PRINCIPLES

CONTRAST AND DISAGREEMENT

prepositions	subordinating conjunctions	coordinating conjunctions	conjunctive adverbs	transitional phrases
after	although	and yet	anyhow	as a matter of fact,
against	even if	but	anyway	at any rate,
before	even though	whether . . . or . . .	certainly, but*	at the same time,
but (= except)	than	yet	conversely,	even so,
despite	though		however,	by contrast,
except	whether		instead,	in contrast,
in spite of	while		nevertheless,	on the contrary,
instead of			of course, but*	On the one hand. . . ; on the other
outside of			otherwise,	hand. . . .
without			regardless (of	on the other side, rather
			something),	The truth of the matter is . . .
			still,	

* To signal a concession before disagreeing.

RELATING WORDS AND ORGANIZING PRINCIPLES

CAUSES, EFFECTS, PURPOSES, REASONS

prepositions	subordinating conjunctions	coordinating conjunctions	conjunctive adverbs	transitional phrases
because of	because	for	actually,	as a consequence,
due to	how	so	consequently,	as a result,
for the purpose of	since		obviously,	for this purpose,
for the sake of	that		surely,	for this reason,
on account of	whereas (formal)		ultimately,	in effect,
on behalf of	why		thus,	in order that
owing to				in order to
				so that
				to this end,
				with this object (*or* purpose) in mind,

RELATING WORDS AND ORGANIZING PRINCIPLES

LISTING AND PROCESS

prepositions	subordinating conjunctions	coordinating conjunctions	conjunctive adverbs	transitional phrases
above all	as	and	again,	among others
along with		and others	also	equally important
		and so forth	besides,	in addition,
		nor	finally,	in the first place, (second place, etc.)
		or	first, (second, third, etc.)	more important,
			last,	more than that,
			likewise,	to begin with,
			moreover,	to enumerate,
			next,	to list a few
			then,	
			too	

RELATING WORDS AND ORGANIZING PRINCIPLES

TIME

prepositions	subordinating conjunctions	coordinating conjunctions	conjunctive adverbs	transitional phrases
about	after		afterward	after a while,
after	as		beforehand	at dawn (dusk, noon, etc.)
around	as long as		earlier	at night
at	as soon as		eventually	at the same time
before	before		henceforth,	in the evening (morning, etc.)
during	once		immediately	in January (February, etc.)
for	since		later	in the meantime,
in	until		meanwhile,	in 1776, etc.
since	when		soon	on Sunday, etc.
throughout	whenever		subsequently	
until	while		suddenly,	
within			then	
			thereafter (formal)	

RELATING WORDS AND ORGANIZING PRINCIPLES

PLACE AND POSITION

prepositions	subordinating conjunctions	coordinating conjunctions	conjunctive adverbs	transitional phrases
above	where		nearby,	adjacent to
across	wherever			in the distance
against				juxtaposed with
along				on the left, (right, top, etc.)
alongside				on the other (opposite) side
among				over the door (window, fireplace, etc.)
around				
at				
before				
behind				
below				
beneath				
beside				
between				
beyond				
by				
down				
from				
in				
inside				

inside of
into
near
next to
off
on
on top of
on the side of
onto
out
out of
outside
outside of
over
past
through
throughout
to
toward
under
underneath
up
upon
within
without (formal)

RELATING WORDS AND ORGANIZING PRINCIPLES

CONCLUDING AND GENERALIZING

prepositions	subordinating conjunctions	coordinating conjunctions	conjunctive adverbs	transitional phrases
			accordingly,	As one can see,
			clearly,	As you can see,
			generally,	in brief,
			hence,	in conclusion,
			obviously,	in general,
			of course,	in short,
			then,	in such cases,
			therefore,	in summary,
			thus,	It follows that . . .
				It is obvious that . . . .
				no doubt,
				on the whole,
				These, then, are some of the reasons . . .
				This indicates that . . .
				This suggests that . . .
				To conclude,
				To sum up,
				To summarize,

rep | # 65. REPETITION

> **Repeat key words to keep your readers on track throughout a paragraph or a writing, but avoid useless repetition of similar words and phrases in the same sentence. Also, make sure one sentence does not merely repeat the one before it and say nothing new.**

EXAMPLES:

wordy repetition:	In today's modern world, electronic technology and hardware change so rapidly and quickly that electronic equipment is almost outmoded before it reaches the market for the general public.
REVISION:	Electronic technology changes so rapidly that hardware is almost outmoded before it reaches the mass market.

SPECIFICS

(1) substitute words: Repetition is necessary when presenting a new idea; using substitute words is effective because it gives the reader different avenues to approach a new idea.

EXAMPLES:
"Many perennial grasses have rhizomes or stolons, horizontal stems that crawl either above or below ground and send out new shoots and roots." (Lauren Brown)

In the example above, the scientific terms *rhizomes* and *stolons,* which refer to roughly the same part of a grass, are equated with the everyday term *stem.* All three words help to explain each other.

(2) pronouns: Especially for familiar words, which do not need to be repeated in simpler terms, substituting pronouns keeps the reader on track. See the example in point (3) below.

(3) parallel sentence structure: When your subject is the same idea in more than one sentence, you can create similar structures by

substituting nouns or pronouns for your main term. In the example below, a prominent writer discusses Americans' missionary impulse.

EXAMPLE:
Americans will probably never wholly understand themselves until they understand (though they may not much like) the missionary impulse so deeply embedded in the American psyche ever since the second Great Awakening of the mid-19th century. The impulse lies behind much in our recent history—behind much of foreign aid, the Truman Doctrine, the Marshall Plan, certainly the Peace Corps; at home, behind the mostly failed good works of the Great Society; at best, behind relief for Biafra; at worst, alas, behind our nightmare, Vietnam. It implies the sense, epitomized in John Foster Dulles, that just as we have arms for export, we also have morality for export—a package deal. It is one reason why we choose our Carters. It is an immensely complex impulse, which speaks now to the best, now to the worst in our national temperament. (John Hersey)

The key terms—*American* and *missionary impulse*—are repeated in nearly every sentence. *American* is repeated as *themselves* and *they*, and later as *our* and *we* in several uses. The term *missionary impulse* becomes *the impulse* and then *it*. The repetition of the pronoun *it* and the noun *impulse* is reinforced by the structure of the last four sentences, which open with subjects, then verbs: *the impulse lies, it implies, it is,* and *it is.* The main idea—that this missionary impulse shows up in our best and worst actions—is stated in the long list of examples and in the summary comment at the end. Finally, for those who know some recent history, the abstract notion of a *missionary impulse* is repeated in concrete terms in the list of examples in the middle of the paragraph.

(For more on parallel sentence structure, see section 4d.)

(4) interlocking paragraphs: Use the devices for repetition when writing a tightly organized expository writing, such as an essay exam, or to give extra guidance for your readers through your writing on a complicated topic. Make your paragraphs interlock by repeating the key terms of your thesis as the subjects of your topic sentences. Use transition statements at the ends of supporting paragraphs or as the opening clauses of topic sentences.

EXAMPLE:

THESIS:	Three current dangers to the ozone layer are atmospheric testing of nuclear weapons, high-flying jets, and fluorocarbons.
TOPIC 1:	Although Russia and the United States no longer test nuclear weapons in the atmosphere, they are not the only nations that possess nuclear weapons.
	. . . .
TRANSITION 1:	At the moment, though, atmospheric testing is only a small threat to the ozone layer worldwide.
TOPIC 2:	A more serious threat than atmospheric testing is the development of supersonic, high-altitude jets, commercial and military.
	. . . .
TRANSITION 2:	Attempts are being made, however, to minimize engine heat in the supersonic transports and hence to minimize the threat to the ozone layer.
TOPIC 3:	The most serious threat, because it is the most widespread, is the use of fluorocarbons as aerosol propellants.
	. . . .
TRANSITION 3:	Although fluorocarbon propellants have been banned in the United States, their worldwide use in aerosols, air conditioners, and refrigeration units poses a constant threat to the ozone layer.
CONCLUSION TOPIC SENTENCE:	The control of nuclear testing in the atmosphere, of jet engine temperatures, and of fluorocarbons demonstrates that mankind can control threats to the ozone layer if it recognizes the danger.

The lines of periods in the example above represent the middles of paragraphs—the supporting details, examples, and statistics that reinforce and explain the topic ideas in more specific terms. Note that the topic is mentioned in the topic sentence that begins a paragraph and in the ending transition statement of the paragraph. The transition sentences wrap up one topic in order to set up the next topic. Note also that each topic sentence echoes one key term from the thesis, one by one. The thesis, then, maps out the entire essay, in this case showing three aspects of the problem in order of seriousness.

EXERCISE 1. REVISING A WORDY PARAGRAPH

Revise the following paragraph by omitting unneeded words. Watch out for extra prepositional phrases, pairs, and series of nouns that repeat common ideas rather than unfamiliar terms. Also omit any clichés you find, or replace them with better phrases.

Today's modern woman is a mixture of ingenuity and cleverness. She not only has taken on more and more responsibility, but she also has allowed today's man to feel as if he is a modern liberated male, too. Visit any office where business and commerce are conducted and carried out; there will be a liberated woman holding court in the midst of the middle of a group of males. At the same time she holds court, the modern woman worker holds a unique and unusual status in the company that needs her. The company needs her because only she has a fresh, new, modern viewpoint and opinions about conducting and carrying on important, significant business in today's ever-changing, shifting marketplace of fads and "new" products.

EXERCISE 2. PRACTICING INTERLOCKING PARAGRAPHS

Examine three aspects of the issue of taxation, such as the collective burden of federal, state, and local taxes on individuals, or the benefits to the city or county of property, income, and sales taxes. Develop a thesis about taxes. (See section 1d for a review of how to develop a thesis.) Develop a topic sentence for each aspect, based on the three-aspect thesis you develop. Write a transition sentence for each aspect. Finally, write a topic sentence for a conclusion that echoes your thesis. You may use a topic other than taxes, but you must include at least three subtopics. Follow the example in point (4) as a model.

EXERCISE 3. WRITING A PLANNED PARAGRAPH

For practice repeating nouns and pronouns and using parallel sentence structure to keep your readers on track, finish one of the paragraphs you planned in Exercise 2.

SPECIAL HINTS

Help your readers keep track of your topic by using substitute words and pronouns; draw parallels of comparable ideas. Review "Relationships" for help in specifying how ideas relate within and between paragraphs. In general, repetition is a way to clarify uncommon ideas. But unnecessary repetition (redundancy) is as unwelcome in writing as is gristle in a hamburger.

resu ‖ # 66. RÉSUMÉ

Write a résumé to play up your strengths and play down your weaknesses, while not giving false impressions.

The basic principles are simple. In any résumé you write for a job, your strengths should be well highlighted, preferably in subheadings. Your weaknesses should either be buried in paragraphs of type or omitted.

66a. Preparing to Write the Résumé

Start by writing for yourself a description of the kind of job you want. Decide whether you are willing to travel or relocate for a job. Then research the companies in the area where you wish to work to see what they are like. For small, local companies, you can call the Better Business Bureau, the Chamber of Commerce, or the college placement office to find out about a company's reputation, customer relations, and civic connections. To find out about a corporation, you can write for the company's annual report or check the company profile in Dun and Bradstreet in the campus library. Also, call the company's general information number to find out who does the hiring for the job you want. For local jobs, keep track of the listings in the local newspaper's want ads, but don't rely on them exclusively. Monitor the job listings in the campus placement office and even discuss particular companies with the placement office staff; watch the posted interviewing schedule for your favorite companies.

Once you have an idea about the job you want and what particular companies are like, you can target your résumé to appeal to a company's interests. By familiarizing yourself with the company's operations and structure, you are also more likely to ask intelligent questions during an interview.

66b. Typical Parts of a Résumé

Make worksheets about each of the following topics:

- your work experience (paid or volunteer) in any field, with beginning and ending dates, official job title (not just "clerk," but "Parts Counter Clerk," for instance), and reason for leaving
- your educational experience, including only high school and college, with dates of graduation and type of diploma or degree earned (you can list expected graduation date and degree)
- community and extracurricular activities (high school and college)
- civic, school, or club offices held
- awards, certificates of completion, or honors
- interests or hobbies
- religious, political, or ethnic heritage activities.

Now look at your worksheets. Put a plus (+) next to everything you have listed that might make a favorable impression about you as an employee, anything that shows reliability, initiative, responsibility, and respect for authority.

Look again. Put a check (√) next to any information that would make a favorable impression about you as a person, anything that shows you're easy to get along with, interesting, assertive (but not pushy or gloating), friendly, able to put up with a lot of annoyances.

Finally, put a minus (−) next to any information that might make a negative impression. Consider carefully the image of the company you have gained from your research.

Write a rough draft of your résumé after reading the next section on organization. For now, decide on how you will list your name (including middle name?), your contact address (you may not want to receive responses from prospective employers at your current business address, if you have one), and your telephone number (include area code if you plan to apply out of town for jobs). You can also decide now whether to include any of the following *optional* information: age, marital status, military experience (including discharge status), number of children, state of health, activities for a "cause." Include such information only if you think it will be to your advantage to do so. Some companies request a photograph along with a separate application form. Keep your worksheets and a copy of your résumé for the application form.

Also jot down the names of three or more people who would be able and willing to report favorably on you as a worker. On your résumé, you may list "References available on request" or "Reference file available at the following placement office" and give the office address. But you should have the references in your file before you send out your résumé. Certainly, you should have the references' agreement that they will endorse you strongly if a prospective employer contacts them. By the way, current law provides that you may obtain a copy of your reference letters, so your letters of recommendation should be as strong as possible. Replace weak letters immediately by negotiating with your reference or by asking someone else to write a letter for you.

66c. Organizing Your Résumé

The crucial sections show your work and educational experience. If you have time gaps in either of these, you probably should not list your information by time. Instead, list the job titles you have held, listing them perhaps in order of impressiveness, most down to least. You might list the companies you have worked for prominently, instead of listing the job titles or the dates as your subheadings. You must make the same decision for education: Do you list dates on the left as your subheadings, or types of diplomas and degrees, or the places where you went to school? The answer depends on which arrangement shows you at your best or is most appealing to the person doing the hiring. (Is your prospective boss a graduate of your school, for instance?) The following sampler lists the three types of arrangements for your subheadings and the corresponding information for your paragraphs at right.

(1.) Time arrangement: start with your most recent experience and work backwards

WORK EXPERIENCE

starting date to present	<u>job title</u>, company name, department; main duties in detail (promotions, if any)
starting date to end (each previous job)	<u>job title</u>, company name, department; main duties (promotions, if any) (reason for leaving?)
starting date to end (earliest relevant job)	<u>job title</u>, company name, department; main duties (promotions, if any) (reason for leaving?)

(2.) Job title arrangement: most impressive to least, or most recent to least

WORK EXPERIENCE

job title	main duties in detail; company name and department (duration? dates?)
job title	main duties (in detail?); company name and department (duration? dates?)

(3.) Company name arrangement: most impressive to least, or most recent to least

WORK EXPERIENCE

company name	<u>job title</u>, department; main duties in detail; (duration? dates? promotions?)
company name	<u>job title</u>, department; main duties (in detail?); (duration? dates? promotions?)

66d. Résumé Format

You must list your name, address, and telephone number. You should list the type of job you want by title. You must list related work experience and education or training. You may list whatever other favorable and relevant information you can present in a neatly typed format. You should end with a list of references, a note telling what placement service has your file, or the note "References available upon request" if you plan to have requests go through you.

The sample cover letter and résumé in "Special Hints" are done in a readable, neat format. The sample also shows how to select and arrange information that presents a job applicant as a good employment risk and an interesting person. A good cover letter should highlight your personal, educational, and employment data most relevant to the position you want and mention other information that could influence an employer to hire you. (See the "Business Letter" section to review envelope address format. Mail your résumé in a #10 white business envelope; use at least 20 lb. bond paper for typing your résumé, white paper only.)

EXERCISE 1. RESEARCH COMPANIES TO WORK FOR

Make notes on companies you would work for. Use the suggestions under "Preparing to Write the Résumé."

EXERCISE 2. WORKSHEETS FOR YOUR RÉSUMÉ

Do worksheets on your own experiences, following the suggestions under "The Typical Parts of a Résumé."

EXERCISE 3. ROUGH DRAFT FOR YOUR RÉSUMÉ

Do a rough draft of your résumé. Select and arrange your information for a particular job in a particular company.

EXERCISE 4. START YOUR PLACEMENT FILE

Find out if your campus placement office keeps recommendations on file for job-hunting students and graduates. How long will the file stay active? Is there a maximum on the number of recommendations one may file? Start your placement file now by filling out the Placement Office forms and by obtaining at least one strong and well-written letter of recommendation.

EXERCISE 5. GATHER YOUR REFERENCES

Keep a list of names and business addresses and job titles of supervisors and teachers who could endorse your work strongly. Start your list now.

EXERCISE 6. PART-TIMING

If you are interested, find out whether the campus placement office helps students find part-time or summer work. Find out from the placement office staff whether you must submit a résumé to qualify for such jobs.

SPECIAL HINTS

For more information on writing résumés, check your campus library or career center for résumé guides, such as this one:

Harold W. Dickhut, *The Professional Resume and Job Search Guide* (Englewood Cliffs, N.J.: Spectrum/Prentice-Hall, 1981).

If you are already employed but thinking of finding a better job or switching careers, check the campus library for the latest edition of this book:

Richard Nelson Bolles, *What Color Is Your Parachute? A Practical Manual for Job Hunters and Career Changers* (Berkeley, Calif.: 10 Speed Press).

Dickhut's book gives advice on slanting your résumé to fit the company; it also contains many sample résumés.

107 Twining Lane
Richmond, VA 23223
February 19, 1983

Mr. James H. Turner III, Sheriff
Henrico County Jail Administration
P.O. Box 27032
Richmond, VA 23273

Dear Sheriff Turner:

  I would be most appreciative for your personal consideration in reviewing my application for the position
which is presently open as a Deputy in Jail Operations.

  At the present time, I am attending J. Sargeant Reynolds Community College in the Administration of Justice
Program, and will graduate on June 21, 1984, with an Associate in Applied Science Degree (AAS).

  During the periods from August 1976 to April 1979, I
was employed as a Correctional Officer with the Virginia
Department of Corrections, working at the Virginia Correctional Center for Women in Goochland, Virginia.
While employed in corrections, I gained valuable work
experience in the field, as well as educational benefits
from the State's Correctional Training Academy in
Waynesboro, Virginia. This experience and training
would enable me to adjust well within the jail facilities while working with county prisoners.

  I will be in the area of the Parham Road Jail during
the first week in March, and I would be grateful if you
could grant me an interview at your convenience.

  Again, thank you for your time and consideration in
reviewing my application.

                              Sincerely,
                              Ellen A. Holt
                              Ellen A. Holt

Enclosure

Ellen Allen Holt

107 Twining Lane
Richmond, Virginia 23223
Telephone: 804-737-5445

**Professional
Objective**

To work in jail operations, continue my
education part-time, and to eventually
move up into an administrative position
in the correction field.

**Education
1983**

Attending J. Sargeant Reynolds Community College in their Administration of
Justice Program, Richmond, Virginia
(full-time)

1978

State of Virginia, Jail Training and
Management Course, Certificate in Jail
Training and Management, 1978.

1977

Virginia Department of Correction
Training Academy, Waynesboro, Virginia
Certificate in Corrections, August
1977—graduated in top five of one
hundred students.

1973-1974

Smithdeal-Massey Business College,
Richmond, Virginia
Professional Secretary Degree, June
1974.

**Employment
1979-1983**

Homemaker and mother of three children.

1978-1979

Unemployment benefits (Workmen's Compensation) due to work related automo-
bile accident with the Department of
Corrections.

Employment   2
(continued)
1976–1979   Virginia Correctional Center for Women,
                 Goochland, Virginia
                 Began working as an officer trainee,
                 then moved up to the position of cor-
                 rectional officer, supervising inmate
                 living quarters, then transferred to
                 the position of transportation officer,
                 supervising the transportation of women
                 inmates outside institution grounds.

1976   J. Sargeant Reynolds Community College
                 (Downtown Campus), Richmond, Virginia
                 Worked in the position of clerk-typist
                 in Veteran Affairs, where I advised
                 veterans and processed their school
                 loans through the college.
                 Transferred to the Department of Cor-
                 rections from this position.

Awards   J. Sargeant Reynolds Community College,
                 Dean's List and Honor Roll, with 4.00
                 average out of a possible 4.00 points.
                 Virginia Correctional Center for Women,
                 Recognition for Life-saving techniques,
                 1978.
                 Received Commendation Letter from a
                 Virginia Commonwealth University (VCU)
                 Police Officer during employment as a
                 correctional officer, 1978.

Activities   High School: Chorus and Art Club
                 Business College: Bowling Team
                 Presently Room Mother, Jacob L. Adams
                 Elementary School.

Interests   Painting, horseback riding, bowling,
                 gardening

References   Available on request.

ro ‖ 67. RUN-ON

> Begin each sentence with a capital letter, and end each sentence with a period (usually), an exclamation mark, or a question mark. These start and stop signals tell readers what information goes together as a sentence. Without these markings, readers find it difficult to pick out any meaning units from the general flow of words.

EXAMPLE:

run-on: Pushkin is often called "The Russian Shakespeare" as Shakespeare did for English, Pushkin influenced the Russian language during a key stage of its development.

REVISED: Pushkin is often called "The Russian Shakespeare." As Shakespeare did for English, Pushkin influenced the Russian language during a key stage of its development.

Notice in the example above that commas signal minor and introductory modifiers, not sentence divisions. (See "Comma Splice.")

SPECIFICS

Here are six ways to fix run-ons.

run-on: The meteor struck the satellite spun out of orbit.

(1)   semicolon: The meteor struck; the satellite spun out of orbit.
(2)   coordinators: The meteor struck, and the satellite spun out of orbit. (*The comma and the coordinating conjunction must **both** be used.*)
(3)   division: The meteor struck. The satellite spun out of orbit.

(4) beginning subordinator: When the meteor struck, the satellite spun
     out of orbit. (*The comma signals the end of a modifying clause, not a
     sentence.*)

(5) ending subordinator: The satellite spun out of orbit because the
     meteor struck it.

(6) semicolon with adverb: The meteor struck; consequently, the sat-
     ellite spun out of orbit.

(For more on sentence structures, see sections 4a and 4c.)

EXERCISE 1. SIX WAYS TO FIX A RUN-ON

Use each of the six methods shown above to fix these run-ons. You will need
to rewrite each run-on six times to make the six revisions. Double-check your
uses of commas and semicolons.

1. During 1982 most banks offered at least sixteen per cent on time-deposits
    some even offered seventeen per cent or more.

2. Pictures of atoms have been taken using a magnification of 15,000,000
    times color enhancement gives different atoms distinctive hues and
    shadings.

3. One moving company promised to supply free packing materials that
    company's estimate was $150 higher than the others'.

4. NASA reportedly planned over 400 Space Shuttle flights therefore, build-
    ing and maintaining a rudimentary space station could be feasible.

EXERCISE 2. SIX WAYS TO WRITE A SENTENCE

Write a pair of sentences on a topic of your choice. Use each of the six
methods above to combine or divide them.

SPECIAL HINTS

Make sure your punctuation clues help your readers keep
bits of information in manageable sizes and recognizable structures. To link ideas, use a subordinating conjunction, use a
semicolon with a joining adverb, or use a comma with *and, but, or,
nor, for, so,* or *yet.*

;/no ; ‖ 68. SEMICOLON

Use a semicolon to do only the following:
(1) **join two base (independent) clauses;**
(2) **join two base clauses with a transitional word or phrase like *however, to be sure,* and others**
(3) **join items in a list of elements that contain commas.**

EXAMPLES:
(1) Mt. Everest is the highest peak in the world; it is over a mile and a half higher than Mt. McKinley.
(2) Mt. Everest is the highest peak in the world; it is, in fact, over a mile and a half higher than Mt. McKinley.
(3) My brother has lived in Denver, Colorado; Short Hills, New Jersey; Chicago, Illinois; and Dallas, Texas.

As examples (1) and (2) show, the usual function of a semicolon is to join independent clauses that are closely related in meaning. Never use a semicolon to join a modifying clause to an independent clause because semicolons are meant to signal a kind of partnership between independent clauses.

EXAMPLE:
misleading: Since she was an accomplished skier, almost a pro; she whooshed down the slope in control but leaving clouds of powder behind.
ACCURATE: Since she was an accomplished skier, almost a pro, she whooshed down the slope in control but leaving clouds of powder behind.

EXERCISE. EDITING SENTENCES: ; or ,

For each sentence below, place a comma or a semicolon in each blank. Use the patterns demonstrated above to help you decide which blanks should be filled with a semicolon.

1. "In 1973___ Hawking turned the theory of black holes inside out when he discovered that some black holes are not completely black___ they can emit particles and eventually even explode___ becoming 'white' holes from which energy and particles gush." (Adapted from Dennis Overbye)
2. "In part because of his scientific accomplishments___ at least dimly grasped by the public___ in part because of his courageous positions on social issues___ and in part because of his benign personality___ Einstein was admired and revered throughout the world." (Adapted from Carl Sagan)

SPECIAL HINTS

As you polish your final draft, make sure that each of your punctuation clues to your readers is accurate, especially your use of semicolons and commas.

sp ‖ 69. SPELLING

You can learn to spell consistently and accurately if you are willing to use your ingenuity, your ability to notice details and patterns, and your determination to help yourself. To be systematic about better spelling you need to:
(1) keep a record of the words you misspell;
(2) learn how to analyze your errors so you can get rid of the causes of errors;
(3) learn to associate troublesome words with some memory-jogging gimmick to help you remember each word;
(4) learn typical spelling patterns or "rules" so you can use them to your advantage.

You may wish to glance at the "Sample Spelling Record" near the end of this section to see where this lesson is going, but study each of the four steps carefully so that you can learn to keep your own spelling record step by step.

STEP 1.   Record words you misspell and single out the letters that you confuse.

Even if you misspell a word, you probably get most of the letters right. So you need to focus on the part of the word that gives you difficulty. The first column on your spelling record should be the correct spelling of the word you need to study. The second column should list the letters in the word that give you trouble.

EXAMPLES:

th*ei*r	ei	t*ho*ught	ho
a*thl*ete	hl	portmant*eau*	eau
re*co*n*c*ile	o,c	ha*vi*ng	vi

STEP 2.   Analyze what you might be doing that causes you to misspell the word and begin learning what makes a word so unusual to you.

You will need a dictionary to help you figure out a word's individual characteristics. If you look up the words listed as examples for step 1 above, you might find out information like this:

Their indicates ownership; *there* indicates position; *thier* is not a word.

Athlete has only two syllables, although some people pronounce it with three.

Reconcile includes an *o* that isn't emphasized when people say it, so it has to be memorized; the second *c* sounds like an *s*.

Thought looks a lot like *through* and *throughout*, but *throught* is not a word.

Portmanteau ends in *eau* because the word came from French, which uses those letters to sound like *o*.

Having doesn't use the letter *e*.

In the third column of your spelling record, then, make a note about what's confusing you—at least make your best guess. Here are some new examples showing column three.

EXAMPLES:

gul*li*ble   lli   There are two *ll*'s because *gullible* = gu*ll* + ible. The *i* isn't accented.

re*cei*ve   cei   Long *e* sound after *c*—check the ie/ei rule.

bur*eau*   eau   French

*pneu*monia   pneu   Greek

STEP 3. Associate the spelling problem for a word with any strange sensory or memory device that you can invent.

To relearn words that you habitually misspell, you need to use your ingenuity to invent a gimmick for each word. Some gimmicks may involve your senses; others may involve things that you find out about how words are made. Here are some guidelines and examples.

SPECIFICS

(1)   talk: Make up a saying for yourself that will help you remember the correct spelling of a troublesome word. If you have trouble remembering the word *there* as a place indicator (some people try to use *their* for place, possession, and even instead of the contraction *they're*), you might make up a nonsense sentence like this one.

EXAMPLE:

th*e*r*e*:   "I shot the elephant where? Right between the e's!"

The stranger the sentence, the longer you will remember it—until you no longer need it to spell your relearned word. The odd sentence for *there* emphasizes the use of two *e*'s separated by a consonant. The *e*'s in *elephant,* the rhyme with *where,* and the punchline pun *between the e's* all emphasize that pattern so *there* cannot be confused with *their,* which doesn't have two *e*'s.

(2) sight: If you're good at doodling or if you remember things best by visualizing them, try making a picture out of a troublesome word. Some people, for instance, put an extra *t* in *throughout*; others leave out an *ou*. But the word has a kind of balance—a *t* at each end and an *ou* on each side of the center of the word. One picture that could help you remember the spelling of this balanced word might be a doodle of the word itself wearing granny glasses—the earpieces hooked over the *t*'s and the *ou*'s showing through the lenses.

Another sight technique is to find "little words in big words." There is a risk with this technique if you forget that you are studying the spelling of a word and start thinking of how the word is said or what it means. Little words you spot in bigger words, however, can help you break the spelling task into chunks.

EXAMPLES:
Thought contains *ought*; *through* doesn't.
Thought contains *thou*; *through* doesn't.

Many people who put an extra *t* on *through* never misspell *ought*. Some people put an *r* in *thought* but would never misspell *thou*.

(3) sound: Sometimes words that rhyme have similar spellings. In these cases you can make a known spelling work for you to help you learn an unfamiliar spelling. One student who knew how to spell *knew* and *screw* but regularly misspelled *threw* made up this sentence to focus on the troublesome letters.

EXAMPLE:
I knew the pitcher threw a screwball.

Another way is to deliberately overemphasize some of the sounds of the words when you say them to yourself. One student could not spell *beautiful* correctly until he thought of this overpronunciation:

EXAMPLE:
BE A U tiful (bee-ah-*you*-ti-full).

By exaggerating the letters he confused, he managed to keep them in the right order.

(4) touch: One way to memorize a word is to trace it. Some would say

that tracing reinforces the feel of the word on your fingertips; it also makes a darker and darker image of the word to help you remember the look of it, its outline, and the order of the letters.

If all else fails, then, try tracing the word several times while saying it to yourself. Then write the word on another sheet of paper and check your spelling. If you confuse letters like *b* and *p* or use two *ll*'s where only one is needed, also trace the outline of the word to point out to yourself how many letters stick up above the line or how many plunge below the line. Finally, retrace just the letters that give you trouble. Then write the word on another piece of paper and check the spelling. (People who type can follow the same steps by retyping over the original word.)

(5) structure: Words that come into English from Latin or Greek are commonly built from standardized blocks of letters. These blocks rarely change in spelling, pronunciation, or literal meaning. Knowing how to spell *circumspect*, then, helps to spell *circumference, circumlocution*, and *circumnavigation*, as well as *spectacular, spectroscope, specter*, and *spectacle*. (See "Dictionary" (4) for another example of word parts.)

(6) source languages: Some combinations of letters are common in languages from which English borrowed words. If you remember, for instance, that *bureau, portmanteau*, and *beau* came from French, you can remind yourself of the *eau* ending. Similarly, if you remember that words like *pneumonia, pneumectomy*, and *pneumatic* are from Greek, you can remind yourself of the silent letter *p* and the *eu* letter combination early in each word when you try to use them in your writing. (See "Dictionary" (4) for more about etymology and a demonstration of how to find out what language a word comes from.)

(7) meaning and function (homonyms and frequently confused words): If you confuse two or three words, you need to know what the words do so you can sort out their spellings.

EXAMPLES:

where:	*Where* was Columbus born? I know *where* he died. (*question word and adverb*)
wear:	For his parents' remarriage he decided to *wear* a tuxedo and a smile. (*verb or verbal showing action.*)
were:	"You *were* running fast!" (*linking verb or helping verb*)
we're:	"We're on our way." (*contraction*)

In the fourth column of your spelling record, then, you should add notes about any of these seven memory aids or any new association you can think up. Here are some examples that show the four columns of a spelling record demonstrated so far.

EXAMPLES:
*wea*ther	wea	confusion with *whether*	We m*ea*sure w*ea*ther.
*whe*ther	whe	confusion with *weather*	two *he*'s in w*he*ther
so*l*d*i*er	i	confusion with *solder*	sold I er (sold-*eye*-err)

STEP 4. Use typical spelling rules to explain the correct spelling of some of the words you need to study.

There are some typical patterns in English spelling. Knowing such patterns can help you avoid troubles with some of the more common words in the language.

SPECIFICS

(1) endings: Many words do not change spelling when they add endings.

EXAMPLES:
king + dom = kingdom   hope + ful = hopeful
contact + ed = contacted   do + ing = doing

(2) final *e* and endings: If a word ends in the pattern of vowel–consonant–*e* and if the ending starts with a vowel, drop the *e* to add the ending because putting two vowels together may change their sound.

EXAMPLES:
bale + ing = baling   *but*   bale + ful = baleful
                                    (*ending starts with a consonant: -ful*)
imagine + ation = imagination   ride + er = rider
                        (*endings start with vowels*)

Dictionaries record the current practice of spelling words when adding the endings *-able* or *-ible*, so you need to look up such words and memorize whether or not an *e* is lost.

EXAMPLES:

defense + ible = defensible
singe + ing = singeing
sing + ing = singing
(<u>Singe</u> keeps its <u>e</u> so it can't be confused with <u>sing</u>.)
judge + ment = judgment
peace + able = peaceable

Many words that end with "soft" *c* (sounds like *s*) or a "soft" *g* (sounds like *j*) end with a silent *e*, such as *peace* and *knowledge*. These words often keep the *e* when they add *-able* so that the soft sound will be kept for the new word, like *peaceable* and *knowledgeable*. The vowels *a, o,* and *u* don't follow soft *c* or soft *g*.

(3) *y* ending: If a word ends in the pattern consonant–y and if the ending being added begins with any letter but *i*, change the *y* to an *i*, then add the ending.

EXAMPLES:

  lonely + ness = loneliness
but study + ing = studying (*ending added starts with* <u>i</u>)
  sly + er = slier
but sway + ed = swayed (*vowel in front of the* <u>y</u>)

If you are forming a possessive, of course, the final *y* will not change. Plurals of words that end in *y*, however, follow the pattern for the *y* ending.

EXAMPLES:

Larry + 's = Larry's (*possessive*)
county + es = counties (*plural*)

(4) doubling ending consonants: If a word ends in the vowel–consonant pattern, if the syllable before the ending is accented, and if the ending being added starts with a vowel, then double the final letter of the word and add the ending.

EXAMPLES:

refer + ing = referring *but*   look + ing = looking
(*two* <u>o</u>'s)

slip + ed = slipped *but*   happen + ed = happened
(*last syllable not accented*)

How the word is said can give you a clue to this spelling pattern. Doubled consonants, even two different consonants, very often follow "short" vowels; single consonants often follow long vowels when endings are added.

EXAMPLES:

long a: taping	short a: tapping
long e: meting	short e: betting
long i: writing	short i: written
long o: sloping	short o: slopping
long u: reducing	short u: reduction

Notice that the examples of "long" vowel sounds above are all made from words that added endings by losing the silent *e*: *tape + ing = taping, mete* (as in "to mete out punishment") + *ing = meting*, and so on.

(5) prefixes: Add prefixes to words without changing the spelling of the prefix or of the word.

EXAMPLES:

re + align = realign	sub + marine = submarine
dis + solve = dissolve	im + practical = impractical

If, for instance, you tend to spell *illegitimate* with only one *l*, look to see if the word isn't made up of another word and a prefix, like *legitimate* and the prefix *il*. You may want to check in a dictionary to see if your word fits this pattern.

(6) ie/ei:

(a) If a word contains a long *e* sound and if you know that the letters that represent that sound are either *ie* or *ei*, use the *ie* spelling after every consonant but *c*.

EXAMPLES:

deceive, receipt, ceiling (*ei after c*)

piece, shield, belief (*ie, no c before the letters that indicate the long e*)

fancier (*ie represents two sounds, not one long e sound*)

(b) If you know that a word is spelled with *ie* or *ei*, use *ei* if the sound represented by these letters is a long *a* sound.

EXAMPLES:

vein, sleigh, eight, weight, freight, reign, Pei, rein, Seine (*even heir, foreign, and peignoir may fit this pattern*)

(c) If you know that a word is spelled with *ie* or *ei*, use *ei* if the sound represented by the letters is a long *i* sound in a word of more than three letters that came from German or Greek.

EXAMPLES:
stein, height (*German*)   eidolon, eidetic (*Greek*)

The last column on your spelling record, therefore, should indicate one of these patterns or a pattern that you discover on your own. Below is a complete sample of a spelling record with new examples.

SAMPLE SPELLING RECORD

STEP 1 word	letters	STEP 2 reason	STEP 3 association	STEP 4 rule
classic	ss	unsure of the double consonant	The class will study the classics.	short *a* sound, so double consonants follow
know	k,w	confuse with *no* and *now*	*Know* when your *k*nees are *k*nocking.	silent *k* before *n* at front of words.
repr*ie*ve	ie	*ie* or *ei*?	*Eve* got no repr*ie*ve.	long *e*, no *c*, so *i* before *e* (none)
than	a	confuse with *then*	than = comparison then = time indicator	

EXERCISE. START YOUR OWN SPELLING RECORD

Begin your own spelling record with the following words used in this section or select fifty words of your own for this term's spelling record. Use only words you need to learn for your writings.

their	wear	thought	no	then
there	where	through	know	than
they're	were	throughout	gnome	though

portmanteau	pneumatic	biography	loneliness
bureau	pneumectomy	bibliography	wilier
beautiful	pneumonia	autobiography	slier
beau	numismatist	autograph	studying

swayed	whether	gullible	taping	sloping
suede	weather	trapped	writing	reduced
baling	singeing	tapping	slopping	judgment
defensible	singing	betting	reduction	written
deceive	piece	leisure	rain	sane
receipt	shield	fancier	rein	seine
ceiling	belief	seige	reign	freight
foreign	peignoir	eidolon	sleight	heir

SPECIAL HINTS

If you can't tell a word's pronunciation from the dictionary, learn how immediately—from your campus reading specialist, your English teacher, or a friend who is willing to show you all of the dictionary's symbols and how to use them. (See "Dictionary," (2) first.)

Check the "Glossary of Usage" for words that are often confused with similar words.

Both your ingenuity and your ability to detect patterns in American spelling, with the help of the guidelines in this section, can help you provide consistently accurate spelling for your readers.

s—v ‖ # 70. SUBJECT—VERB AGREEMENT

‖ **Use an *s* at the end of your subject *or* at the end of your verb.**

EXAMPLES:
unconventional:	Our river catch on fire.
CONVENTIONAL:	Our rivers catch on fire.
unconventional:	Our oil spill onto our beaches.
CONVENTIONAL:	Our oil spills onto our beaches.

Only one verb tense takes the *s* ending, but it is the most frequently used verb tense form. Only the *present* form uses the *s* ending—and only with a subject that is *one* item. In the oil example above, the verb ends with *s* to signify to readers that oil is one commodity. The spilling is a regular or recurring action, so a present verb form must be used. (For more about verb forms and how they change with time and emphasis, see the "Verb Form Chart" at the end of "Passive Verbs.")

SPECIFICS:

(1) words between subject and verb: Sometimes it is difficult to remember the word that works as your subject because other words come between your subject and your verb.

> EXAMPLE:
> unconventional: The current practice of nations seem to be to let businesses police their own waste products for pollution.
> CONVENTIONAL: The current practice of nations seem*s* to be to let businesses police their own waste products for pollution.

Nations cannot be the subject of the sentence since it is already the object of the preposition *of*. Words cannot "moonlight"; they can only do one job in a sentence. *Practice*, then, is the word that determines the present verb *seems* should end with *s* to indicate the single subject.

(2) pronouns: Some pronouns seem so empty of meaning that they can't be the real subjects of sentences, but they are. They occupy the subject position and determine the ending of the present verb, but they also set up prepositional phrases often.

> EXAMPLE:
> unconventional: Each of the rickety railroad tracks are too feeble to carry the load safely.
> CONVENTIONAL: Each of the rickety railroad tracks *is* too feeble to carry the load safely.

The pronoun *each* emphasizes the idea that every one of the tracks was in poor condition. Besides, *tracks* is the object of *of*. Note that there is a separate form of *be* just to signify the singleness of subjects—*is*—and that *is* follows the pattern by being constructed with an *s* at the end.

(Check the "Verb Form Charts" again at the end of "Passive Verbs" to find where *s* endings are used in verb constructions. Look for *is, was,* and *has* in the different time frames.)

(3) compound subjects: Ordinarily, subjects joined by *and* require a verb without an *s* to reinforce that addition. *As well as, like, in addition,* and other words that seem to mean the same as *and* do not have this additive quality. They start subordinate structures, so they cannot add things as equals.

EXAMPLES:

unconventional: Lee, as well as Yang, are famous for their work in subatomic physics.

CONVENTIONAL: *Lee and Yang are* famous for their work in subatomic physics.

CONVENTIONAL: *Lee, as well as Yang, is* famous for his work in subatomic physics.

Notice how *his* is used in the last example to refer to Lee and to reinforce the single real focus of the sentence. Signals about the number of your real focus must be consistent throughout your sentence. (See "Number Shift.")

(4) choice words: Subjects joined by *either . . . or, neither . . . nor, nor,* and *or* take their signal from the subject nearer to the verb.

EXAMPLES:

unconventional: Hitler was faced with a choice—either the V-2 rockets or the atomic bomb were to be fully developed.

CONVENTIONAL: Hitler was faced with a choice—either the V-2 rockets or the atomic *bomb was* to be fully developed.

CONVENTIONAL: Hitler was faced with a choice—either the atomic bomb or the V-2 *rockets were* to be fully developed.

As in the last example above, if a plural alternative is the nearer of the two (or nearest of three or more) subjects, the verb conventionally reinforces that plural. Line up your subjects so that you make a subject–verb match that you are sure shows agreement about the number.

(5) *there* and *here*: At the front of a sentence, *there* and *here* delay the real subject of the sentence until after the verb. The verb, therefore, signals the number of the subject before the readers get to it.

EXAMPLES:

unconventional:	There is faith, hope, and love in the triad of virtues that St. Paul stresses.
CONVENTIONAL:	There *are faith, hope, and love* in the triad of virtues that St. Paul stresses.
unconventional:	Here is the drill bits you ordered.
CONVENTIONAL:	Here *are the drill bits* you ordered.

(6) modals: A special class of verbs overrides the pattern of using *s* to signal the oneness of a subject. Instead, these verbs emphasize opinions to signal to the reader that a sentence is no simple statement of fact. (For a list of modals and their meanings, see "Mood Shift" (4).)

EXAMPLE:

"The EPA's budget *would* not last one week at General Motors," he claimed.

Neither *would* nor *last* uses the *s* signal, even though *budget* is still a single item.

(7) collective nouns as subjects: Sometimes the *s*/no *s* signal is determined by the pronouns you use to stand for your subject word. Words like *jury, committee, faculty, couple,* and others can be thought of as indicating single groups or individuals.

EXAMPLES:

ONE GROUP:	The committee has not made *its* decision yet.
INDIVIDUALS:	The faculty *are* making up *their* minds about the new policy.

Notice that the pronouns later in the sentences reveal that the writer of the first sentence was thinking of a group and that the writer of the second sentence pictured many individual faculty members separately.

EXAMPLE:

INDIVIDUALS:	The faculty *members are* making up their minds about the new policy.

EXERCISE. EDITING A ROUGH DRAFT

Edit the following rough draft to make the subjects and verbs agree about the numbers of things under discussion. Cross out or add *s* endings on subjects or verbs. Remember that pronouns take their number from the nouns they represent. Do not change correct uses of *s*.

The average electronic digital computer system consist of five types of functional units. Each of these units does a specific task. Input devices capable of introducing data and instructions into the memory unit is needed. The memory or internal storage unit is the place in which both instructions and data is kept. The control unit is the part of the central processing unit (CPU) that direct the overall functioning of the other units and controls the flow of data between them during problem-solving. The arithmetic unit, another part of the CPU, perform all the mathematical and logical operations. Output devices accepts data from the memory unit after it have been processed. The control units, the memory unit, and the arithmetic unit is sometimes called the central processing unit (CPU) because they are the control center for the entire computer system.

SPECIAL HINTS: -S PLACEMENT

To make sure that your subject and verb both indicate the same number of persons or things, check to find your real subject. If you have difficulty deciding whether the real subject is singular or plural, see "Plurals."

In a verb phrase, the part nearest the subject reinforces the number of the subject. The chart below demonstrates this pattern using the four most common helping verbs.

WITH SINGULAR SUBJECTS	WITH PLURAL SUBJECTS
Industry *does* police itself.	Industr*ies* *do* police themselves.
Industry *has* policed itself.	Industr*ies* *have* policed themselves.
Industry *is* policing itself.	Industr*ies* *are* policing themselves.
Industry *was* policing itself.	Industr*ies* *were* policing themselves.

Notice that signals of singular or plural often run throughout a sentence and do not just stop at the verb. Notice, too, that the *s* pattern applies when you are writing about something or someone other than yourself or your reader. (This pattern shows up clearly in the chart under "Special Hints" for "Person Shift.")

t ‖ 71. TENSE SHIFT

Avoid mixing the past and present verb forms. Use the "perfect" tenses with their simple tense partners to indicate finished actions.

EXAMPLES:

unconventional: We shipped nerve gas across the country, and we dump it in the ocean. Our rivers caught fire. Our oil spills onto our beaches.

CONVENTIONAL: *At least once* we *have shipped* nerve gas across the country and *dumped* it into the ocean. At least one river in the Midwest *has caught* fire. *More than once* oil *has spilled* onto our beaches.

The conventional use of time in writing does not rely only on verb forms but adds adverbs, prepositional phrases, even some subordinators, perhaps, to indicate the time period for the action being written about.

For a display of the verb forms used to show time—from distant past, through the present, and into the distant future—see the "Verb Form Chart" under "Special Hints" in "Passive Verbs."

Although mixing past and present forms confuses most readers, the perfect tenses (which use *has, have,* or *had* with other verbs) can help the simple tense forms to specify the times of two actions in one sentence.

SPECIFICS

(1) past perfect with past: The past perfect forms indicate the comparatively distant past, usually action completed just before the simple past.

EXAMPLE:

The union *had* negotiat*ed* the new contract just before the strike deadline elaps*ed.*

(2) present perfect with present: The present perfect forms indicate actions that began in the past and are now finished or still in progress.

EXAMPLE:

The union *has* already negotiat*ed* three contracts in this state, but it *is* not "officially" recognized as a bargaining agent. (*The negotiating was completed in the past.*)

EXAMPLE:

The negotiating session *has* last*ed* for fifty hours so far, but neither side *seems* willing to compromise yet. (*The session continues at the present.*)

(3) future perfect with future: The future perfect forms indicate by what time an action will be completed.

EXAMPLE:

By next month, the managers *will have* estimat*ed* their budgets in detail; then we *will* all *know* how the new union contract *will affect* the operation of the company.

EXERCISE 1. PRACTICE WITH THE "VERB FORM CHART": ACTIVE

To study the "Verb Form Chart" under "Passive Verbs" so that you know from first-hand experience how to form the different tenses, write a sentence that uses only one verb. Then rewrite the sentence using all six active voice forms shown on the chart.

EXERCISE 2. PRACTICE WITH THE "VERB FORM CHART": ACTIVE PROGRESSIVE

Repeat Exercise 1 with a sentence of your choice, but practice writing the active progressive forms into your sentence. Use any other adverb or phrase that you think makes sense as time indicators with each of the six verb forms in the active progressive column. (See "Relationships" for a partial list of time indicators.)

EXERCISE 3. ANALYZING TIME FRAMES IN A PARAGRAPH

The paragraph below uses a variety of verb forms (time frames) correctly, even smoothly. After reading the paragraph carefully, list the verbs that apply to the distant past, those that apply to the more recent past, and those that are about or applied to the present time. Use the "Verb Form Chart" under "Passive Verbs" to help you sort out the time frames.

(1) Unlike the Vandals . . . the Anglo-Saxons gave their stamp to the land they invaded. (2) They did not completely exterminate the Britons, some of whom almost certainly remained as a subject class that was gradually absorbed by the conquerors. (3) None the less, Britain is unique among the invaded regions of the western Roman Empire in that it owes more to the Germanic barbarians than to the Romans. (4) During four centuries of Roman rule, Britannia had been far less thoroughly integrated into Roman culture than had provinces like Gaul and Spain. (5) Moreover, the Anglo-Saxons who came to Britannia were still heathen and had been less influenced by Rome than had other Germans. (Crane Brinton, John B. Christopher, and Robert Lee Wolff)

EXERCISE 4. REWRITING TO CHRONOLOGICAL ORDER

For particularly challenging practice, rewrite the paragraph in Exercise 3 by rearranging it into strictly chronological order. In other words, restate the authors' ideas about the most distant past, then restate their ideas about the more recent past, and finally rephrase the comments about the present. Is the result a more sensible arrangement? How does the point of such a strictly chronological paragraph differ from the main idea of the original paragraph?

SPECIAL HINTS

Avoid mixing the simple present forms with the simple past forms. Decide which time frame to make your statement from and stay with it.

Use the perfect tenses to stress finished action, for the most part. Match only those time periods (and their verb forms) that you can fit together logically. Include adverbs, transitional phrases, and subordinate clauses to help specify time.

tsp | # 72. TOPIC SENTENCE PLACEMENT

Use a topic sentence placement that matches your readers' expectations.

Exposition requires clear topic sentences at the beginning of your paragraphs, usually. Description, narration, and persuasion may require topic ideas to be stated up front. (See the "Four Modes" chart in section 3.) At times, however, some of your paragraphs may work best with the topic statement last, in mid-paragraph, or not stated in any single sentence.

EXAMPLES:

1. Ideology is the ideas of a group of people with common interests—a nation, a party, a government, a social or economic class, an occupational group, an industry, etc. The most common tactic of ideology is to show how the interests of the group are "really" the same as the interests of the whole society or of humanity in general. The famous remark of Charles Wilson some years back, "What's good for General Motors is good for the country," encapsulates the root principle of ideology. General Motors, the American Medical Association, the AFL-CIO, the National Rifle Association, garment workers, English teachers, college professors, businessmen—whatever group is organized and conscious of a common interest turns out ideology. (Richard Ohmann and the Amherst Conference on Public Doublespeak)

2. The seminal quest story is Homer's *Odyssey*, which has modern counterparts in James Joyce's *Ulysses* and Nikos Kazantzakis's *The Odyssey: A Modern Sequel*. Jason's quest for the Golden Fleece, as told by Apollonius of Rhodes, is also basic, as is Virgil's *Aeneid*, the record of the quest for a new Troy. Nearly all of the great epics—*Beowulf, Paradise Lost, The Cid, The Divine Comedy*—are quest stories. (David Adams Leeming, *Mythology: The Voyage of the Hero*)

3. It is true that television renders current events with immediacy. It is true that television appeals directly to the senses of sight and hearing. Nevertheless, television has not yet been used to teach in a way that links its immediacy and sensory appeal to challenging

concepts. Such a link would do much to enliven imagination in learners. Aside from a few successes, like *Civilization* and *The Ascent of Man*, television has rarely made that link between sensation and concept that is the essence of learning.

4. In the beginning, his progress was agonizingly slow, his survival often in doubt. But with the passage of the ages and with a cunning constantly sharpened by the struggle for survival, man established himself at the top of the totem pole of life. He went from flint and flame to rocket-powered flight with ever-increasing speed until he had created a veritable juggernaut against nature and, in so doing, against himself. Now that he has forced the lock on Pandora's nuclear tool box, his capacity to tamper with his environment and his destiny is virtually limitless. (From *Man . . . An Endangered Species?* United States Department of the Interior Conservation Yearbook No. 4)

In the first example, the main idea is stated in the first sentence, a typical procedure for a definition. In the second example, Leeming makes his topic generalization in the last sentence. Since the third example shifts from praise to blame, the middle sentence, with its signal "nevertheless," carries the gist or main idea of the entire paragraph. Finally, the fourth example deals with a process that takes place over a vast amount of time. No one sentence carries the gist of the whole process. The topic idea has been implied.

EXERCISE 1. TOPIC SENTENCES IN TEXTBOOKS

Select a passage of several paragraphs from a textbook. Underline the topic sentence in each paragraph. If a paragraph has no stated topic sentence, write a one-sentence summary of the paragraph. Finally, determine the pattern of placement: Do most topic sentences come at the beginning of the paragraph?

EXERCISE 2. TOPIC SENTENCES IN JOURNALS

Repeat Exercise 1 but with an article from a technical journal or professional journal in your major field.

SPECIAL HINTS

Your topic sentence for a paragraph should specify your subject for the paragraph and make a generalization about it. This generalization shows your attitude or your approach to the reader. In most paragraphs written to emphasize logical processes and organization, you should put your topic sentence first to let your reader know your point in advance.

tr ‖ **73. TRANSITIVE, INTRANSITIVE, AND LINKING VERBS**

‖ **Don't dead-end an idea that's in transit. Some sentences must include a subject, a verb, *and* an object to give a complete idea.**

EXAMPLES:
dead-ended:	He bought.
COMPLETE:	He bought *a car*. (*transitive*)
COMPLETE:	It always starts. (*intransitive*)

The key to completeness is the verbs you use and what you use them to mean. Some verbs like *bought* must have an object noun or pronoun to indicate what was bought. Such verbs transmit ideas from subject all the way through to an object. Since the action in the verb makes a complete transit or trip all the way across the sentence, these verbs are called *transitive*. Other verbs like *start* may or may not need objects, depending on how they are used in a sentence.

EXAMPLES:
He starts the car easily every morning.
                |
        object (*transitive*)

The car starts easily every morning.
            no object (*intransitive*)

Since an object would name what was started, *easily, every,* and *morning* cannot be objects. No object is needed in an intransitive sentence because no action is transmitted, as in the intransitive sentence above, in which the owner's part is not specified.

SPECIFICS

linking verbs: The forms of *be* can be followed by nouns and pronouns, but these verb forms, like *is, are,* and *was,* serve more as equal signs than as transmitters of action.

> EXAMPLES:
> I am the man.   *I = man*
> She was my mother.   *She = mother*

Linking verbs just make an equation, a link, between a subject and something that identifies the subject more completely.

Another set of linking verbs should not be modified by adverbs because their main function is to link a subject with a complementary adjective.

> EXAMPLES:
> I feel sick.   *I = ill*
> I feel poorly.   *?*

The second example means, if anything, that the speaker has an inadequate sense of touch. Such verbs can be modified by adverbs, but this use runs a risk of confusion with an adjective.

> EXAMPLES:
>   adjective: He looked hurried.
>   adverb: He looked hurriedly for his keys.

The first example means that the man seemed to be rushed; the second example indicates a rapid search a man made to find a set of keys. The sentences are not interchangeable.

The linking verbs include the following:
forms of *be*:   *am, are, be, been, being, is, was, were*

others: *appear, become, feel, grow, look, prove, remain, seem, smell, sound, taste, turn*
(See "Verbs" (4) on meanings of these verbs.)

EXERCISE 1. TRANSITIVE AND INTRANSITIVE MEANINGS

The following verbs have both transitive and intransitive meanings. Make up one sentence for a transitive meaning (with an object) and another sentence for an intransitive meaning (no object required). Use a dictionary to help you.

1. start	2. follow	3. build
4. finish	5. lead	6. flash
7. ride	8. agitate	9. estimate
10. propagate	11. accumulate	12. bushwhack

EXERCISE 2. SELECT A WORD

Select one completion for each of the sentences below.

1. Since her calculations were correct, she proved ^impossible/the theorem and passed geometry.

2. He had to turn ^quick/quickly to avoid the deer in the road.

3. Paul tasted delicious ^the ice cream/hurriedly in hopes that no one would catch him.

4. Jerrie appeared ^ill/sickly, but she looked ^well/good later on.

SPECIAL HINTS

Many verbs can be transitive or intransitive depending on their meaning in context. (See "Irregular Verbs" for a sample listing.) A few verbs can be transitive, intransitive, or linking verbs, depending on the context, like *grow* and *turn*. Forms of *be* only link subjects with their completers or "complements." Look in a dictionary if you are not sure whether you must use an object after a verb. If your meaning is labeled *vt*, use an object; if it is labeled *vi*, no object is used. Be careful after linking verbs about using adjectives and adverbs to indicate your meaning.

_____ *or* und | ## 74. UNDERLINING

Use underlining in handwritten or typed work to indicate things that would be set in italics if they were printed: titles of newspapers, magazines, professional journals, books, plays, television and radio programs, paintings, sculptures, symphonies, record albums, operas, movies, and epic or long poems. **Also, use underlining to indicate names of vehicles,** such as airplanes, space vehicles, ships, automobiles, trains, and others. **In addition, use underlining to indicate foreign words or phrases not yet accepted as English, terms to be emphasized, and words used as words.**

SPECIFICS

(1) titles: In general, the names of long or separate works are underlined.

EXAMPLES:
newspapers: The Rocky Mountain News
             The Denver Post
(*Locations in newspaper titles may or may not be underlined. If you have a choice between underlining or not, make that choice consistently for all titles of newspapers.*)
magazines and professional journals:
Omni   Analog   Time
Business Week Engineering   Journal of American Psychiatry
other titles:
Future Shock (book)

<u>Cat on a Hot Tin Roof</u> (play)
<u>The Ten Commandments</u> (movie)
<u>CBS Evening News</u> (television program)
<u>The Shadow</u> (radio program/comic strip)
<u>The Last Supper</u> (painting)
<u>Jesus Christ: Superstar</u> (opera/record album)
Grieg's <u>Piano Concerto in A Minor</u> (concerto)
<u>My Fair Lady</u> (musical/movie)
<u>Paradise Lost</u> (epic poem)
<u>The Waste Land</u> (long poem)
Donatello's <u>Mary Magdalen</u> (sculpture)

(2) vehicles: Indicate the personal names, not brand names or types, by underlining.

EXAMPLES:
<u>Columbia</u> (spacecraft)   <u>Queen Elizabeth</u> (ship)
<u>The Zephyr</u> (train)   <u>The Blue Streak</u> (automobile)
<u>Spirit of St. Louis</u> (airplane)
but Boeing 727

(3) words: Underline specialized or foreign terms.

EXAMPLES:
<u>quid pro quo</u> (Latin)
Such an arrangement, known as an <u>oligarchy</u>, ...
(*Specialized terms should be underlined at their first usage but not later uses.*)
The word <u>maser</u> stands for "<u>m</u>icrowave <u>a</u>mplification by <u>s</u>timulated <u>e</u>mission of <u>r</u>adiation."
(*word used as word; letters underlined to highlight how the word* <u>maser</u> *was formed from first letters of the full term*)

EXERCISE. DIALOGUE ON ENTERTAINMENT

The following is a dialogue between two reporters for the college newspaper who write for the entertainment section. They are comparing (and contrasting) their favorite TV programs, movies, books, and songs. You are to underline and supply quotation marks for the second part of the dialogue. (The first part is done as a guide.) You are also supposed to supply the third and fourth parts of the dialogue with standard underlining and use of quotation marks. You may wish to review the section, "Quotation Marks," before you begin.

Part 1: TV programs

"So what's your favorite TV show?" asked Janet.

"I like old movies best, like <u>Casablanca</u>, <u>The Forbidden Planet</u>, <u>Gone with the Wind</u>, <u>Seven Days in May</u>. How about you?"

"But, Bert, those aren't *shows*. Don't you like reruns of <u>Star Trek</u>—I do. I even like <u>The Wonderful World of Disney</u> sometimes."

"Oh, sure," said Bert, thinking to himself "<u>The Wonderful World of Disney</u>? Well, maybe, but is she kidding?" "Say, Janet, aren't we supposed to cover movies, too?" Bert asked. TV made him uncomfortable.

Part 2: movies

(You supply the quotation marks and the underlining.)

Well, yes, Janet responded. Maybe we can get some promotional pictures from local theater managers. Aren't they making another Star Wars trilogy? I heard they had two more trilogies planned.

Yeah, I heard that Darth Vader is coming back for another Star Wars. There's been some talk of another Star Trek movie. Hey, there's an all-night Bogart film festival coming up at the Broadway Cinema next week. Maybe I could get complimentary tickets. I'd like to get a review of The Treasure of the Sierra Madre into the next issue of the Gazette.

Okay, Janet said, seeming to like the idea. We need to cover books and music, too, though.

Parts 3 and 4: books and songs

(You continue the dialogue between Janet and Bert. Make sure they mention at least five titles for each topic.)

SPECIAL HINTS

In your papers you should generally underline titles of separate publications, like books, magazines, newspapers, TV programs, movies, paintings, etc. You should set off with quotation marks titles of parts of such publications or productions, such as chapters from books, articles in magazines, editorials in newspapers, episodes of TV series, etc.

vbl ‖ 75. VERBALS

Use verbals to compress wordy subordinate clauses. Since verbals are formed from verbs, they can take subjects, objects, and complements like verbs do. Unlike verbs, however, verbals do the work of nouns or adjectives in sentences.

SPECIFICS

(1) participles: These words end in *ing* to stress present activity; participles end in *ed, en,* or *t* to stress past motion. (For oddly spelled participles, see the table under "Irregular Verbs.") Participles act as adjectives.

EXAMPLES:
A single *swimming* fish is easy prey for a *marauding* shark.
The *broken* windows stare at me; the *cracked, chipped, split* walls hover over me like *falling* slabs *frozen* in time.

(2) gerunds: Gerunds always end with *ing,* but they act as nouns.

EXAMPLES:
Seeing is *believing.*
Owning a home is a way of life.

(3) infinitives: Infinitives, made up of the word *to* and the present form of a verb, usually act as nouns.

EXAMPLE:
"*To err* is human, *to forgive* divine." (Alexander Pope)

Since an infinitive is a phrase unit, nothing should be used between the two parts of the infinitive ordinarily.

EXERCISE 1. REVISING VERBALS

In the sentences below, change the underlined part of speech to the indicated alternative. Change other words as needed. Number 1 is revised in one way as an example.

1. To swim is invigorating. (*infinitive to gerund*)
    REVISION: Swimming is invigorating.
2. A dream can be horrifying. (*noun to gerund; participle to noun*)
3. They knew the importance of being safe. (*gerund phrase to noun*)
4. Getting to know someone isn't always easy. (*gerund with an infinitive to another infinitive*)
5. A swimming person uses many muscles. (*participle to noun*)

EXERCISE 2. WRITING AND ANALYZING VERBALS

Make up a sentence at least ten words long that uses a gerund. Change the gerund to an infinitive as you rewrite the sentence. Could either sentence be written smoothly using nouns instead of gerund or infinitive?

EXERCISE 3. WRITING AND ASSESSING VERBALS

Make up a sentence of at least ten words that includes a participle. Can the participle be changed to an adjective that is equivalent in meaning?

SPECIAL HINTS

Use gerunds or infinitives to replace abstract nouns, when you use too many, to put some motion into your sentences. If your writing sounds vague, try adding participles and other adjectives to bring it into focus. Also, study how present and past participles are used to help indicate time in verb phrases by referring to the "Verb Form Chart" under "Passive Verbs."

vb ‖ 76. VERBS

Use action verbs to enliven your writing. Use being verbs to equate subjects with qualities or identities. Use helping verbs as parts of verb phrases. Use linking verbs to emphasize sensory impressions and appearances.

SPECIFICS

(1) action verbs: Most verbs show activity, dynamism, motion.

EXAMPLES:
Kings epitomize their times.
The rider leaped from his horse.
Prices rose steadily in heavy trading.

(2) being verbs: The forms of *be* merely place a subject in time, or simply equate a subject with an identity or a quality.

EXAMPLES:

time:	I was here yesterday.
quality:	Sugar is sweet.
identity:	You are the one from the mill.

(3) helping verbs: The forms of *be*, as well as *has, have, had, do, does,* and *did* help make verb phrases quite often. Since they begin verb phrases, their spellings indicate usually whether the subject is singular or plural.

EXAMPLES:
"Finding signals from extraterrestrial civilizations *has been* likened to discovery of the New World by Columbus. . . . Here we *are* talking about news that would *have* taken years to reach us. . . ." (Walter Sullivan)

(See "Irregular Verbs" for a complete display of the helping verbs as verbs. See the "Verb Form Chart" under "Passive Verbs" for a complete display of the uses of *be* forms, *has, have,* and *had* as helpers. See "Mood Shift" (4) for a run-down on modals like *would* and *will*.)

(4) linking verbs: The verbs *feel, smell, sound,* and *taste* emphasize sensory impressions. The verbs *appear, look,* and *seem* emphasize the way things may seem at first but not really be after a closer look. Other linking verbs are *become, grow, prove, remain,* and *turn,* which emphasize change or the lack of change.

EXAMPLES:
Her perfume smelled faintly like roses or azaleas.
He seemed to be happy, but I found out later that he had been faking it.
The rivalry between the companies grew more intense with each set of quarterly figures.

EXERCISE. REVISING FOR ACTION

The paragraph below suffers from weak verbs and an overuse of being and linking verbs. Use the four methods listed under "Special Hints" or ways of your own to revise the paragraph using more action verbs.

I am a weekend tennis player. Although I am not as good as Nastase, I am as temperamental as he is. I am not left-handed like Connors is, but I am a two-handed backhander. I am also one of those players who is "into" the big-headed racket. These butterfly nets are easier to use than I was guessing they would be. Aside from my temperament, my playing style, and my racket, my consistency is not very good. I am one of those players who is able to get the first serve in only when I take speed off of it. Naturally, my opponents are able to kill my serve, and they are only weekend players, too. I am thinking of switching to racquetball—at least shagging for the ball is easier when you are in a box.

SPECIAL HINTS: FOUR WAYS TO SPICE UP YOUR VERBS

Unless you are following the set form of a definition ("Spelunking is. . . ."), locating someone's or something's existence in time or space ("Caesar was. . . ."), or stating a perception ("They seem well rested."), you should favor action verbs over linking verbs and verbs of being. Here are some ways to spice up your verbs:

1. Turn a noun subject into a verb.

   The *location* of Manitoba *is* just north of North Dakota and Minnesota. It sprawls toward Hudson Bay.

   Manitoba *is located* just north of . . . . It sprawls. . . .

2. Turn a noun subject into a participle.

   Located just north of North Dakota and Minnesota, Manitoba sprawls toward Hudson Bay.

3. Use a stronger synonym for a weak verb and an object or complement.

   Pauline *gets angry* easily. (*gets* = *becomes*)

   Pauline *flares up* easily.

4. Drop weak base clauses in order to bring your main idea out of the modifiers and into a strong base sentence.

   It *seems* reasonable that we should try to control our own destinies.

   We should control our own destinies.

ww ‖ 77. WRONG WORD (DENOTATION)

Make sure you call things by their right names. If you are not sure about what to call something, look up your best guess in a dictionary. Double-check your key terms to make sure that your use of them is accurate by looking them up in a dictionary or a textbook.

EXAMPLES:

confused:	I don't hoarse around on the job because I'm cerius about urning a living.
REVISED:	I don't *"horse around"* on the job because I'm *serious* about *earning* a living.
confused:	He tried hopelessly to expound his error.
REVISED:	He tried hopelessly to *expunge* his error.

The first example illustrates a spelling problem; the second example shows a vocabulary problem—a confusion between two similar words' meanings. In both examples, the confusion resulted in a use of words that did not mean what the writer intended.

EXERCISE. SPELLING OR VOCABULARY?

For each sentence below tell if the word pairs being confused seem to represent a problem with spelling or a problem with learning new words (vocabulary). Mark the spelling problems *sp* and the problems with unusual words *voc*. Cross out the incorrect word.

_____ 1. Thought / Throughout history inventions have changed societies.

_____ 2. It is difficult to extrapolate / exculpate from current trends.

_____ 3. I hated to choose ether / either one.

_____ 4. Parapsychology is the study of the supernal / supernatural

_____ 5. My advisor suggested I study some acrobatics / macrobiotics in order to become a nutritionist.

SPECIAL HINTS

Look at your own writings for word confusions. Your instructors may mark the confusions they spot as *sp, voc,* or *ww.* Although the word problems marked may not be evident to you, rely on your instructors' judgments as specialists in word usage. Check in your dictionary, in the "Glossary of Usage," or add the word to your spelling record. Proofread for word problems that have been brought to your attention on previous writings.

glos | 78. glossary of usage:

A COLLECTION OF SHIBBOLETHS

During one of the skirmishes depicted in the Bible (Judges 12:4–6), the men of Gad captured the points along a section of the Jordan River where crossing was safe. When any of the men from Ephraim tried to cross the river at one of these fords, they were challenged by Jephthah's soldiers from Gad to say "Shibboleth." Because they spoke a different dialect of Hebrew, the Ephraimites pronounced "Shibboleth" as "Sibboleth." Anyone mispronouncing this password was killed at the fords of the Jordan as he tried to reach his tribal homeland.

Although you won't be killed for confusing the uses of the words listed in this section, you may jolt some readers and lose others altogether by violating their sense of what is "proper" in written English. Knowing how to use—or to avoid—these shibboleths in your writing will help keep your readers concentrating on what you have to say.

a, an; and
Use *an* before words that begin with vowel sounds. Otherwise use *a*: *an orange* crate, *a c*rate; *an h*onest and *a h*umble woman (Note: and is used to join words; don't confuse *and* with *an*.)

accept, except
Use *accept* to mean *receive*.
> Though surprised by its intensity, the actress accepted the applause of her audience humbly at first, then with increasing assurance.

Use *except* to mean *besides*.
> Everyone except Bill guffawed when the pie hit his face.

Use *except* to mean *exclude*. (formal)
> Excepting a few brilliant scenes, the movie was generally ill-plotted and poorly acted.

affect, effect

Use *affect* when you mean *influence*.
Smoking can affect your health.
Use *effect* to mean *result*.
His speech didn't have the effect he expected.
Use *effect* to mean *achieve* or *accomplish*. (advanced)
The social worker effected a humane solution to her client's problem.
Use *affect* to mean *fake* or *pretend*. (advanced)
For fear of seeming "uncultured" to his new girlfriend, Jake affected a liking for Mozart.
Use *affect* to mean *an emotional response* in writing about psychology or education. (specialized)
The affect of the day's lesson should be increased enjoyment of reading.

allusion, illusion, elusion, delusion

Use *allusion* to mean *reference*.
His allusion to Cheryl's recent success reignited the jealousy of everyone.
Use *illusion* to mean *a false image*.
Magicians are masters of illusion.
Elusion is a rarely used word that means *an escape* or *an evasion*. These two synonyms should be used more often than *elusion*.
Her interrogators quickly realized that her answers were only evasions of the real truth.
Use *delusion* to mean *a misguided belief*.
All Cambodians suffered for their leaders' delusions that a society could be revamped overnight.

a lot

Use *a lot* (two separate words) in informal or even standard writing situations. Avoid using *a lot* in business correspondence and reports and in formal writing. (*Alot* is a misspelling.)
(informal) We enjoyed visiting you last week and hope we can get together a lot more often.
(formal)   We very much enjoyed last week's visit, and we hope we may meet much more frequently.

already, all ready

Use *already* to mean *by now*.
She must have already reached the train station.
Use *all ready* to indicate that every member of a group is prepared.
The packages are all ready for mailing.

among, between

Use *among* to indicate a difference or a similarity that applies to *more than two*.
The fallen dictator shouted at the crowd, "There is not one among you who would have acted differently if he had the power I commanded!"

Use *between* to indicate a difference, a similarity, or a choice of *exactly two*.

> The mutineers had a choice between being castaways thousands of miles from home or returning home to be hanged.

amount, number

Use *amount* to indicate the quantity of something measured in bulk.

> The amount of sand used to fill a sandbox depends on the dimensions of the box and the depth of the sand required.

Use *number* to indicate the quantity of things measured separately.

> A number of people have complained about the shortage of ruled paper.

data

Data may be used as a singular or as a plural. The singular use is especially popular in technical writing.

> The data is reliable, but our interpretation could be disputed.

different

Use *different from*, rather than *different than*, to make contrasts.

> Her opinions are usually different from mine.

etc.

Since the Latin word for *and* is *et*, and since the Latin word for *others* is *cetera*, the abbreviation *etc.* is used to stand for *and others*. The spelling *ect.* mixes the Latin words; the use of "and etc." ignores the meaning of the abbreviation—which already contains *and*. Why not simply use the English wording rather than the Latin abbreviation? Use *and others* or some variation to complete a list.

> He spoke the standard platitudes of grief—"so sorry to hear of your loss," "better off now that it's over," and the other empty phrases—but he didn't seem to care in the least.

farther, further

Use *farther* and *farthest* to refer to physical distances.

> Denver is farther from Chicago than from Phoenix.

Use *further* and *furthest* to refer to mental or figurative distances.

> The memory of the Rockies is further from my mind now than it has ever been.

fewer, less

Use *fewer* to indicate the quantity of countable items.

> Fewer people eat at that restaurant since the former chef retired.

Use *less* to indicate the quantity of items that are not usually or not easily counted individually.

> Can he really run the 100 in less than 10 seconds?

imply, infer

Writers *imply,* hint at, or suggest meanings; readers *infer* meaning or draw conclusions from what they read.

The reporter's selection of details implied wrongdoing by the agency.

After she read his letter, she inferred that things were not as bright as he wanted her to believe.

its, it's

Since personal pronouns do not use an apostrophe to show possession, *it's* can only represent the contraction of *it is. Its* shows what belongs to nonhumans.

It's amazing that the dog could chew through its leash so quickly.

like, as

Use *like* to mean *similar to.*

She dances like a ballerina.

Like me, Charlie wouldn't hurt anyone on purpose.

Use *as* in writing formally to conservative readers.

She dances as a ballerina dances—gracefully, yet with precision.

real, really

Use *really* to mean *very,* or simply use *very.*

I was really tired at the halfway point of the marathon.

Often a comparison based on *so . . . that* should be used instead of the trite *really* or *very.*

I was so tired at the halfway point of the marathon that I felt like I was running through pancake batter.

Real might be used to assure your readers that something is actual rather than imagined.

He faced a real difficulty this time.

reason is because

This construction equates a noun with an adverb clause. Most readers prefer a noun clause starting with *that* after the *is* to make a parallel statement. So avoid using *reason* and *because* in the same statement.

Her reason for excelling is not that she is compensating for being lonely. She excels because she enjoys the work.

than, then

Use *than* to make comparisons.

Algebra is harden for me than chemistry.

Use *then* to indicate time.

I usually get off work at 9:30; then I study for a couple of hours before I go to my night job.

there, their, they're

Use *there* to indicate a place or to postpone a subject in a sentence.

There are ten more cartons over there in the corner.

Use *their* to indicate possession, to mean *of them.*

Their car was reported stolen.

Use *they're* in informal writing to stand for *they are.* In standard and formal writing, as well as business correspondence, spell out *they are.*

(informal) They're going to be at your place soon.

(formal)   They are to arrive at your residence shortly.

to, too, two   Use *too* to mean *also* or *very.*

He's too proud to bend.

She's stubborn, too.

Use *two* to indicate the number *2.*

Two deer used to eat the tops off our tulips every year.

Use *to* as the preposition.

We went to the mountains on our last two vacations.

used to   Most readers expect to see a *d* on *used.* In formal writing, substitute the word *accustomed* for *used.*

He used to be an energetic singer.

They were accustomed to taking long drives on Sunday afternoons, but that habit has been broken.

EXERCISE 1. USING A DICTIONARY FOR DICTION

Use a hardbound dictionary to help you select the correct word to complete each sentence below.

1. She always refused to accept my (advise, advice).
2. The constant tapping thoroughly (aggravated, annoyed) me.
3. Ignoring his limp, he claimed to be (all right, alright) after the fall.
4. We were (altogether, all together) too tired to continue.
5. The sheriff treated his men (bad, badly) and kept them underpaid.
6. Cannons are sometimes fired off at the (climactic, climatic) moment of Beethoven's *1812 Overture.*
7. The (continual, continuous) rumble of the train eventually lulled me to sleep.
8. The stockbrokers were glad to (council, counsel) Uncle Bill on how to convert his inheritance into stocks and bonds.
9. His story about the UFO was almost (credible, credulous).
10. He (hanged, hung) his coat in the closet.
11. He turned himself (in to, into) the police.
12. Can a hen (lay, lie) more than one egg per day?
13. Whenever my brother became sullen, we would simply (leave, let) him alone for a few hours until he regained his good spirits.
14. "Geometry isn't hard," she claimed. "(Loosing, Losing) a friend is hard."
15. The train was going (almost, most) a mile a minute when it hit the bus.
16. They (past, passed) us going the wrong way!
17. "A yellow light means to slow down and (precede, proceed) with caution," he recited.

18. One of the (principal, principle) reasons for her nervousness was the series of nightmares about her debut over the last several nights.
19. She was so weak that she could hardly (raise, rise) from the sofa.
20. The lawyer and the accountant were accompanied by a legal researcher and a tax economist, (respectfully, respectively).
21. "(Sit, Set) down by the fire and tell me about your trip," she cooed.
22. The dusty bones of those who had tried to cross the desert were strewn (though, through, throughout, thought) the arid flatlands.
23. (Who's, Whose) child is this?
24. Home is (where, were) you know you are welcome.
25. It seems like it's just the information you need that is the last thing (your, you're) likely to find out.

EXERCISE 2. RESEARCHING USAGE: SIX PROBLEMS

The three dictionaries of usage listed below are those that were consulted in preparing this glossary. Use one of them or some other usage dictionary in your college library to solve the usage problems given for this exercise.

Copperud, Roy H. *American Usage: The Consensus* (New York: Van Nostrand, 1970).

Follett, Wilson, and others. *Modern American Usage* (New York: Hill and Wang, 1966).

Morris, William, and Mary Morris. *Harper Dictionary of Contemporary Usage* (New York: Harper & Row, 1975).

Usage Problems

1. What would a fiction writer be trying to indicate about a character if the writer has the character use phrases like *could of* and *should of*?
2. Why is *try and* regarded as informal usage and *try to* regarded as "standard" or "educated" usage?
3. Is there a significant difference in meaning between the words *disinterested* and *uninterested*?
4. When should you use *good* and when should you use *well* in formal writing and business writing?
5. Are there legitimate uses for the words *kind, sort,* and *type,* or are they just "filler"?
6. Is there a difference between the uses of *shall* and *will* in formal writing?

An interesting perspective on singling out words as usage problems is developed in Jim Quinn's *American Tongue and Cheek: A Populist Guide to Our Language* (New York: Pantheon, 1980), a book that is both fun to read and filled with surprising information about our language.

index